Dalits Rights / Human Rights

Dalits Rights / Human Rights

Debi Chatterjee

RAWAT PUBLICATIONS
Jaipur • New Delhi • Bangalore • Guwahati • Kolkata

ISBN 978-81-316-0427-4

Reprinted, 2016

Published by
Prem Rawat for **Rawat Publications**
Satyam Apts, Sector 3, Jawahar Nagar, Jaipur 302 004 (India)
Phone: 0141 265 1748/7006 Fax: 0141 265 1748
E-mail: info@rawatbooks.com
Website: www.rawatbooks.com

New Delhi Office
4858/24, Ansari Road, Daryaganj, New Delhi 110 002
Phone: 011 2326 3290

Also at *Bangalore, Guwahati* and *Kolkata*

Typeset by Rawat Computers, Jaipur
Printed and bound in India.

Contents

Acknowledgement

It is indeed a pleasure to be able to place the present work in the hands of the readers. My long years of interest in dalit studies and human rights questions made it amply clear to me that dalit rights need to be asserted as human rights. In the human rights discussions and debates, dalit rights till recently hardly found a place. Only since the 1990s a measure of limited attention has been given to the question of dalit human rights. The assertion of dalits themselves and the cooperation of human rights bodies, both national and global, have significantly contributed towards this development. Yet, it can be described as 'too little, too late'. Much more needs to be done, and on an urgent basis.

The ideas of many thinkers, dalit activists and friends have gone into the making of this book. It is indeed difficult to lay out a complete list of such indebtedness. However, very specifically, I would like to thank those who have given their valuable suggestions towards the writing of the book. I would also like to record my immense gratitude towards my former teacher and colleague, late Professor Jayantanuja Bandyopadhyaya, who till his last days constantly encouraged me and gave his valuable suggestions on the book. I am extremely grateful to the staff of the National Library of Kolkata as also the staff of the central and departmental libraries of Jadavpur University for their assistance. The book is likely to benefit all those interested in dalit studies, human rights and sociology.

Debi Chatterjee

Chapter 1

The Global Human Rights Discourse

The global concern for human rights is today universally recognised. Its legitimacy has evolved over time, traversing what have come to be widely known as the three generations of human rights.[1] The first-generation human rights dealt essentially with liberty, epitomised in the Universal Declaration of Human Rights (UDHR). The second-generation human rights reflected the concern for socioeconomic issues focusing on equality. Besides the UDHR, they were codified in the International Covenant on Economic, Social and Cultural Rights. The third-generation human rights are those rights that go beyond the mere civil and social, and include group and collective rights, such as the right to self-determination, right to economic and social development, right to a healthy environment, right to natural resources, right to communicate, right to participate in cultural heritage and the right to intergenerational equity and sustainability. The term "third-generation human rights", however, remains largely unofficial, and covers an extremely broad spectrum of rights.

By the mid-1990s every state had signed up to at least one international human rights instrument – the vast majority of states being well entrenched among the interlinking declarations, protocols and other tools of international human rights law.[2] India is no exception.

Despite the universal concern for human rights, the human rights discourse has remained entrapped in the "politics" of human rights, making for disagreements, disputes, controversies and discontent. As the vulnerable lament their vulnerability, political power games are played around them converting them into pawns. Questions like "What are human rights?", and "How can such rights be safeguarded?", often arise. As liberal political philosophers emphasise what they project as positivistic, scientific, neutral, objective and deontological approaches, particularities of human conditions, are avoided.[3]

The Roots of the Discourse

Today's global human rights discourse stretches far back into history, to ancient laws such as the Hammurabi Codes of Babylon, the Greco-Roman doctrines, the French and American Declarations, the traditions of natural law and natural rights and the term "The Rights of Man".[4] Ideas pertaining to rights operated at different levels for many centuries. Sometimes they were primarily moral codes, at other times legally structured norms. They reflected and defined variously the relations between the ruler and the ruled.

Prior to the emergence of the global human rights discourse, "rights" assured to citizens by different states were diverse. The concerned state was itself the reference point, the ultimate authority and arbiter of such rights. There were no uniform standards globally asserted or acknowledged with regard to the rights. Positive law along with the idea of positive rights dominated the scene, with the notion of natural law and natural rights being more relevant in the domain of protest.

It was actually with the events leading up to the Second World War and the war itself that concern for human rights came to the fore. The Nazi atrocities in Germany and the horrors of the war were the major causes of concern. Across the world there were fears of such history being repeated, perhaps in a worse form. Against such a backdrop, it was felt that human rights needed to be standardised on an urgent basis. The concern was voiced by representatives of 26 nations that were fighting the Axis Powers in the declaration of the United Nations in 1942. In the Document, the signatories spoke of the need to "preserve human rights and justice in our lands as well as in other lands".

At the end of World War II in 1945, as representatives of 50 states met at San Francisco to draft the United Nations Charter, they incorporated as one of the purposes of the UN the obligation to "achieve international cooperation … in promoting and encouraging respect for human rights and for fundamental freedoms of all without distinction as to race, sex, language or religion". Article 55 of the UN Charter stated that the UN would promote "universal respect for, and observance of, human rights and fundamental freedoms for all without distinction as to race, sex, language or religion". By the following Article 56, the members pledged themselves to "take joint and separate action in cooperation with the organisation for the achievements of the purposes set forth in Article 55". Significantly, despite these commitment, the Charter did not answer one key question; what rights and freedoms should exactly be upheld?

It was with the adoption of the UDHR in 1948 that the question was taken up, though partially. Article 68 of the UN Charter mandated the UN Economic and Social Council to set up a Commission "for the promotion of human rights". Based on it, the Commission of Human Rights was formed. And, it was that Commission that played the key role, devoting nearly three years of intensive study, undertaking heated debates and delicate negotiations, in ensuring the adoption of the UDHR.[5] In view of the continuing debates on the draft declaration, the President of the General Assembly on 10th, December 1948, called upon the member-states of the UN to vote on the proposed declaration. While 48 countries voted in favour of it, eight abstained and two were absent. As such, the UDHR was adopted without dissent. Much of the credit for this goes to the hard work put in by the Commission on Human Rights, which at the time was headed by Eleanor Roosevelt. Needless to say, prior to the adoption of this document, there had been no equivalent powerful instrument for the promotion and protection of human rights. True as the statement of Roosevelt is, the UDHR has proved to be a living document as it has grown over the years through numerous conventions and statutes and has been reflected in the constitutional law of numerous countries. It represented the first of the three stages of a programme designed to achieve an international Bill of Rights, based upon universally binding obligations of states and reinforced by effective administrative machinery. The three stages visualised were to be: (i) declaration defining the human rights that ought to be respected; (ii) series of binding covenants on the part of states to respect those rights; and (iii) measures and machinery for implementation.[6] The adoption of the International Covenant on Civil and Political Rights and the International Covenant on Economic, Social and Cultural Rights (1966) were part of the second stage.

The year 1968 saw the organising of the International Conference on Human Rights in Teheran to mark the International Year for Human Rights. Delegates, assembled there to review the progress that had been made in the field of human rights and prepare the future course of action, observed that "since the adoption of the Universal Declaration of Human Rights, the United Nations has made substantial progress in defining standards for the enjoyment and protection of human rights and fundamental freedoms". They went on to observe that, "During this period, many important international instruments were adopted but much remains to be done in regard to the implementation of those rights and freedoms".[7] Thus, protection of human rights came in for focussed attention.

On 25th June 1993, representatives of as many as 171 states adopted the Vienna Declaration and Programme of Action at the close of the two-week World Conference on Human Rights held at Vienna. It marked, inter alia, a renewed effort to strengthen and further implement the body of human rights instruments that had been constructed so far on the foundations of the UDHR. The Vienna Declaration called for the creation of the position of a High Commissioner for Human Rights – a post that was subsequently created in December 1993 with Jose Ayala Lasso being nominated by the Secretary General as the first High Commissioner.[8]

Major Debates and Controversies

Despite all these developments, however, many of the pressing debates were hardly resolved. As a matter of fact, quite a few of the criticisms got reinforced over time and new controversies and conflicts have surfaced in recent times. Euro centrism was a major criticism levelled against the rights documents from the very beginning and questions were raised about the "representativeness" of the representatives who participated in drafting the basic rights documents. It was alleged, for example, that those who participated in the drafting of the UDHR were not representatives of the various cultures and creeds of the world at the time of drafting, and had hence lacked credibility on that ground. It was pointed out that even though there were representatives of India, China, Iran and France, they came as experts in their fields, not as national or cultural representatives.[9] In more contemporary times, there has been a resurfacing of arguments from the standpoint of ethical and cultural relativism interrogating the politics of universality of human rights to make possible the toleration of extensive human and social suffering.[10] It is also alleged that the human rights movement has virtually got converted into the human rights market with the paradigm of the UDHR getting transformed into a trade-related, market-friendly paradigm of human rights ushered in by globalisation, ideologies of "economic rationalism", "good governance" and "structural adjustment".[11]

Post-1990s, in particular, with the collapse of the Soviet Union, "human rights" has more blatantly become the excuse of the US-led western states to impose their ideological and cultural domination across the world – particularly in the developing countries – in the guise of humanitarian interventions. The plight of the Palestinian, Afghan and Iraqi people reveals such shocking (mis)use of "human rights" in the name of its protection and the claim of liberating the people from so-called undemocratic, rogue regimes. The ideological overtones that had remained somewhat covert, and had been in check in the face of concerted pressures from the developing countries articulated through various international fora, such as the UN General Assembly, Non-aligned Movement, Organisation of African Unity, etc., have now gained ascendancy in the wake of the altered international realities. Not surprisingly, the alarm bells are ringing and human rights norms and practices are under attack from human rights activists at an altogether different level and on a never before visualised scale.

Yet, we can hardly deny the fact that even as the very concept of human rights remains problematic, it is a reality that "human rights languages ... remain perhaps all that we have to interrogate the barbarism of power".[12] Thus, not unexpectedly, the practice of human rights has come to shelter diverse ranges of politics of desire-in-dominance and *politics of desire-in-insurrection,*[13] and the concept of rights, including human rights, continue to "defy easy identification" and in fact "too many images crowd consciousness of human rights".[14]

However, even as difficulties plague the human rights discourse, the importance of standard setting and codification attempts at the international level have undoubtedly had positive results. In certain fields at least, such as women's rights or rights of racial equality, to mention but a few, the contributions of the international human rights regime can hardly be brushed aside. At the same time, it is necessary to place on record the fact that human rights activism outside the UN frame, prior to and after the establishment of the UN contributed in no mean sense to the UN centric moves. Taking for example, the case of the women's issues, the cumulative pressures of the women's movement right from the early struggles for suffrage through the different waves of feminist concerns were significant in activating the UN into devoting its attention to the question of women's rights. Similarly, the national liberation struggles being undertaken in the different colonies were clearly catalytical in stimulating the UN's concern for racial justice. In these circumstances, and notwithstanding the myriad difficulties, the human rights discourse developed over the years under the aegis of the UN. This comes in as a point of reference in efforts to address the issue of dalit marginalisations and dalit rights.

Caste in the Global Human Rights Discourse

It is pertinent to note that caste-based discrimination did not figure in the UN human rights discourse till as late as the 1990s. While varied forms of rights violations were being addressed, rights violations generated by caste discrimination and the obnoxious practice of untouchability went virtually unnoticed. In

1948, as the UDHR listed a whole range of different rights, it failed to speak of rights against caste discrimination. Likewise, neither did the CERD nor any other international human rights treaties take it up. For years, UN treaty based bodies such as the International Covenant on Civil and Political Rights (ICCPR), International Covenant on Economic, Social and Cultural Rights (ICESCR), Committee on the Elimination of Racial Discrimination (CERD), Committee on the Elimination of Discrimination Against Women (CEDAW) and the International Labour Organization (ILO) examined different problems affecting India, such as illiteracy, poverty child labour, bonded labour, gender discrimination and human rights violations without addressing caste discrimination as a major root cause of the problems. The caste dimension of discrimination was in fact overshadowed by other dimensions of discrimination more familiar to the world outside India.

It was only in 1996 that the CERD Committee came forth to make its first explicit reference to caste discrimination, untouchability and the Scheduled Castes. The reference came in the context of the Government of India's posture as expressed in the 1996 State Report stating that caste discrimination was not within the purview of the CERD since caste was not the same as race and "descent" referred to in Article 1 meant only descent based on race. Opposing this contention, the CERD Committee observed:

> ... descent mentioned in Article 1 of the Convention does not solely refer to race. The Committee affirms that the situation of the Scheduled Castes and Scheduled Tribes falls within the scope of the Convention.[15]

In 1997, the UN Human Rights Commission first noted the serious shortcomings in the Government of India's performance in guaranteeing the basic human rights of the dalits:

> Despite measures taken by the government, members of the Scheduled Castes and Scheduled Tribes ... continue to endure severe social discrimination and to suffer disproportionately from many violations of their rights under the Covenant ... .[16]

In a resolution adopted on 9 August 2000, the UN Sub-Commission on the Promotion and Protection of Human Rights had noted:

> ... discrimination based on occupation and descent has historically been a feature of societies in different regions ...
>
> ... discrimination based on occupation and descent is a form of discrimination prohibited by international law.[17]

This came in the context of discussions preparatory to the Durban Conference Against Racism, which was to take place in 2001.[18]

Rumblings from dalit activist groups and human rights bodies, which began decades earlier, turned into loud protests in the nineties. The already established international human rights regime was, from the late nineties, to become their reference point for measuring the state of dalit existence. Further, international human rights institutions were also to become their arena of struggles as will be seen in Chapter 9.

India's Commitment to Human Rights

The concerns for rights and articulation of demands in different forms goes back into the ancient past.[19] However, organised articulation of rights concerns developed largely in the interwar period and in the context of the struggles for freedom. In the last 60 years or so a public vocabulary of human rights has gained prominence by becoming more egalitarian and people oriented, and reaching out to an international network.[20]

In the 1940s, as vigorous constitution drafting exercises were underway, it was hoped that human rights would be written into the Constitution as a Code of Fundamental Rights that would establish precise limitations on governmental powers, which were to be enforced by an independent judiciary.[21] In the much discussed and much debated final draft of the constitutional document that was adopted, the goals of human rights were written into the Preamble, Part III of the Constitution dealing with Fundamental Rights and Part IV titled "Directive Principles of State Policy".

The Preamble to the Constitution is seen as laying down the basic structure of the Constitution with its focus on democracy, secularism, liberty, equality and dignity of the individual.

A reading of Part III of the Constitution dealing with Fundamental Rights reflects a rich content of human rights commitment. The incorporated rights are for all citizens. Caste does not stand in the way. In fact, for members of the traditionally oppressed castes, special concern is reflected in the form of prohibition of untouchability and the authorisation of special provisions.

However, on a careful reading of this part of the constitutional document, it becomes equally evident that the commitment to the protection of rights has a strong bias in favour of the civil and political rights. Economic, social and cultural rights are pushed to the next part, i.e., Part IV of the Constitution, under the caption, "Directive Principles of State Policy". Under this part we find Article 46, which asserts that it shall be the duty of the government to promote with special care the educational and economic interests of the weaker sections of the people, particularly the Scheduled Castes and Scheduled Tribes. It further states that the government shall protect these communities from social injustice and all forms of exploitation. Here, however, the rights are not justiciable and thus much is left to administrative whims and judicial activism.

Nonetheless, it is a fact that on the basis of the Directive Principles of State Policy a number of Acts related to human rights have been enacted. Periodically, schemes have been formulated exclusively for the benefit of members of these communities and monitoring mechanisms established.

In line with constitutional provisions supplemented by statutory Acts, a number of commissions have been set up over the years to look into the conditions of the weaker sections of society and suggest necessary remedial measures as also to ensure the protection of human rights of all people, including dalits. These include at the national level the Commissioner for Scheduled Castes and Scheduled Tribes, the National Commission for Scheduled Castes and Scheduled Tribes, the National Human Rights Commission, and the National Commission for Women. In fact, from the 1990s there has been a spurt in human rights legislations in India. The National Commission for Women Act (1990) led to the formation of the National Commission for Women. In 1992, the National Commission of Minorities Act was passed. And, in 1993, the Protection of Human Rights Act led to the creation of the National Human Rights Commission and State Commissions in different states. In a note that the Ministry of Home Affairs circulated, three specific objectives of the establishment of the National Human Rights Commission were mentioned, namely, (i) to strengthen the institutional arrangements through which human rights issues could be addressed in their entirety in a more focused manner; (ii) to look into allegations of excesses independently of the government, in a manner that would underline the government's commitment to protect human rights; and (iii) to complement and strengthen the efforts that have already been made in this direction.[22]

It is pertinent to note that much of this post-1990s activism came in the wake of internationally expressed discontent pertaining to the human rights scenario in the country. In fact, reacting sharply to the decision to set up the National Human Rights Commission, Justice V.R. Krishna Iyer had noted:

> It is a reaction in panic, a shame that we should think in terms of a Commission on Human Rights only because Sweden or the United States Congress or some other country tells [us] ... you are not respecting human rights. Therefore, have a Commission if you really want help from us. The mendicancy to which this nation is reduced not merely financially but even in regard to human rights ideology is a matter of pity. We may be proud of our judiciary, we may be proud of our Press but I am not proud of international mendicancy which originates from Delhi.[23]

As of the nature of the Human Rights Commission, he went on to state that it is:

> An optical illusion, cosmetic coloration, opium for the people at home and brown sugar for countries abroad, a legislative camouflage, a verbal wonder which conceals more than it reveals. An ineffectual angel which beats its golden wings in the void in vain.[24]

Other dimensions of human rights questions apart, India has shown extreme resistance to international criticisms of caste-based discrimination in the country. Despite all her impassioned statements on human rights concerns across the globe, India seeks to keep caste and caste-based discrimination outside the purview of international debates and discussions. The apprehension of successive governments has been all too evident. When, since the 1990s, UN bodies started making references to caste generated problems and at different levels of discussions analogies were being attempted between caste and race seeking to incorporate discussions of caste alongside race within the ambit of the provisions of CERD at the Durban Conference Against Racism in 2001, the Government of India persistently opposed it. Its general line of assertion was that (i) "caste" and "race" were clearly different and could not therefore be clubbed together, and (ii) India had her own mechanisms of addressing the issue and international moves on the matter were uncalled for. At that point of time, there was a pro-Hindutva, BJP-led government at the Centre in India. The governmental position on the matter could, under the circumstances, be explained in terms of its Hindu moorings. However, years later when, in April 2009, the Durban Review Conference (popularly referred to as Durban II) was held at Geneva to review the progress and assess the implementation of the Durban Declaration and Programme of Action produced at WCAR, the Indian government's position had hardly changed. This, despite the fact that now the central government was not a BJP-led government, but a Congress-led UPA government.

Notes

1. The division of human rights into three generations was initially proposed in 1979 by the Czech jurist Karel Vasak at the International Institute of Human Rights in Strasbourg.
2. David P. Forsythe, *Human Rights in International Relations,* Cambridge University Press, Cambridge, 2000, p. 4.
3. Cf. Anthony J. Langlois, "The Narrative Metaphysics of Human Rights", *The International Journal of Human Rights,* Vol. 9, No. 3, September 2005, p. 369.
4. Ibid., p. 370.
5. http://www.udhr.org/history/overview.htm
6. J.G. Starke, *An Introduction to International Law,* Butterworth & Co., London, 1958, p. 269.

7. http://www.unhchr.ch/html/menu3/b/b_tehern.htm
8. DPI/1394/Rev.1/HR–95–93241, April 1995.
9. See Daniel Bell, "Which Rights are Universal?", *Political Theory*, Vol. 27, No. 6, December 1999.
10. Upendra Baxi, *The Future of Human Rights*, Oxford University Press, New Delhi, 2008, p. 5.
11. Ibid., pp. 5–6.
12. Ibid., p. 4.
13. Ibid., p. 11.
14. Ibid., p. 12.
15. http://www.dalits.org/perspectiononcaste.html
16. CCPR/C/79/Add.81
17. Resolution of the UN Commission on Human Rights, Sub-commission on the Promotion and Protection of Human Rights, 52nd Session, 9th August 2000. E/CN/Sub2/2000/L14.
18. See Chapter 9 for discussion on Durban Conference.
19. See Debi Chatterjee, *Ideas and Movements Against Caste in India: Ancient to Modern Times*, Print-o-Graph, Calcutta, 1998.
20. Chiranjivi J. Nirmal, "Setting an Agenda", Chiranjivi J. Nirmal, ed., *Human Rights in India: Historical, Social and Political Perspectives,* Oxford University Press, New Delhi, 2006, pp. 235–36.
21. As this was done, Ivor Jennings preferred to criticise it as a lawyer's paradise. Sir Ivor Jennings, *Some Characteristics of Indian Constitution*, Oxford University Press, New Delhi, 1953, p. 50, cited in ibid., p. 237.
22. T.K. Thommen, "Human Rights Commission", *Cochin University Law Review,* Vol. XVII, Nos. 1 and 2, March–June 1993, pp. 67–68.
23. V. Vijayakumar, "The Working of the National Human Rights Commission: A Perspective", Chiranjivi J. Nirmal (ed.), op. cit., p. 217.
24. Ibid.

Chapter 2

The Indian Social Scenario

For thousands of years India has enthralled and mystified travellers and scholars coming from around the world. They have been fascinated by her mountains, rivers, forests and innumerable varieties of flora and fauna. Her people and their lifestyles have for centuries fascinated many across her borders. Those who have made efforts to understand the multifarious social patterns have noted the variety of cultural, religious, linguistic, ethnic forms, the diversity of mores and traditions. They also become acquainted with the complex trappings of power relations; the interplay of religious discourses and social practices to justify much that remains otherwise unjustifiable.

Today, India presents the picture of a large multireligious, multiethnic, multilingual culturally variegated state. A democracy, nay, the largest democracy in the world. She has the lengthiest written constitution, an array of rights assured therein for all her citizens irrespective of caste, creed, religion, sex, etc., apart from the justiciable fundamental rights. The vision of socio-economic justice to be ensured over the years is enshrined in the Directive Principles of State Policy of the Constitution of India. The independent judiciary stands to safeguard the guaranteed rights. The impact of the UDHR in the formulation of the rights is clearly visible as is evident even to a lay reader of the constitutional document. Yet, society remains essentially caste stratified, far from the holistic democratic vision.

Emergence of the Brahminical System

Stratification of Indian society along caste lines has a long history. It developed over time, with its origin going back some thousands of years in history. Based on the Hindu Brahminical philosophy of *varnashrama dharma* it has entrenched the sociocultural and economic marginalisation of the low, "untouchable castes", who form the core of the dalit population, and the adivasis.

This inegalitarian social order germinated in the late Vedic period. In course of time, through the *Sutras* and *Shastras* it got firmly structured, resulting in the social marginalisation of a vast section of the population. There were those who were low down in the caste hierarchy, those who were outside the system, which included the tribals and those professing other religions referred to by the derogatory term *Mlechchas*, and of course there were the women of all castes and creeds who were deemed to be no superior than the *Shudras*.

Even as details of the emergence of the caste system remain shrouded in obscurity, and different theoretical propositions compete for recognition, it may be said with a measure of certainty that, as per the dominant view, the system grew out of a process of conflict and interaction between the Aryan immigrants and the already existing non-Aryan inhabitants of the region. Needless to say, it was intended to structure socioeconomic relations to the convenience of the Aryan victors.

The Aryans are believed to have entered the region from the north west around 1500 BC. It appears that for centuries they remained in constant conflict with the indigenous people whom they shunned as culturally inferior and ritually unclean. Not long after the Aryans made an entry into the region, they composed the first *Rigvedic* hymns. It was probably some time between 1500 and 1200 BC. From then onwards, through the *Yajurveda, Samaveda* and *Atharvaveda*, the Aryans built up, step-by-step, an elaborate philosophical system, which by further consolidation, interpretations, additions and alterations through the *Sutras* and *Shastras* and a host of other literature gave birth to the brahminical system. The latter could well be described as "a system of ideas, beliefs and ritual practices associated with the social dominance of the brahmins, the class that has provided a fairly well-defined and coherent interpretation of normative social and religious behaviour and thought throughout the centuries."[1]

The *Vedas* are among the "holy books" of the Hindus. In a loose and broad sense the word *"vedas"* is popularly used to describe all "sacred" Hindu books including the *Brahmanas, Upanishads* and the traditional *Sutras*. One of the few essentially binding duties of a true Hindu is not to dispute their authority.[2] Conversely, any sect that denies the authority of the *Vedas* is, from the point of the orthodoxy, not fit to be called "Hindu".[3] Acknowledging the authority of the *Vedas,* as demanded by the orthodox Hindu, means in effect acknowledging the rank station of its leaders, the brahmins.[4]

The Hindu religious injunctions codified in the *Laws of Manu,* explicitly placed the injunction that a servant – that is one belonging to the *Shudra* category – was not to amass wealth even if he had the ability, since a servant who amasses wealth annoys the priests, i.e., the brahmins. The pursuit of knowledge, too, was placed beyond his reach. The only recommended activity for the servant was to serve the priest as whatever he did beyond that would bear him no fruit. It is these *Shudra* communities who formed the mass of the labour force working under conditions of intense social stigma and inhuman economic exploitation. Religious sanctions legitimised the exploitation and indignity. Their labour thus extracted helped in the sustenance of a numerically minuscule parasitic upper caste. The scriptures sanctioned their marginalisation, society endorsed it and implemented it.

Historically speaking, members of the untouchable castes were victims of perpetual brahminical oppression as they were stigmatised as polluting to the upper orders of society. They were relegated to perform demeaning tasks, socially humiliated, and educationally deprived, and all in the name of religion. Over and above all and subsuming all, they have been denied through generations the very basis of human rights – human dignity. Members of these castes were frequently abused, insulted, beaten up, and even massacred. It is they who form the core of India's dalit population.

Untouchability, as aptly observed by Robert Deliege, cannot be reduced to a question of ritual, nor could untouchables be regarded as merely necessary complements of brahmins.[5] The issue is indeed complex. Agreeing with Oommen,[6] Deliege would prefer to see the problem as one of "cumulative deprivation". Socioeconomic dependence, material poverty, social deprivation and lack of political power combine with ritual pollution to make untouchables a social category clearly set apart from the rest of society. Yet, they are not completely cut off from the rest of society. They are marginalised only up to a point as for many aspects of life they remain an integral part of Indian society. That is, they are "both outside and inside the system".[7]

Economics of the Caste Order

Even as concepts of purity and pollution occupied a very central position in caste ideology, the economic content of the system can hardly be missed. From its very early days the system had a clear economic content.

As Aryan society moved from nomadic pastoralism to a settled agrarian economy, specialisation of labour and crystallisation of the caste system came along with it, even though it is possible that the castes in the initial period may not have been hereditary.

The economics of the caste system becomes clearly evident if we note that, as per caste norms certain occupational functions were to be rightly performed by members of certain castes and not others. Brahmins were to teach, act as priests and occupy administrative positions under the state. *Kshatriyas* were to live by administration and the profession of arms. Agriculture, trade and pastoral pursuits were placed within the ambit of activities of the *Vaishyas* and the *Shudras* were to serve the three upper castes. It was the dirty work, unremunerative and involving hard physical labour, which was earmarked for the untouchables.

Serving the brahmin, learned in the *Vedas,* was depicted by Manu as the highest duty of the *Shudra*. If this duty was humbly and sincerely performed, the *Shudra* could attain highest status in the next life after his rebirth.[8] Whatever exists in the universe was deemed to be rightfully the wealth of the brahmin and he was entitled to take without hesitation the property of the *Shudra* for purposes of sacrifice, as the latter had no business with sacrifices.[9]

During the period of the *Dharmashastras*, the *Shudras* were socially subject to increasing degradation and it came to be clearly established that they were doomed to perpetual servitude. They were not to acquire wealth, attain education or learn the art of warfare. The noted Hindu grammarian, Patanjali had identified categories of *Shudras*. First, there were the *Shakas* and the *Yavanas* who resided outside the *Aryavarta*. Second, there were the *Chandalas* and the *Doms* living within the limits of the towns and villages of the Aryans though their food vessels could not be used by the latter even after purification. Third, there were groups such as the carpenters, washermen, blacksmiths and weavers whose food vessels could be used by the Aryans after appropriate cleansing though they could not be permitted to attend the sacrificial sessions and rituals. Fourth, by implication there were the Shudras, the specific illustrative groups being not named by Patanjali who could attend even sacrificial sessions and rituals. Fifth, there were those living outside the limits of the Aryan villages and towns.[10]

From a cursory glance at the above scheme it becomes more than obvious that the caste of a person, which was determined by birth, fixed his role in the social division of labour. It was decisive in determining whether the person would or would not participate in physical labour, have access to wealth and knowledge. It was decisive in determining whether a person would live off the surplus produced by the labour of others or whether he would have to live a mere hand-to-mouth existence while the surplus produced by him was unashamedly expropriated by others.[11] The economics of caste relations was clearly brought out by the noted historian, Irfan Habib in the following words:

> The menial castes were deprived of any pretension to setting up as tillers of land themselves, they could, therefore, form a vast reservoir of landless labour with exceptionally depressed wages. This would in turn correspondingly enlarge the surplus that the ruling class could derive from the peasant. At the same time that share in the surplus could obtain for the ruling class a larger return in terms of goods and services because of the larger productivity from 'special skill' transmitted through the system

of hereditary occupation while wages could be further depressed owing to the low station assigned to artisan castes.[12]

Maintenance of the Social Hierarchy

Hundreds of rules regulate inter-caste and intra-caste functioning. Interactional norms vary from caste to caste. Even for members of the same caste variations of locale spell differences. In addition are the constant adjustments necessitated by changing economic and technological factors.

Down the centuries there developed in India a unique system that is today known as the *jajmani* system. It is a system of complementary relationship between dominant castes on the one hand and the service and artisan castes on the other. In essence, it was based on the organisation of production and distribution around the institution of hereditary occupational castes, the non-agricultural castes being recompensed by traditionally determined fixed shares of the village produce.[13] The *jajmani* system ensured an adjustment between the brahmin's egoistic non-participation in the social economy and his beneficial integration to those groups that wielded effective power in society and controlled the collection and distribution of the available social wealth.[14] It was anything but a harmonious arrangement among the various castes.

It is possible that with the rise of the town-centric economic order brahmins started taking up residence in the towns and cities in order to get a share of social goods and powers of which the towns were becoming the most effective centres. It appears from the *Grhyasutra* passages that despite probably an initial resistance, they accepted the urban way of life making necessary adjustments as required. Along with it, and in keeping with it, brahmin theorists made more and more allowances for those of their caste who associated with urban trades and clientele.[15] Persistent attempts were made by the gift-seeking brahmins to revive the values of gift exchange in decaying towns by declaring them to be important *tirthas* and promoting religious journeys to those places.[16]

By the fifth century AD, the system of land grants became an integral feature of the rural economy. This, on the one hand, neutralised the effects of a reduced *jajmani* subsistence and on the other hand heralded the beginnings of a new basis of *jajmani* relationship between the ruling aristocracy and its priestly appendage.[17] The introduction of the *dana* system came to ensure for the brahmins a dependable and adaptive means of sustenance and effective sources of social authority.[18] Through *dana*, the *jajmana* could buy *punya* and the brahmin could obtain his sustenance. Greater the *punya* sought to be acquired, greater would the *dana* have to be; this in turn implied, greater would the earnings of the brahmin be !

Traditionally, maintenance of the system was the combined responsibility of the secular and religious authorities. Brahmin law writers took great pains to constantly theorise on social relationships and behaviour patterns to ensure their own position of superiority. Whilst the religious authorities pronounced on the norms and interpreted them, in the early period of Indian history as well as in the middle ages, the state authorities were in charge of ensuring their smooth continuance.[19] Manu, the great Hindu lawgiver, had enjoined that taking into account the laws of castes, districts, guilds and families, a king who knows justice should establish the particular law of each.[20] Enforcing *varnashrama dharma* was thus the basis of *rajdharma* ! The king was expected to ensure that the various castes observed the caste rules. He was expected to differentiate between different castes by means of appropriate marks of distinctions. While enacting a law he was to see that it was not at variance with the customs of castes and before settling disputes the king was obliged to look into the laws of castes.[21] Vasistha, quoted by A.T.M. Jackson in his *Note on the History of Caste System*, had laid down:

> Let the King, paying attention to all the laws of the countries, castes and families, make the four Varna fulfil their particular duties. Let him punish those who stray.[22]

It is significant to note that the *Manusmrti* emphasised at length the necessity of alliance between the brahmins and *Kshatriyas* but, in the course of it, was careful to remind that the brahmin must always stand as the superior partner.[23]

It may be stressed that during the medieval period, temples functioned as the principal power centres alongside the palaces from where the kings reigned. Throughout the period, the alliance forming a social bloc was dominant in terms of religious, intellectual and political authority and leadership. [24]

Both overt and covert violence went into the maintenance of the system. Imposition of fines, social ostracism and even physical violence, legitimised by social sanction, were not uncommon. Digression from the stipulated norms called forth a host of penalties depending on the caste of the digresser and the nature of the offence. Needless to say, when the offender hailed from the lower ranks of society the penalties were much harsher than when the violator hailed from the upper castes. According to Kautilya, a *Shudra* who dared to call himself a brahmin was to have his eyes destroyed by poison or be made to pay a heavy fine of eight hundred "panas". If he violated a female he was to be burnt to death, whereas, if he criminally assaulted a brahmin, the offending limb would be cut off.[25] These are just a few of the many types of harsh penalties that could be imposed on the *Shudras*. The leniency in dealing with the brahmin is equally perceptible. The killing of a *Shudra* by a brahmin was, for example, to be viewed as no more serious than the killing of a cat, a mongoose, a frog, a dog, a lizard, an owl or a crow.[26]

All-powerful caste *panchayats* at the local level acted as regulators of the functioning of the caste groups and the repositories of caste values. In fact, traditionally, castes were kept in their place by a combination of factors such as religious and moral sanctions, division of labour, kinship affiliations, physical force and political authority.[27]

As of the continuance of the caste system, the noted historian Romila Thapar noted:

> The continuance of caste was secured by its being made hereditary: the primitive taboo on commensality (eating together) became a caste law, and this in turn made it necessary to define marriage limits, leading to elaborate rules of endogamy and exogamy. The basis and continuance of the caste system depended not on the four fold division but on the vast network of sub-castes, which was intimately connected with occupation.[28]

While the social barriers had begun to harden by the Maurya period, even during the time of the Guptas the regulations were by no means rigid.[29] It was only in the late medieval period that exogamy and inter-dining became impossible.[30]

Understanding Caste

The process of evolution of the caste system has been a long and complex one. Originating probably as the four *varnas,* today, several thousand groups claim caste status. For all practical purposes the numerous existing sub-castes or *jatis* today reveal the characteristics of caste groups. Thus, while the *varnas* remain relevant in terms of academic interest, contemporary reality tends to revolve around the *jati* system. In tune with such dictates of social reality, the term caste is hence widely used to include those groups, which technically speaking should be referred to simply as "sub-castes".

There have been quite a few attempts undertaken by scholars at classification of the caste system. While we shall not go into the details of the varied classifications attempted, we shall here refer to the classification of Moffatt,[31] in view of its importance in terms of attempting to incorporate the phenomenon of untouchability. Moffatt's model is largely appreciated by Deliege.[32] Moffatt distinguishes three types of approaches to untouchability. He terms them as the outcaste model, model of diversity and model of unity. The first two emphasise the separation or disjunction between the untouchables and others. The difference between the outcaste model and those of the model of diversity is, in Moffatt's assessment, slight. Whilst the first stresses the untouchables' lack of a separate culture and their exclusion from the dominant culture, the second regard untouchables as bearers of an "alternative culture". The third model, to which Moffatt himself largely subscribes, emphasises "conjunction" – the consensus that unites untouchables with Indian society at large.[33]

British Colonial Rulers and the Indian Social System

The initial British policy on assumption of power in India had by and large been one of non-interference in the internal affairs pertaining to Indian society. They intervened only when and to the extent that Indian customs and institutions conflicted with imperial interests and ideas of governance. Beyond that they were not interested in intervening. This was all the more true of the caste system. Nonetheless, over the years British imperial policy had multiple ramifications that affected and transformed the caste system in a variety of ways. In many respects, the interventions of British policy even when indirect, were significant.[34]

With the passage of time, British policy came to impact on the "citadels of caste". As the British courts were set up and an uniform criminal law sought to be administered, many matters that were till then considered to be within the purview of caste and the caste *panchayats* were removed from such purview. Thus, questions of assault, adultery, rape, etc. were taken up by the British courts and to that extent the caste councils lost their former independence.[35]

In British India, in the nineteenth century, increasingly rule-by-contract came to be replaced by rule-by-status.[36] Rule-by-contract operated as a pyramid, with the East India Company at the apex and the myriad "little republics" of village communities at the base. Rule-by-status, by contrast, operated as an inverted pyramid, with the individual at the nadir, identified by his caste, and "India", the sum of all castes, at the top, governable because the individual himself was known to be governed by the laws, customs and rules accorded his status.[37]

At the time of the first census in 1871–72 itself, attempts were made by the British authorities to collect caste data – an exercise that was further developed through the subsequent census operations. During the 1901 census, the British authorities in India had attempted to settle the rank ordering of the then existing castes. The attempt, which at the time stirred up a hornet's nest was not repeated thereafter.[38]

To the British officials, religion and caste were the keys to understanding Indian society and the Indian people – essential tools for effective governance. Not unexpectedly, most of the basic works on the Indian caste system written between 1880–1950 were by persons who had held important administrative positions in relation to the census operations. It was rightly noted by G.S. Ghurye and several other leading analysts of Indian society that the census operations launched by the British authorities had an impact on the caste system, affecting caste consciousness and opening the doors for the use of the census for validation of claims to new status within the caste system.[39]

It is pertinent to note that with the introduction of railways and modern industries, new relations of production came into being. These were incompatible with the hereditary divisions of labour, the basis of the castes. Caste, in order to survive, had to adapt itself to these new realities. At the same time, the imperial interest of procuring cheap labour and raw material necessitated the continuance of pre-capitalist extra economic forms of surplus extraction and the caste system was conducive to such extraction.[40]

Towards the close of the colonial period, the possibilities of transfer of power set in motion a chain process of hard bargaining. By then, the untouchables had found in Ambedkar a powerful champion of their interests. Their political activism of the period earned for the lesser castes the identity of "Depressed Classes" and the constitutional recognition of a variety of rights and safeguards.

Caste and Indian Democracy

As India attained independence, under her newly framed constitutional system, the promises of justice, liberty and equality were upheld. The Preamble to the Constitution spoke of it all. The chapter on Fundamental Rights, largely reflected the values of the Universal Declaration of Human Rights. Citizens were equal before the law and assured equal protection of the law (Article 14). Alongside, the principles of non-discrimination were espoused (Articles 15 and 16). And, the obnoxious practice of untouchabilty was prohibited (Article 17).

Side by side, the Constitution recognised the need to extend special support to the socially marginalised sections. As such, provisions for positive discrimination for certain backward sections of the population were incorporated; not to be seen as contraventions but as supportive of the overall principle of equality. Among those identified for special attention are the Scheduled Castes, the Scheduled Tribes and the socially and educationally backward classes.

The President's Constitution (Scheduled Castes) Order No. 19 of 1950 identified the castes that were to be considered as Scheduled Castes. While it was originally decided that "no person who professes a religion different from the Hindu religion shall be deemed to be a member of a Scheduled Caste", an amendment of 1956 included the Sikhs and another later in 1990 incorporated the Buddhists.

The measures that the Scheduled Caste members or those of the formerly called untouchable castes were assured of were primarily of three types. First, a system of "reservations" for members of these communities in legislative bodies, in government-run and government-aided educational bodies and in employment; second, a set of measures involving financial support from the state in the form of loans, scholarships, land grants, etc; and third, a number of special measures undertaken by the state in the form of campaigns against untouchability, special steps to free bonded labour, etc.

In accordance with these constitutional provisions a number of measures have been initiated by the government for providing protection to untouchables (Scheduled Castes). These measures are both protective and developmental. In the "protective" sphere untouchability was legally abolished and its practice in any form forbidden by the Protection of Civil Rights (Anti-Untouchability) Act of 1955.

Nearly two decades later, protections for the Scheduled Castes were reviewed to make them more stringent and effective in the Bonded Labour (Abolition) Act 1976. In 1989, the Government enacted yet another Act, namely the Scheduled Castes and Scheduled Tribes (Prevention of Atrocities) Act in order to prevent continued atrocities against the Scheduled Castes and Scheduled Tribes. The need for this additional Act was felt because under the circumstances, PCR 1955 and normal provisions of the Indian Penal

Code had been found to be inadequate to provide safeguards to Scheduled Castes and Scheduled Tribes against several crimes.[41]

By the end of the 1980s, a measure of improvement became quite evident in different respects. Parliamentary democratic institutions, reservations in legislatures, educational institutions and jobs, impact of socialist ideas and the Mandal Commission Report all created conditions for greater dalit assertion. Over and above all, the democratic political empowerment of the low castes and the power of the "vote" as it may be referred to in summary form, undoubtedly had an impact on Indian society.

At the time when India attained independence, India's national politics, not unexpectedly, was dominated by urban politicians well-versed in English and trained in law. Most of these leaders during the fifties hailed from upper caste backgrounds and many had been trained abroad. At the level of state and local politics even as a "vernacular" elite and agrarian domination was apparent, the political leadership tended to come from the upper castes at least in northern India. In southern India, however, the picture was somewhat different as by the fifties the politicians were drawn increasingly from the lower castes.[42] In 1957, for the first time the Communist Party came to power in Kerala primarily resting on *Ezhava* support. The *Ezhavas* were basically a low caste, toddy-tapping community engaged in the production of indigenous liquor. In the 1960s the Dravida Munnetra Kazagham (DMK) came to power in Tamil Nadu as an anti-brahmin party. By the 1950s and 1960s in southern India the low castes had already developed their own leaders and parties, while by contrast in the northern region of the country the model of mobilisation was top down with the lower castes dependent on the upper castes in a clientelistic relationship.[43] In the 1980s and 1990s northern India, too, saw the rise of a low caste political elite. Repeatedly the names of Laloo Prasad Yadav, Kanshi Ram and Mayawati made news.[44] The political relevance of the low castes was not confined to the states but affected national level politics as well. Between 1989 and 1991 and again between 1996 and 1998 Delhi had primarily low caste coalitions in power.[45] The fact was that the relevance of the lower castes and their concerns had started to make a dent in

Indian politics. But then, to what extent was the overall human rights situation of the dalit population changing, or was it changing at all?

Notes

1. "Introduction", Ainslie T. Embree ed., *Sources of Indian Tradition,* Penguin, New Delhi, 1992,Vol. 1, p. 3.
2. Max Weber, *The Religion of India, The Sociology of Hinduism and Buddhism,* translated by Hans H. Gerth and Don Martindale, The Free Press, Illinois, 1960, p. 26.
3. Ibid.
4. Ibid.
5. R. Deliege, *The Untouchables of India*, Berg Publishers, Oxford, 1999, Translated from the original French by Nora Scott.
6. T.K. Oommen, "Sources of Deprivation and Styles of Protest: The Case of the Dalits in India", *Contributions to Indian Sociology,* (NS) 18, 1984, p. 46. cited in R. Deliege, ibid., p. 7.
7. R. Deliege, op. cit.
8. *Laws of Manu*, translated by Buhler, IX, pp. 334–5.
9. Ibid., p. 13.
10. G.S. Ghurye, *Caste and Race in India*, Popular Prakashan, Bombay, 1969, p. 88.
11. Debi Chatterjee, *Sociology of National Integration,* Minerva Associates, Calcutta, 1993, p. 29.
12. Irfan Habib, "Theories of Social Change in South Asia", *The Journal of Social Studies*, 33, 1986, pp. 34–54.
13. Tapan Roychaudhuri, "The Mid-eighteenth Century Background", Dharma Kumar ed., *The Cambridge Economic History of India*, Orient Longman, New Delhi, 1991, p. 21.
14. Ramendra Nath Nandi, *Social Roots of Religion in Ancient India,* K.P. Bagchi, Calcutta, p. 4.
15. Ibid., pp. 8–9.
16. Ibid., p. 12.

17. Ibid.
18. Ibid.
19. J.H. Hutton, *Caste in India,* Oxford University Press, 1983, p. 47.
20. See Debi Chatterjee, *Sociology of National Integration*, Minerva Associates, Calcutta, 1993.
21. G.S. Ghurye, *Caste and Race in India,* Popular Prakashan, Bombay, 1969, p. 95.
22. Cited in J.H. Hutton, op. cit., p. 93.
23. Ramendra Nath Nandi, *Social Roots of Religion in Ancient India,* K.P. Bagchi, Calcutta, pp. 5–6.
24. S. Selvam, "Sociology of India and Hinduism", S.M. Michael ed., *Dalits in Modern India: Vision and Values,* Vistaar, New Delhi, 1999, pp. 180–1.
25. Kautilya, *Arthashastra,* translated by R. Shamasastry, 1915, pp. 238, 275–6, 285.
26. *Laws of Manu* (tr. By Buhler) IX.
27. G.S. Ghurye, op. cit., p. 88.
28. Romila Thapar, *A History of India,* Vol. 1, Penguin, London, 1986, p. 40.
29. A.L. Basham, *The Wonder That Was India,* Rupa, New Delhi, 1994, p. 149.
30. Ibid.
31. M. Moffatt, *An Untouchable Community in South India: Structure and Consensus,* Princeton University Press, Princeton, 1979.
32. R. Deliege, op. cit.
33. Ibid., p. 29.
34. Debi Chatterjee, *Sociology of National Integration*, Minerva Associates, Calcutta, 1993, p. 32.
35. G.S. Ghurye, *Caste and Race in India*, Popular Prakashan, Bombay, 1969, p. 271.
36. Richard Saumarez Smith, 'From Village to Community", Ishita Banerjee-Dube ed., *Caste in History,* Oxford University Press, New Delhi, 2008, p. 67.

37. Ibid.
38. Max Weber, *The Religion of India, The Sociology of Hinduism and Buddhism,* translated by Hans H. Gerth and Don Martindale, The Free Press, Illinois, 1960, p. 47.
39. Bernard S. Cohn, "The Census, Social Structure and Objectification in South Asia", Ishita Banerjee-Dube ed., op. cit., pp. 30–1.
40. Debi Chatterjee, op. cit., p. 32.
41. http://www.indiatogether.org/combatlaw/issue4/hinduorder.htm
42. Ashutosh Varshney, "Is India Becoming More Democratic?", *The Journal of Asian Studies,* Vol. 59, No. 1, February 2000.
43. Ibid.
44. Ibid.
45. Ibid.

Chapter 3

Dalits in Contemporary India

Who is a Dalit?

"Dalit" has come to mean things or persons who are cut, split, broken or torn asunder, scattered or crushed and destroyed. The great Marathi social reformer and revolutionary, Mahatma Jyotirao Phule (1826–1890), used it to describe the outcastes and untouchables, the oppressed and victims of India's caste ridden society. The word "Dalit" was used in the 1930s as a Hindi and Marathi translation of "Depressed Classes", the term that was used by the British to refer to the untouchable castes. In 1930, there was a depressed classes newspaper being published from Pune called *Dalit Bandhu* (Friend of Dalits).[1] Under the leadership of B.R. Ambedkar (1891–1956), this term gained greater importance and popularity as he used it in his Marathi speeches.

During the 1970s, the followers of the Dalit Panther Movement of Maharashtra gave currency to the term "dalit" as a constant reminder of their age-old oppression, denoting their state of deprivation. For the people concerned, the term is not merely a name or title: for them it has become an expression of hope, the hope of recovering their identity. The term has gained a new connotation with a more positive meaning. It must be remembered that dalit does not mean caste or low-caste or poor; it refers to the deplorable state or condition to which a large group of people has been reduced by social convention and in which they are now living.[2]

The dalits have been called by different names at different times and in different parts of the country. Most of these names were attributed to them by the caste Hindus as expressions of contempt. They include: *Dasa, Dasyees, Raksasa, Asura, Avarna, Nisada, Panchama, Chandala,* Harijan, Untouchable. Each of the names has a history and background. These names carry within them the two-term contrast of "we – the pure" and "you – the impure". In response to these insulting labels, the untouchables have chosen to give themselves a name and this is "dalit", which refers to the hardship of their condition of life. If today the dalits are reduced to a life of abject poverty and treated as polluted human beings, it is the non-dalit that must be seen as the agent of their dehumanisation. By the British, the dalits were named "the Depressed Classes" and "the Scheduled Castes", in the Scheduled Caste Act of India, 1935. Gandhi named them *"Harijans"*, which means "children of God": but this term was not welcomed by the dalits because it did not adequately describe their condition,[3] and had in fact derogatory connotations.

It would be wrong to think that today those who are known as dalits are themselves equally content with the "dalit" nomenclature. While some are, some are not so satisfied. The latter are mostly those who belong to the Buddhist religious frame. Rather than being called dalit, they prefer to identify themselves simply as Buddhists. They passionately put forward their arguments in favour of a "Buddhist" rather than a "dalit" identity. Such a position, of course, has its problems. Whether it irks the dalit Buddhists or not, the fact of the matter is that all dalits (the term is being used in the absence of any other suitable term), are not Buddhists. In fact, as of now, only a minority of the dalits are Buddhists. Even if for the sake of argument it is conceded that dalits' conversion to Buddhism is desirable (it may, or may not be), to refer to those who are not Buddhists as Buddhists is factually wrong.

Untouchability in History

It may be noted that, in the *Vajasaneyi Samhita,* composed around the tenth century BC, the words *Chandala* and *Paulkasa* can be found. However, there was an indication to suggest that they were untouchables.[4] In the *Chhandogya Upanishad* it was stated that, persons whose actions were low, will quickly attain an evil birth, the birth of a dog, or a hog or a chandala.[5]

The origin of the *chandalas* was sought to be explained for the first time in the *Gautama Dharma Sutra*. There, the chandala was described as the offspring of a male *Shudra* and brahmin woman and the worst of pratiloma relations. Gautama referred to the pratiloma castes as dharmahina or devoid of religion.[6]

Apastamba Dharma Sutra prescribed that after touching a chandala one should plunge into water, on talking to him one should converse with a *Brahmana*, and on seeing him one should look at the luminaries of the sky such as the sun, moon or stars.[7] The *Sutras* were composed around the sixth century BC.

In the *Manusmrti* that was composed sometime between the second century BC and the second century AD, it was ruled that the chandalas and the shvapakas should live outside the village.[8] It was further stated by Manu that an *antyavasayin* should be employed in a cemetery.[9] In the *Parashara Smrti* it has been opined that if a chandala or a dog touches a twice-born person while taking his food, the rest of the food should be abandoned.[10] If a brahmin drinks water from a well touched by a chandala, Parashara stated, he should take barley water prepared in the urine of a cow for three days.[11] There were elaborate instructions in the *Parashara Smrti* on what should be done in the event of pollution of a house by the entry of a chandala. The house would have to be washed with water mixed with cow dung; the earthenware should be thrown away; family members as well as the servants of the house should bathe thrice a day and take curd with cow urine for three days; barley water with cow urine for the next three days, milk with cow urine for the next three days, then he should take all these things for one day each. Thus, the purification regimen was of twelve days. Bronze and bell metal utensils would have to be cleaned with ashes; the *kusunbha, guda,* cotton, salt, oil and ghee would have to be burnt outside the house, followed by a feast of 21 Brahmins and a gift of 20 cows and one bull to them.[12] Identical measures have been recommended if a washerwoman, a shoemaker's wife, a hunter's wife or a bamboo worker's wife live in the house. All of these castes were deemed to be untouchable and said to cause pollution according to Parashara.[13]

Narada called the *Shvapaka, Meda* and *Chandala, mala* or human waste and stated that they should be punished with corporal punishment and not with fines, since a fine from them would be unacceptable as even their wealth happens to be impure.[14]

The above is simply a cursory view of the behaviour that the brahminical society recommended be meted out in relation to the untouchable. It amply demonstrates how over the years, and not just in the context of a single scriptural text, untouchability was built into the rubric of Hindu society.

Scholars have presented diverse analyses of the emergence of untouchability in the region. J.H. Hutton, the eminent anthropologist, located the origin of caste in the taboos and division of labour in the pre-Aryan tribes of India as well as in their efforts at self-preservation in the face of invasion. Untouchability, according to him, was the result of ritual impurity. To put it in his own words, "the origin of the position of the exterior castes is partly racial, partly religious, and partly a matter of social custom. There can be little doubt that the idea of untouchability originates in taboo".[15] Another noted anthropologist, Christoph von Furer-Haimendorf, presented an altogether different angle. He located untouchability in terms of urban development and the rise of unclean and ritually impure occupations. Emerging in the urban and semi-urban settlements, according to him, the practice spread to the villages.[16]

Protecting the Dalits: Legal Safeguards

The Preamble to the Indian Constitution assures the people of the country justice, liberty, equality and fraternity. But, given the fact that traditionally Indian society had been essentially inegalitarian marked by stark injustice and lack of liberty and fraternal feelings, where social exclusion adversely affected the low stigmatised castes, it was agreed that unequals would first have to be brought up to a position of equality, before they could be treated as equals to the others. The point had been repeatedly emphasised by Ambedkar as member of the Constituent Assembly and Chairman of the drafting committee of the Constitution. With dogged persistence, he had fought for the incorporation of the special rights for the depressed sections of the society in the Constitution. His efforts were fruitful to the extent that measures for compensatory discrimination were embodied in the Constitution to uplift, among others, the untouchable castes. These castes, members of which were identified for the benefits, came to be referred to as the Scheduled Castes, the names being listed in a "Schedule".

It is important to note that the term Scheduled Castes had been coined by the Simon Commission. It had been embodied in the Government of India Act of 1935 and the first listing of the untouchable castes in a "Schedule" came about in 1936 in order to give effect to the provisions of the 1935 Government of India Act.

Identification of the untouchables for purposes of listing in the "Schedule" was, however, not an easy task. It posed difficulties from various angles. The many dimensions of the problem had come up for discussion in the pre-independence days in the points raised before the Indian Franchise (Lothian) Committee. The majority of the members of the Committee felt that denial of access to temples, causing pollution by touch or approach were the "generally accepted tests of untouchability". The Committee reiterated its conviction that the depressed classes should include only untouchables and not "those Hindus who are only economically poor and in other ways backward but not regarded as untouchables".[17] The Franchise Committee (1918–19) recommended nomination from the depressed classes to the Provincial Councils. The Act of 1919 accepted the recommendations but leaders of the depressed classes were not satisfied with mere nominations; many continued to demand separate electorates.[18]

Based on the framework of the Constitution, an elaborate legal network of special assistance for the members of the Scheduled Castes has come into existence. At its core has remained the provision of "reservations". Controversies, however, have plagued the "reservations" from the very beginning. Needless to say, the criticisms come from the powerful upper caste lobby that had traditionally been enjoying disproportionate advantages made possible by the hierarchical structuring of society. Critics have tended to emphasise what they believe to be the costs of the positive discrimination policies. They point out that, such policies tend to lead to an increase in caste differences, compromise on merit and thereby adversely affect quality of work, and lead to sense of devaluation of the beneficiaries. The identified benefits revolve around aims at countering the marginalisation of the dalits and facilitating the greater integration of these people into the services and elite professions, ensure a spread of social capital, motivate the dalits to aspire for advancement and serve the purpose of redistribution of resources and opportunities.[19]

It is pertinent to remember that caste-based reservations rest on the wider logic of social justice and democracy, where "reservation" policy acts as one of the tools of countering the age-old exclusion of the dalits. It suggests a conscious and deliberate effort to restructure the social order in a manner whereby those of the traditionally marginalised groups get adequate opportunities to realise their potential and get their due share of resources. These reservations are thus to be seen not as ends in themselves, but rather as a set of means to achieving a just and democratic society.

Even as the existence of social exclusion is widely recognised and the need for correctives in the form of public interventions acknowledged at least professedly by many, the criticisms against reservations remain loud. As a matter of fact, in such a milieu other forms of affirmative action have now and then been spoken of. Sophisticated techniques highlighting more complex deprivation index incorporating a range of criteria for which differences in access to facilities exist, rather than focussing only on caste, have been suggested.[20] However, it must be conceded that as attempts are made to incorporate a variety of criteria, the system tends to become very complex, costly and uncertain in terms of outcome.[21]

Dalit Woes: Tales of Marginalisation and Violence

In 2001, dalits made up around 16 per cent of India's population. A mere glance at the statistical evidence pertaining to their economic and educational conditions as it has prevailed over the years reveals the extent of their exclusion and the odds under which they have to labour. Table 1 given below demonstrates the general occupational pattern of the Scheduled Castes as compared to others, revealing their overall deprivation. Two-thirds of the dalit population is still illiterate, 75 per cent live below the poverty line; only 7 per cent have access to safe drinking water, electricity and toilets. In India, among the millions of bonded labourers – estimates ranging from 20 to 65 million in 2001 – 85 per cent are dalits or from low castes and these include a large number of children. Many are engaged in traditional occupations such as flaying and scavenging.[22]

Table 1

Occupational Pattern: Scheduled Castes and Others

(in percentage)

Occupational Category	*1987–88*		*1993–94*		*1999–00*	
	SC	*Other*	*SC*	*Other*	*SC*	*Other*
		Rural				
Self-Employed in Agriculture	18.90	43.3	19.12	42.42	16.4	41.1
Self-Employed in Non-Agriculture	11.0	13.8	10.32	3.89	12.0	14.8
Self-Employed (Total)	29.8	57.1	29.49	56.3	28.4	55.9
Agricultural Wage Labour	51.7	23.2	50.6	22.37	51.4	19.0
Non-Agricultural Wage Labour	11.4	09.7	10.22	6.67	10.0	6.3
Rural Wage Labour (Total)	63.1	31.1	60.28	29.14	61.4	25.3
Others	06.9	11.5	9.67	14.62	10.2	18.7
		Urban				
Self-Employed	28.0	35.2	24.08	35.05	27.3	35.5
Regular Wage/Salaries	39.4	45.0	39.27	43.11	37.6	46.5
Casual Labour	26.0	10.3	26.96	10.57	26.5	7.4
Others wage	08.5	09.2	9.67	11.25	8.5	10.5

Source: NSS survey data cited in Sukhadeo Thorat, *Economic Exclusion and Poverty*, p. 18, http://www.ifpri.org/2020ChinaConference/pdf/ manilac_Thorat.pdf

Judged by all social indicators, dalits are clearly in disadvantageous positions in comparison to the general population. Upper caste Hindus still dominate the entire range of public institutions, the skilled professions and the media. Their overwhelming presence in major areas of decision-making tend to reinforce upper caste monopoly and perpetrate the overall exclusion of the dalit population. This exclusion becomes evident if we note the following facts. In 2000, of the total Scheduled Caste households in rural areas, about 17 per cent pursued cultivation as an independent (self-employed) occupation. About 12 per cent were employed in some kind of non-farm self-employment activities (or business). In rural areas thus, about 28 per cent of SC households had acquired some access to fixed capital assets, (agricultural land and non-land asset). This was still a very low proportion compared with 56 per cent for other households (non-SC/ST households). In urban areas also as compared to other households (35.5 per cent), the access to capital assets by SCs was low (27 per cent).

Inadequate access to fixed capital assets leads to exceptionally high dependence of the SC household on manual wage labour. In 2000, the wage labour household account was 61.40 per cent of all SC households in rural areas and 26 per cent in urban areas, compared to 25.50 per cent and 7.45 per cent for other households. In urban areas 38 per cent of SC households also depend on regular wage and salaried jobs. Thus, about 62 per cent of the SC household in rural and 63 per cent in urban areas continued to depend on wage employment and only about 28 per cent had acquired some access to fixed capital assets. Even those who have acquired access to fixed capital assets, are mostly small and marginal farmers and petty business holders.[23] With high incidence of wage labour associated with high rate of underemployment and low wage earning, the SCs household suffer from low income, and high incidences of poverty. This is reflected in the proportion of persons falling below a critical minimum level of consumption expenditure, what is called the poverty line. In 1999–2000 about 35.43 per cent of SC population were below the poverty line in rural areas as compared to 21 per cent among others; in urban areas the gap was slightly larger, 39 per cent of SC and only 15 per cent among others.[24]

Analysing data from the 38 (1983), 50 (1993–94) and 55 (1999–2000) rounds of the National Sample Survey, S. Madheswaran and Paul Attewell noted that, "though the occupational placement of caste groups varies across India, a common feature is the sharp contrast in status and income between Scheduled Castes (SCs) and Scheduled Tribes (STs) on the one hand, and so-called forward castes on the other".[25] The main conclusions reached were that (i) discrimination causes 15 per cent lower wages for the Scheduled Castes and Scheduled Tribes compared to equally qualified others, (ii) Scheduled Castes and Scheduled Tribes are discriminated against in both the public and private sectors, but the discrimination effect is much larger in the private sector, and (iii) discrimination accounts for a large part of the gross earnings difference between the two social groups in the regular salaried urban labour market, with occupational discrimination (unequal access to jobs) being considerably more important than wage discrimination (unequal pay in the same job).[26]

Data pertaining to ownership of agricultural land by the Scheduled Castes in rural areas provide some insights. There is low proportion of self-employed cultivators among the SC households in rural areas. In 1991 about 13 per cent of SC households were landless and 87 per cent owned some land. Among the latter (that is, land-owning households), about 56 per cent owned less than one acre (of which 47.50 per cent owned less than half acre). Thus, the landless and near landless (that is those owning less than one acre) accounted for nearly 70 per cent of the total SC households in 1991. Evidence of a more recent year, 1999–2000 from alternative sources namely NSS Employment Survey puts the figures of landless and near land less among the SCs in the vicinity of 75 per cent.[27]

It is estimated that, even today, every two hours, two dalits are assaulted, everyday three dalit women are raped and two dalits are killed. The 2005 annual report of the National Crime Records Bureau reported a total of 26,127 cases – 8,497 cases under the Protection of Civil Rights Act and 291 cases under the SC/ST (Prevention of Atrocities) Act of 1989 (Atrocities Act) – for crimes against the Scheduled Castes. Although the average charge sheeting rate for the crimes against the Scheduled Castes was 94.1 per cent, the average conviction rate was only 29.8 per cent. A total of 46,936 persons (82.4%) out of 57,804 persons arrested for crimes committed against Scheduled Castes were charge sheeted but only 28.3 per cent were convicted consisting of 12,691 persons out of 44,842 persons against whom trials were completed.[28] As the dalits assert the rights, they face increased violence. But their complaints are seldom registered. The enactment of the SC/ST Act in 1989 became necessary after the earlier Civil Rights Act was found to be ineffective. The purpose behind this specific legislation to give greater protection to dalits has been neutralised by the police and judicial machinery by not applying the empowering sections of the law when such crimes are committed. Institutionalised bias (casteism and communalism) prejudices the criminal justice system against dalits and the religious minorities further. A report of the Home Ministry that between 2000–2001 there was a 16.5 per cent rise in reported rape cases was alarming.[29] Table 2 below gives an overview of the enormous magnitude of the human rights violations to which the dalit are subjected to.

Table 2

Incidence of Crime Against Scheduled Castes During 1998 to 2001

Crime Head	*1998*	*1999*	*2000*	*2001*
Murder	516	506	526	763
Rape	923	1000	1083	1136
Kidnapping and abduction	253	228	268	400
Dacoity	49	36	38	41
Robbery	150	109	108	133
Arson	346	337	290	354
Hurt	3809	3241	3497	4547
Against protection of civil rights	724	678	672	633
Crimes under POA Act	7443	7301	7386	13,113
Other crimes	11425	11657	11587	12201
Total	25638	25093	25455	33321

Source: Crime in India, 2000, National Crime Records Bureau, Ministry of Home Affairs, New Delhi, 2003, cited in Prakash Louis, "India Untouched: A Discursive Discourse from Dalit Perspective", *Voice of Dalit,* Vol. 1, No. 1, 2008, p. 5.

The National Commission for Scheduled Castes and Scheduled Tribes in its report in 2004 analysed the violence against Scheduled Castes and Scheduled Tribes between 1997 and 2001, as published by the National Crime Record Bureau under the Ministry of Home Affairs. It shows that between 1997 and 2001, 1,27,933 atrocities against Scheduled Castes were committed which gives an average figure of 25,587 per year.[30]

The extent of violence perpetrated against the dalit population and the dismal record of convictions in such cases will be clearly visible from Table 3 given below:

Table 3

Cases Registered for Various Crimes on Scheduled Castes and Scheduled Tribes

Total Cases	8,029	115,878	116,131
Cases Disposed	—	8,673 (7.5)	12,956 (11.2)
Convictions	125 (1.6)	700 (0.6)	982 (0.9)
Acquitals	1,367 (17.0)	7,420 (6.4)	11,605 (10.0)
Cases Pending	6,537 (81.4)	107,204 (92.5)	100,891 (86.9)

Note: Figures in brackets give the percentages.

Source: National Commission for Scheduled Castes and Scheduled Tribes, Reports, 1991, 1999–2000, 2000–2001.

N.D. Kamble, in his book *The Scheduled Castes*, gives a rather lengthy and horrifying list of the different kinds of atrocities to which the people of the untouchable communities are subject to across the country. They include:

(i) locking up families in their homes and then setting the house on fire;

(ii) burning alive these people either individually or collectively;

(iii) murdering on ground of untouchability;

(iv) sacrificing them in the name of the Hindu deities;

(v) setting houses on fire;

(vi) stripping women naked, beating them, violating their modesty, parading them naked in broad daylight through the village and raping them;

(vii) throwing excreta into their drinking water wells;

(viii) belabouring and threatening them with death;

(ix) destroying the standing crops in their fields;

(x) compelling them to perform duties laid down by tradition that are against their interests; and

(xi) preventing them from exercising rights as citizens and compelling them to refrain from exercising individual freedom, denying them access to eating houses, public drinking water wells, obstructing their marriage and other processions, denying them access to temples, etc.[31]

The scenario as it exists in Tamil Nadu is worth noting as an example of the varied and multiple manifestations of the continued prevalence of the practice of untouchability. Its vivid depiction is as follows:

> In Tamilnadu, the old *paraceri* where the Paraiyars have to live has always been built away from the *ur*, the main quarter of the village where high castes as well as 'backward castes' (another denomination for OBCs) reside. Worse, even the new 'colonies' (the local modern euphemism for dalit quarters) built up by the government for Scheduled Castes are still generally erected apart.
>
> Temple entry is still prohibited in the *ur* for the *ceri* dwellers, and the age-old compulsions concerning funerals and rituals calling for the *paraimelam* (the 'Pariah orchestra') are still expected to be fulfilled. Tea stalls and *arak* shops do serve dalit patrons, but usually keep two sets of glasses so that Untouchables may not 'pollute' the glasses used by others. Despite recent changes, the usual perception of dalits amongst high castes and even backward classes remains derogatory: ... *Paraiyars* continue to be stereotyped as ritually impure, 'uncivilised,' uncultured, unsophisticated and quarrelsome. Mixed marriages of dalits with other castes are rare in town.
>
> They would not be accepted in the villages. The socioeconomic status of most dalits is still very depressed. Most of them (72 per cent) are landless agricultural laborers. Dalits account for 23 per cent of the rural population in Tamilnadu, but own only 7 per cent of the land, ...

> Besides raw brutality and open murders, one must not forget the silent violence of everyday life, the violence of poverty, debt and bondage, the violence of discrimination, the humiliation Dalit men, women, and children experience.[32]

Needless to say, the picture is similar, if not identical, in many other parts of the country.

In the report of the Commissioner of SC/ST in 1988 (28th Report) the Commissioner attributed the violence related to dalits to three causative factors. One, unresolved land disputes related to allotment of government lands or distribution of ceiling surplus lands to SC/ST persons. Two, tension and bitterness on account of non-payment or underpayment of prescribed minimum wages. Three, resentment of upper castes over the manifestation of awareness among the SCs and STs about their rights and privileges as enshrined in the Constitution and various other laws relating to their welfare.[33]

Caste-based fragmentation has been one of the major problems of the untouchables. Untouchables could have wielded far greater political weight had they formed a homogeneous group. Unfortunately however, they have remained split into hundreds of groups scattered across the country.[34] There is no single organisation that could be said to truly represent all the groups. At most organisations are able to barely bring together two or three castes, not more.

Dalits in a Globalising World

Needless to say, today, globalisation has generated new threats for the already marginalised dalits. As it is, the world over, it has been noticed that the processes of globalisation have led to rising disparities between the rich and the poor, with the latter becoming increasingly impoverished and marginalised.

In India, as we are well aware, dalits are among the weakest sections of the population. They had traditionally suffered centuries of socioeconomic exclusion because of their caste. Their percentages in terms of being below the poverty line as also in terms of illiteracy are still far higher than the rest of the population. As such, their susceptibility to the adverse impact of globalisation is also undoubtedly much greater. They are among the most vulnerable. And, it is feared that with increasing emphasis on privatisation and the growing discrimination against the rural, agricultural and informal sectors, the socioeconomic exclusion of the dalits is all set to be reinforced.

The simultaneous abdication by the state of its responsibilities in the social sector especially in areas of health, education and provision of food security, and the adoption of economic policies that have increased unemployment in the formal sector and aggravated job insecurity in the informal sector have led to an acute crises in the field of subsistence agriculture and intensified commercialisation of agriculture.

It is by now well established that in India globalisation has actually increased rural indebtedness, landlessness, food insecurity, unemployment, child labour, casualisation of work, wage gaps between skilled and unskilled workers, etc. Given the fact that the price of illiterate labour is close to zero in industrialised nations, it means that the illiterate population of developing countries will tend to get more and more impoverished. In India, where illiteracy rates are extremely high in general and more so amongst the dalit population, globalisation can only contribute to increasing poverty and inequality.[35]

Curtailment of the State's Service Sector: Dalits as Victims

Like in other third world countries, when India went in for the structural adjustment policies, alongside privatisation and liberalisation came the progressive curtailment of the state's service sector. Subsidies were withdrawn, social service expenses increasingly curtailed and in many cases abolished. It may be noted that state expenditures on social sectors as a proportion to total budget expenditure have shown a declining trend in almost all social services in recent years. Welfare services, which the state was previously extending to the people, free of charge were now either being withdrawn from the purview of the state or made available only on payment of a charge. Needless to say, it is the dalit population, living largely in rural areas and low cost residential areas of the cities that relies heavily on the social services extended by the state. It is beyond their capacity to access expensive medical centres or send their wards to expensive public schools. Withdrawal of the state's helping hand simply means that most of the dalits would have to dispense with those services.

The Effects of Health Sector Reforms

One of the worst hit areas is that of health. Health sector reforms have clearly indicated the option for cuts in welfare inputs, a techno centric approach and commodification of health care, fragmentation and privatisation of the existing infrastructure through introduction of user fees and the opening up of public sector institutions, especially hospitals to private investments.[36]

It may be noted that at the national level both policy and planning have been extensively guided by the representatives of global capital. The policy document prepared by the World Bank for India in 1992 entitled *India: Health Sector Financing,* had proposed privatisation of health care and opening up of the medical market for capital to move in, irrespective of the costs for the marginalised sections. Without acknowledging influence, the Ninth Five-Year Plan chose to plan basic health services mainly for the marginalised, while secondary and tertiary medical care was left in the hands of the private sector.[37] The inevitable implication of this is that the poor dalit population would have to remain content with the extremely limited facilities offered by the primary health centres. The doors of specialised treatment would remain shut to the dalits who are in no position to bear the costs of referral treatment. Such treatment would be the exclusive monopoly of the better off sections of the population.

Shrinkage of the Public Sector: Implications for the Dalits

Alongside the shrinkage of the public sector, the constitutionally guaranteed special provisions aimed at distributive justice are heading for a natural death. Even though the system of special representation of the dalits in the services over these fifty years has not been able to ensure their satisfactory presence in the higher services, the little that has been won through the system is bound to come to a halt with the advance of the process of privatisation. Under the new arrangement, wholly private educational institutions and offices would be under no obligation whatsoever to introduce such reservations for SC/STs. And, there is little doubt whether the government would be in a position to bargain. Under the circumstances, the few jobs, which the SC/STs were earlier in a position to lay hands on, would most certainly go out of their reach, forcing them into unemployment and petty jobs in the unorganised sector.

The deep penetration of globalisation into the Indian industrial sectors have resulted in fundamental changes in the manner in which capital is handled, production organised, decisions taken, goods delivered and workers managed.

Layoffs, retrenchment, Voluntary Retirement Schemes (VRS), closure, social benefit cuts, delayed payments and contractualisation are the norms of the day in the public sector and government departmental undertakings, not to speak of the private sector. Till 31 March 1998, a total of 2,27,133 employees of the Government of India had to step aside, whilst public sector employment, which was 194.18 lakh in 1997 went down to 175.59 lakh in 1998.[38]

Banking and the Rural Credit Structure: The Shifting Focus

The establishment of the Reserve Bank of India in 1934 and the subsequent nationalisation of banks in 1969 had all aimed at the institutionalisation of the rural credit structure. The effort was to liberate the rural poor from the exploitative moneylenders. With nationalisation the idea was to bring the banks under the control of the government and ensure lending for fulfilment of social objectives. After nationalisation, the banks had introduced innovative schemes in their operations such as the widening of the bank network in the rural areas through branch expansion in the rural and semi-urban areas, establishment of specialised branches for farm lending, lead bank schemes and district credit plans, differential rate of interest scheme, village adoption scheme and service area approach. Efforts were also made to extend banking to unbanked regions of rural areas.

Later, National Bank for Agriculture and Rural Development (NABARD) was established to take up the role of a leader in the entire rural credit system in the country.[39] The Reserve Bank even stipulated that 40 per cent of the advance of commercial banks be earmarked for what was the priority sector; it incorporated firm sub targets such as 18 per cent for agriculture and 10 per cent for the weaker sections, etc. Several anti poverty credit cum subsidy programmes like the Integrated Rural Development Programme (IRDP) were also launched with banking mediation. A significant section of beneficiaries of these schemes were the SC/STs and women. Today, under the new regime of liberalisation, the trends have clearly been reversed. It may be noted that the trends in the numbers of beneficiaries under the IRDP and PMRY (Prime Ministers Rozgar Yojana) have fallen significantly. The number of beneficiaries (in lakhs) of the IRDP during 1994–95 was 22.15. By 1998–99 it had almost halved to 12.68. In the case of the PMRY, the 1994–95 figure was 1,58,863; by 1998–99 it had declined to 1,46,525.[40]

Though the members of the Scheduled Castes and Scheduled Tribes mostly reside in the countryside and derive their livelihood by working on the land, they remain the most disadvantaged with respect to land. The bulk is agricultural labourers with minuscule holdings, sharecroppers or other types of insecure tenants. A majority of the SC/ST population is landless and without any productive assets and sustainable employment opportunities. Those who do hold land belong to the category of small and marginal farmers. In a nutshell, it can be said that the poorest amongst the poor hail from these groups.[41]

It is alarming to note that in India the absolute number of poor has sharply risen by almost 50 per cent during the decade of liberalisation. In the rural areas the level of underemployment has increased; casualisation has increased, probably at the cost of self-employment. Besides, open rural unemployment too has been on the rise.[42] The number of persons employed per 1,000 persons in rural areas declined from 444 to 417 and unemployment rates increased in the case of rural males and females from 56 and 67 respectively in 1993–94 to 72 and 73 respectively in 1999–2000; thus demonstrating that despite a fairly high GDP growth rate during this period, rural employment declined sharply.[26] It may be noted that the agricultural sector is today the most neglected. Public sector investment in agriculture has declined in the 1990s, while private sector investment during the period has showed only a moderate rise.[43] Agricultural labourers who constitute nearly one-third of the rural workforce and 80 per cent of labour force do not enjoy any social security cover such as maternity benefits, provident fund, gratuity and leave benefits. They are the most exploited section of society living in abject poverty and under inhuman conditions and belong almost totally to the dalit categories. With rising unemployment and hardships in the village areas, these sections of the population are particularly victimised.

In fact, the dalit population in India is today under a double pressure. One, from the brahminical societal structuring and the age old sufferings associated with it. The other is from the new wave of imperialism that capitalism in the present world is generating in the name of "globalisation". In the dalits in India imperialism has found a ready source of cheap labour, and in their common property resources a mine of wealth ready for extraction. The overall exclusion of the dalit population is visible at different levels.

Against this backdrop of globalisation, efforts are being made by the dalits to bring in new issues into focus in the course of their struggles, develop new tools and techniques of struggles to supplement the existing ones, and to search out new support bases. Even as varied forms and levels of struggles within the state are waged vigorously through political parties, pressure groups and in the form of spontaneous protests against atrocities and indignities, mobilisation at an altogether different plane is seen to be unfolding. That is at the international level and in relation to that level. A section of the new dalit elite has undertaken to structure dalit struggles in terms of the general human rights discourse and to generate the UN's and the international community's support in favour of their struggles for human rights.

Notes

1. Atul Chandra Pradhan, *The Emergence of the Depressed Classes,* Bookland International, Bhubaneshwar, 1986, cited in John C.B. Webster, "Who is a Dalit?", S.M. Michael ed., *Dalits in Modern India: Vision and Values,* Vistaar Publications, New Delhi, 1999, p. 68.
2. http://www.dalitchristians.com/Html/dalitmeaning.htm
3. Ibid.
4. Shrirama, "Untouchability and Stratification in Indian Civilisation", S.M. Michael, ed., op. cit., p. 40.
5. Ibid.
6. *Gautama Dharma Sutra*, 1966: IV.20, cited in ibid.
7. *Apastamba Dharma Sutra,* 1960: II.1.2 8–9, cited in Shrirama, op. cit.
8. *Manusmrti,* translated by Wendy Doniger and Brian K. Smith, Penguin Books, New Delhi, 1992, X.51, cited in Shrirama op. cit.
9. Ibid.
10. *Parashara Smrti,*1973: edited by Mahamahopadhyaya Chandrakanta Tarkalankara, Asiatic Society, Calcutta, VI.66, cited in Shrirama, op. cit.
11. *Parashara Smrti*, 1973: VI.26, cited in Shrirama, op. cit., p. 41.
12. *Parashara Smrti*, 1973: VI.411–12d in Shrirama, op. cit., p. 41.
13. *Parashara Smrti,* 1973: VI.43–45, cited in Shrirama, op. cit., p. 41.
14. *Narada Smrti,* 1980 translated by Ganesh Vasudeo Tagara, Motilal Banarsidass, Delhi, cited in Shrirama, op. cit.
15. J.H. Hutton, *Caste in India*, Oxford University Press, Oxford, 1963, p. 207.

16. Cited in S.M. Michael, "Introduction", in S.M. Michael ed. op. cit., p. 14.
17. Marc Galanter, *Competing Equalities: Law and the Backward Classes in India*, Oxford University Press, New Delhi, 1984, p. 131.
18. See Ghanshyam Shah, "Introduction: Dalit Politics", Ghanshyam Shah ed., *Dalit Identity and Politics*, Sage, New Delhi, 2001, p. 31. It may be noted that not all Depressed Classes leaders were in favour of separate electorates. M.C. Raja of Tamil Nadu and several others from different parts of the country wanted more representation for the Depressed Classes but were not in favour of a separate electorate.
19. Thomas E. Weisskopf, "With Reservations", *The Little Magazine*, Vol. VI, Issue 4 and 5.
20. The inspiration largely comes from the nature of the Affirmative Action as it exists in the USA. For an examination of such proposals see Purushottam Agrawal, "The Call of MIRAA"; Jayati Ghosh, "In Praise of Bluntness", *The Little Magazine*, Vol. VI, No. 4 and 5, pp. 69–70.
21. Jayati Ghosh, ibid., p. 70.
22. For a detailed discussion of manual scavenging and the legal discourse see Saptarshi Mandal, "Through the Lens of Pollution: Manual Scavenging and the Legal Discourse", *Voice of Dalit*, Vol. 1, No. 1, 2008, pp. 91–102.
23. Sukhadeo Thorat, *Economic Exclusion And Poverty: Indian Experience of Remedies Against Exclusion*, http://www.ifpri.org/2020ChinaConference/pdf/manilac_Thorat.pdf
24. Ibid.
25. S. Madheswaran and Paul Attewell, "Caste Discrimination in the Indian Urban Labour Market: Evidence from the National Sample Survey", *Economic and Political Weekly*, October 13, 2007, p. 4146.
26. Ibid.
27. Ibid.

28. 2005 Report of National Crime Records Bureau, Ministry of Home Affairs, available at http://ncrb.nic.in/crime2005/cii-2005/CHAP5.pdf
29. http://www.newint.org/features/2005/07/01/combatting_caste/ the data is compiled from India Human Rights Report, www.ncbuy.com/reference/country/humanrights toc.html?code=in, National Sample Survey Organisation, India, 1997, and J. Muthumary, "Dalit Women in India", www.ambedkar.org/Worldwide*Dalits*/*dalit*women*in*India.htm
30. http://planningcommission.nic.in/reports/publications/rep_dce.pdf
31. N.D. Kamble, *The Scheduled Castes,* Ashish Publishing House, New Delhi, 1982, pp. 46–7.
32. Jean-Luc Racine and Josiane Racine, "Dalit Identities and The Dialectics of Oppression and Emancipation in a Changing India: The Tamil Case and Beyond", *Comparative Studies of South Asia, Africa and The Middle East*, Vol. XVIII, No. 1 (1998), p. 7. http://web.archive.org/web/20070629160620/http://cssaame.com/ issues/18_1/RACINES.pdf
33. *Report of the Commissioner for Scheduled Castes and Scheduled Tribes*, 1988, 28th Report, New Delhi.
34. See R. Deliege, op. cit., p. 5.
35. Kaushik Basu, "India and the Global Economy: Role of Culture, Norms and Beliefs", *Economic and Political Weekly*, October 6, 2001, p. 3840.
36. Imrana Qadeer and Alpana Sagar, "Health", in *Alternative Economic Survey, 2000–2001, Second Generation Reforms: Delusion of Development*, Rainbow Publishers, Lokayan, Azadi Bachao Group, New Delhi, 2001, p. 122.
37. Ibid.
38. J. John and Souparna Lahiri, "Labour Against Liberalisation", *Alternative Economic Survey, 1998–2000, Two Years of Market Fundamentalism,* Rainbow Publishers, Lokayan and Azadi Bachao Andolan, Delhi, 2000, p. 118.

39. Veerashekharappa, "Rural Credit in VIP Districts: A Study in Uttar Pradesh", *Economic and Political Weekly*, September 28, 1996, p. 126.
40. M.A. Oommen, "Financial Sector", *Alternative Economic Survey, 1998–2000, Two Years of Market Fundamentalism*, Rainbow Publishers, Lokayan and Azadi Bachao Andolan, Delhi, 2000, pp. 59–61.
41. See B.B. Mohanty, "Land Distribution Among Scheduled Castes and Tribes", *Economic and Political Weekly*, October 6, 2001, p. 3857.
42. Milindo Chakraborti and Samar K. Datta, "Agriculture", *Alternative Economic Survey: 1998–2000*, Rainbow Publishers, Delhi, 2000, p. 38.
43. Ibid., p. 73.

Chapter 4

Dalit Working Children

Whither Human Rights?*

It is estimated[1] that in India 12.6 million children are engaged in hazardous occupations. As a matter of fact, India has the largest number of child labourers under the age of fourteen years in the world. Particularly susceptible are the children of the weaker sections of the population. For many such children, food, clothing and shelter remain elusive, not to speak of education and human dignity. Although poverty is often cited as the cause underlying child labour, other factors such as discrimination, social exclusion, as well as the lack of quality education or existing parents' attitudes and perceptions about child labour and the role and value of education need also to be considered.[2] The UNICEF was forthright in stating that, evidence suggests that children in need of special protection belong to communities suffering disadvantage and social exclusion such as Scheduled Castes and Scheduled Tribes, and the poor.[3]

The United Nations and Children's Human Rights

With the setting up of the UN in 1945, promotion and protection of human rights per se came in for systematic international attention. It was recognised that all human beings have a right to a life of dignity and basic human rights. Codification of the basic rights was first attempted under the aegis of the UN through the

---

*An earlier version of the paper had been presented at The Asiatic Society of India, Seminar on Marginalisation in Urban and Rural Contexts of India, March 8–10, 2007 at Kolkata and is scheduled for publication in the seminar volume.

adoption of the Universal Declaration of Human Rights in 1948. Thereafter, through a continuous process, human rights concerns were expressed in different fields, assured through the adoption of different Declarations and Conventions.

The adoption of the Convention on the Rights of the Child in 1989 brought into focus the need for acknowledging the importance of child rights. And, going by the number of ratifications, it could easily be considered to be one of the most successful UN Conventions. As it is, the ILO had been adopting Conventions relating to child labour from as early as 1919 and the Declaration of the Rights of the Child had been adopted by the UN General Assembly in 1959 highlighting the need for recognising a range of rights for the child. In 1992, the ILO launched the International Programme on Elimination of Child Labour (IPEC).

India's Commitment to the Child

In independent India, the commitment of the government to the cause of children manifests itself through constitutional provisions, policies, programmes and legislation.

Article 21 of the Constitution guarantees the right to life and liberty, and as interpreted by the Supreme Court, it includes inter alia, the right to free movement, the right to eat sleep and work at will, freedom from inhuman and degrading treatment. Article 23 prohibits the practice of debt bondage and other forms of slavery, trafficking in human beings and the practice of begging being treated as punishable offences.

The Constitution of India in Article 39, under the category of the Directive Principles of State Policy, pledges that "the State shall, in particular, direct its policy towards securing … that the health and strength of workers, men and women, and the tender age of children are not abused, and that citizens are not forced by economic necessity to enter a vocation unsuited to their age or strength, that children are given opportunities and facilities to develop in a healthy manner, and in conditions of freedom and dignity, and that childhood and youth are protected against exploitation, and against moral and material abandonment".[4]

As a follow up of this commitment and being a party to the UN Declaration on the Rights of the Child 1959, India adopted the National Policy on Children in 1974. The policy reaffirmed the constitutional provisions and stated, "it shall be the policy of the State to provide adequate services to children, both before and after birth and through the period of growth to ensure their full physical, mental and social development. The State shall progressively increase the scope of such services so that within a reasonable time all children in the country enjoy optimum conditions for their balanced growth".[5]

As the responsibility of children's nurture and proper growth is bestowed on the government, children's programmes have occupied a prominent place in the national plans for human resource development. Successive Five-Year Plans have provided the basics of dealing with these issues. Dramatic technological developments since the 1990s, particularly in the areas of health, nutrition, education and related spheres have opened up new vistas of opportunities for the cause of children.

The Government of India ratified the Convention on the Rights of the Child on 2 December 1992. As a follow up, the government is taking action to review the national and state legislation and bring it in line with the provisions of the Convention. It has also developed appropriate monitoring procedures to assess progress in implementing the Convention, involved all relevant government/ministries/departments, international agencies, nongovernmental organisations, and the legal profession in the implementation and reporting process, publicised the Convention, and sought public inputs for frank and transparent reporting.

Besides being a signatory to the Convention on the Rights of the Child, India is also a signatory to the World Declaration on the Survival, Protection and Development of Children of 1990. In pursuance of the commitment made at the World Summit, the Department of Women and Child Development under the Ministry of Human Resource Development has adopted a National Plan of Action for Children in 1992. Most of the recommendations of the World Summit Action Plan are reflected in India's National Plan of Action[6].

The National Plan of Action was formulated professedly keeping in mind the needs, rights and aspirations of 300 million children in the country and set out quantifiable time limits for India's Charter of Action for Children by 2000 AD. The priority areas in the plan are health, nutrition, education, water, sanitation and environment. The plan gives special consideration to children in difficult circumstances and aims at providing a framework, for actualisation of the objectives of the Convention in the Indian context. The National Plan of Action also lists out activities to achieve these goals. To make the aims and activities of the plan more need-based and area-specific, the Central Government has urged the state governments to prepare plans of action for children for their states, taking into account the regional disparities that may exist.

It may be noted that the first Act in India relating to child labour had been adopted far back in 1933. It was the enactment of the Children (Pledging of Labour) Act of February 1933. Thereafter, numerous legislations have been adopted seeking to impact on the problem of child labour. The present regime of laws pertaining to child labour in the country largely rests on the International Labour Conference resolution of 1979. The Central Act aiming to deal with the child labour issue is the Child Labour (Prohibition and Regulation) Act, 1986. It seeks to prohibit the employment of children under fourteen in hazardous occupations. Through a notification issued on 26 May 1993, the working conditions of children have been regulated in areas of employment not prohibited under the Child Labour (Prohibition and Regulation) Act. In August 2006, a Ministry of Labour notification banned the employment of children in residences and the hospitality sector.

Basically, government's policy framework for addressing child labour ranges between what could be termed as the "preventive approach" and the "facilitative public interventions" approach. The former involves suitable legal interventions for checking and regulating the entry of children into the labour market, whilst the latter seeks to create a congenial environment for the withdrawal of children from the labour market.[7]

The Vision and the Reality

Notwithstanding the constitutional provisions, laws, administrative decisions, etc., the realities continue to be grim. According to the census of 1991, there were some 11.28 million children under the age of fourteen years in India who were engaged in hazardous occupations. By the time of the 2001 census, the figures had risen to 12.6 million. The actual figures are likely to be much higher. Voluntary groups put the numbers at a whopping 60 million – including both the formal and informal sectors.[8] It is pertinent to remember that the law excludes children engaged in home-based activities and, significantly 90 per cent of child labour is so engaged. The existence of a huge informal sector in India implies the presence of a large workforce and widespread extraction of cheap labour. Unable to fend for themselves, children remain one of the major sources of such cheap labour. Moreover, dalit children make up the majority of those sold into bondage to pay off debts to dominant caste creditors.[9]

Over half the working children are engaged in agriculture (54%), while most others are employed either in construction (15.5%) or household work (18%). About 5 per cent are in manufacturing jobs, and remaining (about 8%) are scattered across other forms of employment.[10] It may be noted that child workers make up about 20 per cent of the labour in the tea gardens, 25 per cent in gem polishing and 30 per cent in the carpet industries of Mirzapur. The industries most notorious for employing child labour include carpet weaving, fireworks and match manufacturing, "bidi"-making, glass and bangle manufacturing, construction work and rag-picking, not to mention child prostitution.

A glance at Table 1 reveals the social composition of child workers in several of these industries:

Table 1
Religious/Caste Composition of Working Children in Select Industries

Industry	*Religion*	*Caste*
Lock Making (Aligarh)	M – 62.1% H – 37.7%	SC – 87.5% BC – 63.1%
Carpet (Mirzapur)	M – 13.8%	SC – 38.01%
	H – 86.2%	ST – 1.02%
		BC –45.93%
		UC – 2.35%
Glass (Ferozabad)		SC – 45.17%
		BC – 30.35%
		UC – 9.86%
		MC – 14.62%
Match and Firework (Sivakasi)	H – 98%	SC – 40.8%
Tea Plantation (Assam and North Bengal)		SC/OBC – 50.9%
		ST – 46.8%
		UC – 0.4%

M – Muslim, H – Hindi, UC – Upper Caste and MC – Middle Caste

Sources: cited in http://www.cwa.tnet.co.th/Publications/Newsletters/vol11_2–3/v11_2–3_child-labour.html

1.Operations Research Group, *Child Labour in Different Industries: Consolidated Report,* Madras 1993

2.For Tea Industry see Vasanthi Raman's study "Child Labour in the Tea Plantations of North India", Ministry of Labour, Government of India, unpublished, 1992. Cited in "Reckoning with Child Labour", *Child Workers in Asia Newsletter,* Vol. 11, No. 2–3 (April–September, 1995).

About 18 per cent of children do not go to schools and form the potential pool for child labour. Table 2 below will demonstrate the hard realities of the scenario:

Table 2

Activities of Children

Activities	*Children of Age Group (5–14 years)*					
	Number of Children (%)			*Number of Children (in 100's)*		
	Boys	*Girls*	*Total*	*Boys*	*Girls*	*Total*
Children engaged in economic activities	4.18	3.86	4.02	52967	45618	98392
Attended domestic duties only	0.30	3.15	1.67	3770	37208	40788
Attended domestic duties plus free collection of goods, tailoring, weaving for HH only	0.25	1.92	1.06	3178	22693	25897
Children at work	4.73	8.93	6.75	59915	105519	165077
Attending schools	72.98	61.45	67.44	925350	725964	1651186
Children neither at work nor at school	17.26	20.42	18.80	218889	241255	460205

Source: Pradeep Narayanan , 01 July 2006. Pradeep Narayanan is Manager, Research at Child Rights and You (CRY). The data in these tables have been compiled from official sources. http://www.indiatogether.org/photo/2006/chi-labour.htm

Despite the government's efforts at universalising education through the *Sarva Siksha Avijan*[11] and reducing drop out rates through encouragements provided by schemes such as the midday meals, etc., the dropout rates of dalit children remain higher than that of others as is evident from Table 3:

Table 3

Drop out Rates by Social Composition, 2004–05

(per cent)

Categories	*Primary (I–V)*			*Elementary (I–VIII)*		
	Boys	Girls	Total	Boys	Girls	Total
SC	32.7	36.1	34.2	55.2	60.0	57.3
ST	42.6	42.0	42.3	65.0	67.1	65.9
All	31.8	25.4	29.0	50.5	51.3	50.8

Source: Selected Educational Statistics, 2004–05, cited in http://www.education.nic.in/plan/XIPlandocument.pdf

Some Observations

For the employer, employing child labour is clearly an economic gain. Children can often be paid at a lesser rate for the same type of job performed by an adult. They are more readily exploitable, less likely to protest low status, low pay, the tedium and monotony of the work. To the employer, the child labourers appear more docile, less troublesome and of course unaware of and incapable of agitating for their rights in an organised way. Needless to say, to the employer the social costs are irrelevant. Sandhya Barge, Richard Anker and M.E. Khan have listed some of these and other non-pecuniary reasons for hiring child labour.[12]

Investigations undertaken by the Madras Institute of Development Studies (MIDS), too, have brought out the non-economic advantages accruing to companies through the use of child labour. In a report on the Sivakasi match industry published in 1985, MIDS researchers observed of children as a docile group:

> Docile workers will not protest if they are used like instruments of production, moved from operation to operation as the demands of the manufacturing process dictate. They will work as long as the management requires, particularly when they are on piece-rated occupations. Most important of all, they will not have the capability and experience to organise mass protests against wages and working conditions, even though their knowledge of their situation may be acute. They leave the management's authority untouched.[13]

Much of these observations would hold good for other industries as well.

The brahminical system gets reinforced through the exploitation of child labour. The continuance of child labour ensures the continuance of the supply of a pool of cheap exploitable labour not only in terms of children, but also adults. Children who are compelled to join the workforce at an early age and are thus denied the chances of educational attainments, are left with little choice on attaining adulthood but to work in low paid, stigmatising menial jobs – work that Manu had stipulated for the lowdown castes ! Thus, through child labour, the socially stigmatised marginals remain marginal and their marginality remains entrenched within the modern state's discourse frame. The brahminically-induced mindset of people makes a vast majority of even the "socially conscious" elite virtually oblivious to the problem. The voices of protest are thus mute. In fact, the problem hardly becomes an "issue" – a rallying point for agitation for deep-rooted social change.

For the working children, most of who come from low caste dalit families, the losses are massive. They involve the denial of basic human rights. The harm suffered by children in some of the specific industries that may be noted gives us barely a glimpse of the abhorring scenario. It has been recorded that those working in the lock industries of Aligarh and the metal industries of Moradabad, Varanasi and Delhi, have to labour from dawn to dusk on the hand presses, buffing machines, electroplating and spray painting units. Continuous chemical fumes and the white hot flames from which they have no protection, slowly destroy their respiratory system and eyesight. In the carpet weaving industry, bent over the looms in dark sheds all day with little ventilation or seating space, the children are doomed to a lifetime of respiratory diseases, joint and finger pains and emaciation. In the glass bangle and glass blowing industries, tuberculosis is widespread and lifespan short. Children are compelled to work with furnace temperatures of 700 to 1800 degree centigrade, and often for 24-hour shifts with cyanide and silica fumes.[14] Many die young, many others are left to lives of perpetual morbidity. For most, the future has little to promise. The laws, government schemes, court rulings touch barely the fringes. For the vast majority who are not fortunate enough to be noticed either by NGOs or the government or both, their legal rights mean little.

The fact remains that with the higher incidence of wage labour associated with high rate of underemployment the SCs suffer from low income and consumption and resultantly greater levels of poverty.[15] For the dalit families living below the poverty line there appear to be limited options other than using the child as labour. Either the child is sent to work outside the home, which brings in perhaps a meagre remuneration or at least offloads the family of the horrendous task of having to feed the child; or, the child is used as "labour" in the family to perform the domestic chores so that the elder family members can be relieved of some of their time to work for an income. Either ways, the labour of the child ensures short-term material gains for the family, as a result of which there is often a reluctance to act otherwise but to extract the child's labour.

From the long-term point of view the losses incurred by the family are no doubt painful. The overburdened and exploited "crippled" child inevitably develops in course of time into a "crippled" adult, both physically and emotionally. The family can hardly expect to avail of the benefits accruing out of the development of the full potentials of such a member. Untimely ageing, disease, morbidity and death terminate many a hope that the family may have nurtured.

Nevertheless, where existence is on a day-to-day basis, a child's income a critical input to the survival of the entire family, the tomorrow fraught with immense uncertainties, long-term losses, which child labour entails for the family, hardly count as relevant.

For India, the continued prevalence of child labour tarnishes her image and belittles her claims to a democratic identity. With all the promises made in becoming a signatory of the Convention on the Rights of the Child, India's credibility in terms of protecting her children is badly at stake. The child labour problem in India has already drawn the attention of international bodies and the UN has expressed concern as also rights bodies like Amnesty International and Human Rights Watch.

As already noted, child labour reinforces caste in India. And, as the destructive caste system, with all its negative bearings, gets reinforced, it cuts at the roots of all efforts to combat the social evil. Child labour, bonded labour, trafficking in children, the continued practice of untouchability and social marginalisation form a vicious circle – impenetrable to the ideological influences of democracy, human rights and social justice.

Last, but not least, it corrodes the infrastructure of the country by causing irreparable damage to the human resource of the future – the children. This is bound to have long-term negative effects on diverse fields such as health and education of the population, economy of the country as well as national security.

Over years, dalit struggles for survival, dignity and human rights have flowed through different streams. In terms of antiquity, the struggles for rights and dignity go back into ancient times – almost as ancient as the caste system itself. Sometimes the untouchables struggled for religious space, sometimes for social justice, at other times they fought for their economic rights. Time and again the struggles met with renewed oppression.

Nevertheless, since India's independence, parliamentary democratic institutions, reservations in legislatures, educational institutions and jobs, impact of socialist ideas and the Mandal Commission Report all created conditions for greater dalit assertion, which became clearly evident in the rise of dalits to political prominence at the levels of national and state politics. On the one hand, dalit pressure groups and political parties rose to prominence. Particularly noticeable was the rise of the D-S 4 and from it the Bahujan Samaj Party with assertive leaders like Kanshi Ram and Mayawati. On the other hand, in relation to the other political parties the growing strength of the dalit lobby was evident both through the cooption of dalits to leadership positions and the attention given in speeches, programmes and manifestoes to dalit issues.[16]

From the 1990s, very clearly articulation of the dalit interests within the paradigm of the international human rights discourse has been under way.[17] International conferences have been held by dalits at Kuala Lumpur (1998), London (2000), New Delhi (2001) and Vancouver (2003) to mobilise and struggle for dalit human rights. The National Campaign on Dalit Human Rights has been formed (1998) to spearhead efforts of mobilising international public opinion through the UN against the gross violation of dalit human rights and the continuance of the obnoxious practice of untouchability in India. And, at the UN's Third World Conference Against Racism held at Durban in 2001 dalit activists did succeed in drawing the attention of the international community to the obnoxious practice of untouchability and caste discrimination as prevailing in India.[18] All these, and much more have, however, failed to address the problem of human rights of the working dalit children. Barring occasional references, a screen of silence continues to conceal their tears. Their problems are unspoken of, their issues go unnoticed. The concerns of activists remain confined to the world of adults. Ironically, perhaps because the children are neither able to lobby for themselves nor are they voters forming precious vote banks !

On another plane, the Government of India, UN, different international donor agencies, NGOs and civil society organisations have repeatedly expressed their concerns about the continuance of child labour and professed their unflinching commitment to human rights. Yet, child labour and violation of the basic human rights of children are alarmingly on the rise.

There is no denying the fact that the majority of child workers and victims of rights abuse come from the socially marginalised sections. This is a reality indisputably substantiated by facts and widely recognised not only at the national but at the international level as well. Just as it has been taken note of by the Government of India, international rights bodies like Human Rights Watch and international organisations like the UNICEF have alluded to it.

For children of the Scheduled Caste families, educational backwardness, economic deprivation and social marginalisation form a persistent vicious circle. It is pertinent to remember that most dalits continue to live in extreme poverty, and, barring a small section, they are without land, remunerative employment options or a suitable education. Constitutional eradication of untouchability, schemes for their uplift, quotas notwithstanding, the roots of the caste system on which dalit distress rests, are yet to be shaken. Faced with discrimination based on caste, these families are left with very limited options but to use their children as "labour".

Understandably, thus, against the backdrop of the problem of child labour, the issue of children's human rights in the Indian context can hardly be meaningfully addressed without reckoning with the caste factor. It is simply not enough to recognise the fact that amongst other identity groups, Scheduled Castes are particularly vulnerable to the exploitation of child labour. It is also not enough to recognise the links between the multiple types of marginalities to which they are victim. Addressing the problem effectively calls for addressing the roots of the problem. And, here the roots lie in the caste system itself. Hence, any meaningful condemnation of the practice of child labour in the Indian context must rest on an outright condemnation of the caste system and the drawing up of a suitable, time-bound action plan for the dismantling of the Brahminical social structure. The government, international agencies, civil rights organisations and dalit activists, despite their growing human rights awareness, have so far failed in pursuing such a line of action. It is a race against time that could easily be lost as the dalit child's human rights remain a far off dream.

Notes

1. 2001 Census of India, Government of India, New Delhi.
2. http://www.unicef.org/india/child_protection_152.htm
3. Ibid.
4. See *Constitution of India,* Government of India, New Delhi.
5. http://www.indianembassy.org/policy/Children_Women/rights_children.html
6. Ibid.
7. Rajeev Malhotra, Arvinder S. Sachdeva and S.V. Ramana Murthy, "Child Labour in India: Nature and Policy Options", in G.K. Lieten, Ravi Srivastava and Sukhadeo Thorat eds., *Small*

Hands in South Asia: Child Labour in Perspective, Manohar Publishers, New Delhi, 2004

8. "Ban or no, they're labouring on", *The Times of India*, Kolkata, 12 June, 2007, p. 8.
9. http://www.ncdhr.org.in/ncdhr/general-info-misc-pages/oodhrs
10. http://www.indiatogether.org/photo/2006/chi-labour.htm
11. Sarva Siksha Avijan is the principal programme for Universalising Elementary Education and is the culmination of all previous endeavours and experiences in implementing various education programmes. It has very successfully brought down the numbers of out of school children from 32 million in 2001–02 to 7.0 million in 2006–07. See http://www.education.nic.in/plan/XIPlandocument.pdf
12. "Child Labour: Economic Gain or Social Cost?", in G.K. Lieten, Ravi Srivastava and Sukhadeo Thorat eds., *Small Hands in South Asia: Child Labour in Perspective*, Manohar Publishers, New Delhi, 2004, p. 156. See also Lakshmidhar Mishra, *Child Labour in India*, Oxford University Press, New Delhi, 2000.
13. MIDS, "Match Industry in Sivakasi, Sattur: Towards Removal of Child Labour", Report of a Study presented to the Ministry of Labour, Madras, Madras Institute of Development Studies, 1985.
14. See *The Hindu*, 26.1.03
15. For a detailed discussion see Sukhadeo Thorat, "Oppression and Denial: Dalit Discrimination in the 1990s", in *Economic and Political Weekly*, 9 February, 2002.
16. Debi Chatterjee, "Dalit Situation in India Since the 1990s: An Examination of Certain Issues and Trends," *Socialist Perspective*, Quarterly Journal of the Council for Political Studies, Kolkata, Vol. 33, No. 1–2, June–September, 2005, pp. 53–67
17. Debi Chatterjee, *Up Against Caste: Comparative Study of Ambedkar and Periyar*, Rawat Publications, Jaipur, 2004. See also Ambrose Pinto, "Caste Discrimination and UN.", *Economic and Political Weekly*, 28 September 2002, p. 3989.
18. Ambrose Pinto, "Caste Discrimination and UN.", *Economic And Political Weekly*, 28 September, 2002.

Chapter 5

Dalit Women and Human Rights Concerns

Throughout the world women face innumerable obstacles and are victims of massive rights violations. The subordination of women is a visible feature of most stages of recorded history and is widely prevalent across the world; however, the social, economic and cultural environment in which women have been placed has conditioned its extent and form. For India, this is particularly true.

Gender Exploitation in Historical Perspective

Historically viewed, women in India have been persistently victims of brahminical oppression. The classical Hindu scriptures had relegated them to a distinctly inferior position compared to their male counterparts. On strict control of their sexuality rested the basics of caste stratification – caste endogamy. To ensure that intermarriage amongst different caste members did not take place, strict separation of the sexes was advocated and control over women's bodies formed the crux of it. The notion of chastity, child marriage, and perpetual supervision were some of the many devices to render them incapable of treading the path of "sin". Independent functioning was taboo. The tutelage first of the father, then the husband and finally the son were the destiny of women.

Caught in the vortex of caste and patriarchal norms, women en mass have been victims of persistent oppression. To put it in the words of the feminist historian, Uma Chakravarti, "It is ironical therefore that brahminical patriarchy's obsessive concern with controlling female sexuality and ensuring the reproduction of pure blood – the earliest evidence we have for an abhorrent form of genetic engineering – has survived across all caste groups, high and low, in a way that changes in legal forms and even liberal ideologies have not been able to break. What is tragic is that the lower castes too, especially in North India, strongly monitor female sexuality for purposes of exogamy but also more generally, thus reproducing the biogenetic map of inequality, without being conscious that these norms are derived from the very structures that oppress them in other ways".[1]

The UN Efforts

Equality of rights for women is a basic principle of the United Nations as the preamble to the UN Charter sets forth as one of the organisation's goals, the reaffirmation of' faith in fundamental human rights, in the dignity and worth of the human person, in the equal rights of men and women.

The Universal Declaration of Human Rights adopted by the UN General Assembly in 1948 codified basic rights, which individuals, irrespective of sex could enjoy.

1975 was declared by the UN as the International Women's Year and the decade from 1975–85 as the United Nations Decade for Women. At least four international conferences were held between 1975 and 1995 focussing directly on the issues of women's empowerment. The first-ever world conference on women was held in 1975 in Mexico, followed by the second at Copenhagen in 1980 and the third at Nairobi in 1985. The fourth World Conference on Women was held at Beijing in 1995. The issue of women's political empowerment came to the forefront at the Beijing Conference on Women held in 1995. Henceforth, it continued to remain centre stage at all discussions on gender justice and equality. Women were also at the centre of discussions on such varied issues as population, environment and peace. These efforts resulted in bringing the issue of women's empowerment, equality and development on the national political agenda of most countries of the world.

The single most important and comprehensive Convention dealing with the question of women's empowerment has been the Convention on the Elimination of All Forms of Discrimination Against Women adopted by the UN in 1979. It defines discrimination, identifies its sources, and pinpoints the responsibilities of the state in ensuring gender justice.

A strong reiteration of women's rights was made at the 1993 World Conference on Human Rights at Vienna where it was stated that "the human rights of the women and of the girl child are inalienable, integral and indivisible part of the Universal Human Rights. The full and equal participation of women in political, civil, economic and cultural life at the national, regional and international level and eradication of all forms of discrimination on grounds of sex are the priority objectives of the international community".[2]

The Beijing + 5 Review (2000) at Geneva clearly pointed out that the injunctions of the Beijing Platform for Action were still to be taken serious note of in many countries. The Outcome Document adopted by the UN General Assembly, recognised that "despite general acceptance of the need for a gender balance in decision-making bodies at all levels, a gap between *de jure* and *de facto* equality has persisted ... the actual participation of women at the highest levels of national and international decision-making has not significantly changed since Beijing 1995 and gross under-representation of women in decision-making bodies in all areas, including inter alia politics, conflict prevention and resolution mechanisms, the economy, the environment and the media hinders the inclusion of a gender perspective .... Women continue to be under-represented at the legislative, ministerial and sub-ministerial levels ..."

Over the years, UN agencies, mainly the UNIFEM,UNDP, ILO, UNICEF, etc., have been involved in supporting governments of different countries, NGOs and other organisations in running programmes for women's development.

The Indian Scenario: The Law and Reality

In independent India, the Constitution granted equality to women as a fundamental right and empowered the state to adopt affirmative discrimination in favour of women. The Constitution assured equal protection of the law, equal opportunities in public employment and prohibited discrimination in public places. As universal adult suffrage added women to the electoral rolls making them politically relevant, political parties pledged their commitment to women's issues. Even though due to strong opposition from the conservatives in the Congress, the Hindu Mahasabha and the Jan Sangh the Hindu Code Bill could not be passed as envisioned by Ambedkar to improve the position of women, a series of laws passed in the fifties did succeed in bringing about certain significant changes in Hindu Personal Law aimed at greater empowerment of women in terms of property, succession and matrimonial rights. Four Acts reforming various aspects of Hindu family law were passed. These were the Hindu Marriage Act, The Hindu Succession Act, The Hindu Adoption and Maintenance Act and the Hindu Minority and Guardianship Act.

By the introduction of Universal Adult Suffrage under the Constitution of independent India women got the right to vote on equal terms with men – a right that in many of the western countries women won after prolonged struggle. But nevertheless, women's representation in legislative bodies remained poor. While in the first Lok Sabha elections the percentage of women elected to the legislative body was barely 4.41 per cent, by 1998 it rose to only 7.92 per cent. Even when they did manage to get portfolios in the ministries they were given what may be termed as the lesser important portfolios or the soft portfolios as they are often called. They do not get portfolios like defence, finance or home !

In 1971, the Ministry of Education and Social Welfare appointed a committee under the chairpersonship of Phulrenu Guha, "to examine the constitutional, legal and administrative provisions that have a bearing on the social status of women, their education and employment" and to assess the impact of these provisions. The move came in response to a UN request to all countries to prepare reports on the status of women for the International Women's Year scheduled for 1975. The report of the Committee was published in 1974. The findings were startling. The Indian government's commitment to equality was seriously challenged in that report titled *Toward Equality*. The report was the first major work to point out the extent to which constitutional guarantees of equality and justice had not been met for women. The authors of the report charged that women's status had not improved but had in fact declined since independence. The report noted that social change and development in India had adversely affected women.[3]

During the International Decade for Women there were a lot of activities on several fronts. The approach to women shifted from being "welfare-oriented" to "developmento-riented". A variety of schemes in different ministries for the advancement of women were initiated or existing schemes intensified particularly relating to skill development, education and income earning capabilities. Focal points in ministries and departments were designated as "women's cells" to exclusively monitor programmes for women. State level Women's Development Corporations were established to finance development programmes for women. In 1993 India ratified the CEDAW. In the same year an Act of Parliament established the long awaited National Commission for Women. State level commissions were also set up in course of time in several states, including West Bengal.

The Government of India made empowerment of women one of the principal objectives of the Ninth Five-Year Plan (1997–2002). The professed aim was to make efforts to bring about such an enabling socioeconomic and psychoemotional environment in which women would be able to greatly exercise their rights as equal partners of men. Also, all efforts were sought to be undertaken to empower women as agents of social change. 2001 was declared by the Indian government as the Year of Women's Empowerment.

However, despite all the bustle of activities, dalit women seem to have fallen between the crevices as neither feminism, nor the theorising by dalit activists and theorists till recently, have taken serious note of the persistent, ongoing violation of their human rights. They are dalits and they are at the same time women. As women, they were perhaps deemed inferior to the male dalits and, as such, seen to be unfit for focused attention by the dalit rights activists. At another level, as dalits they were perhaps considered unfit for being given adequate space in the feminist discourse – a discourse that, in India, was largely shaped by, and consciously or unconsciously revolved around issues of concerns of the non-dalit, caste Hindu women. The problem was very passionately expressed by M. Swathy Margaret in an article written in *Countercurrents.* Identifying herself as a "dalit-middle-class, university educated, Telugu-speaking Dalit-Christian-Woman",[4] with all these identities having a role in the way she perceived herself and the world, she noted that on the one hand the dalit ideologues like Katti Padma Rao, Gopal Guru and Gaddar seem to be less sensitive to the internal patriarchy of dalit communities, and on the other the lack of understanding of the caste gender dynamics is reflected in the works of some important upper caste feminists like Volga, Vasantha Kannabhiran, Kalpana Kannabhiran, and Chhaya Datar.[5] Unfortunately, she laments, these intellectuals do not, for a moment, think of dalits who are also women. To them, all women are seen as dalits. However, the reality is that "the social status of upper caste women has never been like that of dalit men or women. Patriarchy, as it operates within and between different castes is determined by the caste identity of individuals. Politics based on difference should be sensitive not only to the difference that matters to them, which they perceive as important but also to other differences".[6]

It has to be conceded that the plight of dalit women call for special attention as they suffer from multiple dimensions of discrimination. They are discriminated against because they are women (basis of gender), because they are dalits (basis of caste) and as dalit women, by their own men folk (bases of gender and caste). In India caste and gender discrimination is perpetrated in its worst forms on dalit women. Their vulnerability is exposed at different levels and in different fields. They are easy targets of sexual harassment and violence at the hands of upper caste Hindu males; prevalence of the *devadasi* and *jogin* practices provide a religious dimension to and legitimise their physical exploitation. Low educational status, economic deprivation and high unemployment increase their vulnerability.

Dalit women's labour is labelled as unskilled, and, therefore, unrecognised, underpaid, and even unpaid. About 85 per cent dalit women work in the agricultural sector, which is unorganised and does not have facilities of social securities, found in other organised sectors, such as maternity benefits, medical support, etc. Dalit mothers have to bring their infant children with them to work in the fields, where there are no child care facilities. Sometimes they are not allowed to do this, and lose their jobs in the agricultural sector. Land "pattas" are never in dalit women's names. Education is minimal.[7]

In urban areas, too, dalit women work more in the unorganised, sector. They work as hawkers, scrap collectors, petty traders and domestic servants. Or, they may be seen as earning wages as construction workers, or working in *beedi/agarbatti* manufacturing, candle making, garment/*jari*, embroidery works, etc. In some areas dalit women work as night soil removers, without any considerations of hygiene, for as little as one *roti* per day. All these sectors of employment are characterised by low wages, irregular work and wage, absence of social security, sexual harassment and dependency on the whims of middlemen and employers.

Almost all dalit women workers enter the labour market at an early age. 31 per cent of all girl children from dalit communities are child workers. Girls' labour is needed, in agriculture and for household work and poor people choose not to spend money on the education of girls. Thus there is a higher drop out rate for dalit girls at all levels, and over 83 per cent drop out of school at the secondary stage. In addition, women are the ones who mainly take responsibility for cleaning, maintaining and running a household, and in fact, 70–75 per cent of dalit households are female-headed.

Since on an average, 70 per cent of dalit households have no electricity and more than 90 per cent have no sanitation facilities, dalit women (and girls) have to spend a great amount of energy on doing household labour, walking long distances to collect food, fodder, fuel materials and water. Incidents are regularly reported in various newspapers, in different states of India, illustrating the systematic manner in which dalit women are subjected to extreme inhumane treatment, as punishment for asserting their rights, or standing up to dominant castes. Often police stand by, or do nothing to prosecute the perpetrators.[8]

The main areas of violation of rights relate to life and security, torture or to cruel, inhuman or degrading treatment or punishment (UDHR, Article 4,5 and 12), right to work and conditions of work (UDHR, Article 23).

Dominance, resting on resource ownership is intertwined with notions of ritual status of the different castes. As such, it is not uncommon to find that low caste women are sexually assaulted by land owning, upper caste men. Sexual assault and rape manifests itself as an assertion of power. Low caste men not only fail to prevent such assaults from their economically and socially superior masters, there is almost a tacit acceptance of it in many cases as the assertion of dominance is accepted as a matter of right of the upper castes. The instance of Uttar Pradesh may be cited as a sickening instance where it is said that, just as a she-goat may be milked at any time at one's own will, so can a *Chamar* woman be enjoyed at any time at one's discretion.[9] In Vidarbha, *Kunbi* landowners on the prowl for *Mahar* women working in the fields comment, "Give her a few measures of grain and she will be quiet".[10]

Men of dominant castes, including Rajputs, have been found to have mistresses from even low castes. The ritual status of such men are not questioned as long as they do not seek to set up a family and eat food cooked by the mistress. In fact, they have various institutional mechanisms to escape the incurrence of pollution resulting from intercourse with the low caste woman.[11] Thus, the sexual exploitation of dalit women by caste Hindu men continue to be perpetrated.

Protesting Gender Exploitation over the Years: The Non-Brahmin Tradition

In India's non-brahmin ideological tradition, women on the whole enjoyed a relatively better status. This was evident in the *Lokayata, Sahajiya* heritage, the *Tantras* and the Phule-Ambedkar-Periyar's non-brahmin ideological stances.

The *Bhakti* movement in India had thrown up a large number of people challenging the orthodox brahminical values. The *Varkari* tradition of Maharashtra, a part of the thirteenth century larger *Bhakti* movement, rested on notions of equality and produced a long line of female saints hailing from different castes and regions who produced a rich body of literature. Janabai, Muktabai, Gonai, Rajai, Ladai, Kanhopatra and Bahinabai are well known names in this respect. Interestingly, even the male saints of the *Varkari* tradition supported the cause of women, Eknath being one of the four pillars of this tradition.[12]

Tarabai Shinde's now famous essay on *"Stree-Purush Tulana"* ("A Comparison of Men and Women") was, first published as a booklet in 1882, almost a century before Simone de Beauvoir's *The Second Sex*. Tarabai had inherited the revolutionary social tradition of critiquing brahminical hegemony that flourished under the leadership of Jotirao Phule (1827–1890). Her work was undoubtedly an extremely original and brilliant critique of patriarchal oppression far ahead of her times. It is in all likelihood, the first fully worked out analysis of the ideological fabric of Hindu patriarchal society.[13] Shinde had written the piece in response to an article that had been published in *Pune Vaibhav* relating to a hotly discussed incident whereby a young widow had been sentenced to death by the court for committing infanticide. The article published in the *Pune Vaibhav* had made a vicious attack on the concerned woman and women in general for their "modernistic" and "loose" morality. Tarabai refuted each and every argument in her writing and demonstrated how men are invariably the perpetrators of the vices that they so often locate in women.[14] Tarabai's text was written from within the *Satyasodhak* tradition. It launched an attack not only on brahminical patriarchy, but also the patriarchies existing amongst the *Kunbi* and other non-brahmin castes.[15]

It is ironical that, barring Phule, no one even in his movement took serious note of Tarabai's work.[16] In fact, Krishnarao Bhulekar, a close associate of Phule and the number two person in the *Satyasodhak* movement launched a violent attack on the book along with personal abuse.[17] The booklet subsequently was virtually left to be forgotten. Only in 1975 was it rather accidentally found by a reputed scholar of Marathi literature, S.G. Malshe.[18] Till then, only a reference of it in one of the essays of Phule had been all that existed.[19]

Jotirao Phule's Concern for Women

One of the major critiques of the brahminical position on gender in the nineteenth century had come from Jotirao Phule, the great non-brahmin social reformer of Maharashtra. In his rejection of brahminism, Phule was able to reject the ideology of brahminical patriarchy and thus adopt a far more progressive position on the gender question as compared to many of his contemporaries. Phule passionately believed in the power of education and sought to use it as a tool for the liberation of the downtrodden. At the age of 21 in 1848 – significantly, the year in which the Manifesto of the Communist Party was being published – Phule set up his first school in Poona. It was for low caste untouchable girls. His efforts at disseminating education continued against much odds and criticisms that have been elaborately outlined by his biographers. His wife, Savitribai stood by him in his efforts and took up the task of teaching the girls in the face of difficulties in finding teachers. Apart from education of the low caste girls, another major area of intervention of Phule in terms of gender was in relation to the humiliation imposed upon brahmin widows. The material and sexual consequences of enforced widowhood were responsible for a large number of pregnancies in young widows, the attempts to conceal the fact and their consequent excommunication in the event of its becoming known. Phule and Savitribai extended their support to such widows by setting up an orphanage for the children born to the brahmin widows. They thus picked on one of the most vulnerable spots of brahminism – enforced widowhood and its consequences.[20]

Women and the Ambedkar Movement

In the Ambedkar movement women had played important roles. At the time of the historic Mahad Satyagraha (1928), women had not only participated in the procession from the conference site to the pond in question but had also participated in the deliberations of the subject committee meetings in passing resolutions about the claims for equal human rights.[21] They also participated in hundreds in the five-year long Nashik Satyagraha organised between 1930–5 to enter the Kalaram temple.[22]

In the early years of his struggles Ambedkar, while organising conferences, saw to it that simultaneously women's conferences were organised. By the 1930s, women were independently organising meetings. Important women leaders at such conferences included Minambal Shivraj, Sulochana Dangre, Shantabai Dani and Radhabai Kamble. Women's conferences were held at Nagpur in 1942, Kanpur in 1944, Bombay in 1945 and in Calcutta in the following year, i.e., 1946. The demands raised at these conferences mainly pertained to free and compulsory education for girls, women's representation in state legislatures and local bodies, training for self-protection (karate, stick wielding, etc.), prohibition of child marriage, rescuing women from prostitution and reforming the marriage system.

Ambedkar's commitment to the women's cause was clearly evident in his passionate commitment to the Hindu Code Bill. It may be recalled that in 1941, the Government of India had appointed a Hindu Law Committee with B.N. Rau as its Chairman. The Committee had recommended the codification of Hindu law in stages. The Hindu Code Bill could be seen as part of that exercise towards codification. The proposed Bill sought to introduce four new points in the existing law. They were in relation to (i) abolition of the doctrine of rights by birth, (ii) absolute rights over property given to women, (iii) a share to the daughter, and (iv) provisions for divorce. [23] Ambedkar had taken a deep interest in the passage of the Bill. Speaking of its significance, he noted:

> No law passed in the Indian legislature in the past or likely to be passed in the future can be compared to it [Hindu Code] in point of its significance. To leave inequality between class and class, between sex and sex, which is the soul of Hindu society untouched and to go on passing legislation relating to economic problems is to make a farce of our Constitution and to build a palace on a dung heap. This is the significance I attach to the Hindu Code.[24]

Lengthy discussions on the bill took place in Parliament, only to be aborted. Ambedkar lamented that the Hindu Code Bill was introduced in Parliament on 11 April 1947 and after a life of four years it was "killed and died unwept and unsung, after four clauses of it were passed".[25] During this period, Ambedkar was the Law Minister. In 1951, the disheartened Ambedkar resigned from his position.

While different aspects of Ambedkar's ideas and movements have come into focus, his gender sensitivity and the role played by women in the movement remained sidelined over the years. Only recently, it was brought into focus by the research undertaken by Meenakshi Moon and Urmila Pawar, which was published in 1989 under the caption, "We Made History Too". The work was in Marathi and first published from Pune.

Periyar and the Self-Respecters' on the Women's Question

Perhaps the most radical critique of patriarchy from an anti brahminical perspective in modern India was developed by E.V.Ramasami. As he carried forward his crusade against the gods, priests and the brahminical order through his *Cuyamariyadai* or Self-Respect Movement in the first half of the twentieth century, he firmly stood for women's rights.

Periyar worked through different notions of identity and sexuality.[26] To him, the worst victims of caste society, the lowest of the low, were the adi dravidas and women. Their emancipation was possible only through the destruction of the brahminical structure. He extolled the women to stand firmly against their exploitation; to challenge the existing notions of gendered role models. Periyar criticised the ideal of female chastity and argued against a sexual ethic that legitimised male promiscuity while reproving of and rendering illegitimate female desire. Periyar urged women to give in to the claims of a free, self-validating desire, take on lovers, choose a life of economic self-sufficiency and abjure the responsibilities of motherhood.[27]

Extremely significant for the women associated with the Self-Respect Movement was the Self-Respect Marriage. It rendered marriage a matter of mutual contract amongst equals, based on reason and respect, free from the shackles of rituals and customs that tended to strap the women to domestic servitude. Minus the trappings of the brahminical mantras and the overarching presence of the priest, these marriages lent space for inter-caste alliances as well as marriages of widowed women.

Periyar succeeded in inspiring a committed band of Self-Respecters to take up cudgels for women's emancipation and in favour of the Self-Respect Marriages. Thus, over time a large number of articles on these and related questions were published in the organs of the Self-Respect Movement – *Kudi Arasu, Puratchi, Paguttharivu* and *Samadharmam.* Women themselves wrote enthusiastically about these matters. In many of these writings, even as common cause was made of the exploitation of all women, the particular concerns of the adi dravida women were not lost. A very typical reflection of this can be found in an article written by Meenakshi, a regular contributor to the *Kudi Arasu,* as she urged her nationalist sisters to practice a different sort of non-cooperation and civil disobedience,

> You may offer satyagraha, ... for the sake of our devadasi sisters who are being coerced by their parents into the profession of their forebears. Offer satyagraha in front of the homes of your sisters who disdain to grant our adi dravida sister's rights of access to the common well ... .[28]

Focusing the Dalit Women: The Rise of Dalit Feminist Concerns

A rather brief article written by the dalit scholar and Professor of Delhi University, Gopal Guru, titled "Dalit Women Talk Differently", which was published in the *Economic and Political Weekly* of 14–21 October 1995, stirred up a hornet's nest. Drawing attention to the need to give attention to the peculiarities of the dalit women's question in terms of the women's movement he observed in the article,

> Over the last several decades women's issues have become a part of global public agenda. While it is due to their ceaseless struggles that women have acquired visibility at the global level, women's assertion assumes particular expression by operating on a particular terrain shaped by forces of a particular country. The scenario of the women's movement in India, particularly in the context of the Beijing Conference, is characterised by simultaneous mobilisation of women by different autonomous feminist groups and by groups affiliated to formal political formations .... The organisation of dalit women around the notion of difference is bound to be a logical outcome.[29]

A series of discussions around the paper were organised by different feminist groups of which special mention may be made of a two-day seminar organised by Alochana, Centre for Research and Documentation of Women in June 1996. [30]

In 1987, the first national meeting of dalit women was held in Bangalore. A leading role in initiating the move was taken by Ruth Manorama,[31] a noted activist in the field. 1994 saw the formation of the All India Dalit Women's forum and in the following year, i.e., 1995, the National Federation of Dalit Women and Dalit Solidarity was set up. It was this body that came forth to speak up for dalit women at the UN Conference at Durban in 2001.

In March 1994, a "Public Hearing on Atrocities Against Dalits with Specific Reference to Dalit Women" was organised by Women's Voice, Bangalore, and Asian Women's Human Rights Council, Manila.[32] Through the testimonies and evidences presented there, it was clearly evident that the major offences against dalits had been perpetrated by the police themselves in violation of the law or else they had colluded through indifference and inaction. The atrocities followed a pattern. Houses and crops were burnt, people were murdered tortured and beaten up, there were lockup and custodial deaths, molestations, beating and rape of women and girl children.[33]

At the All India Democratic Women's Association (AIDWA)-s Convention Against Untouchability and Dalit Women's Oppression held on 20 December 1998, at Delhi, a thousand-odd dalit women were assembled from Punjab, Haryana, Rajasthan, Himachal Pradesh, Uttar Pradesh, Bihar and Madhya Pradesh along with several guest speakers and AIDWA activists and sympathisers. Hailing from different backgrounds, belonging to different age groups and having varied degrees of consciousness of their socioeconomic conditions and legal rights, the dalit women spoke with different degrees of passion, of their problems and experiences of struggles.[34]

At the state level in Maharashtra, the Maharashtra Dalit Mahila Sanghatana was formed in 1995. In the previous year, the women's wing of the Bharatiya Republican Party and the Bahujan Mahila Sangh set up the Bahujan Mahila Parishad.[35] In December 1996 a Vikas Vanchit Dalit Mahila Parishad was organised at Chandrapur and it was proposed that 25 December – the day Ambedkar set fire to the *Manusmrti* – be commemorated as Bharatiya Stree Mukti Divas. Dalit Christian women in 1997 set up the Christi Mahila Sangharsh Sanghatana. Despite their diverse ideological stances, these organisations worked together on several issues such as the celebrations of the Bharatiya Stree Mukti Divas and reservations for OBC women in parliamentary bodies.[36]

At the international level, the Hague Conference on Dalit Women's Rights, the first international conference of its kind, was held on 20–21 November 2006. It was a joint venture of NGOs including Justitia et Pax, Cordaid, CMC (Mensen met enn Missie), Dalit Network Netherlands (DNN) and National Campaign on Dalit Human Rights (NCDHR – India). Most of the participants were dalit women from India, Nepal, and Pakistan. They shared stories about the violence they endured and discrimination they faced at the hands of non-dalits and police departments who did not stand by the victims. During the conference, participants were organised into groups to discuss issues such as atrocities and criminal justice administration, participation in government, land rights and state budget allocation, employment, education and health rights. The outcome of the discussion was the Declaration on the Human Rights and Dignity of Dalit Women incorporating recommendations for the governments of Nepal, India, Pakistan, Bangladesh and Sri Lanka as well as the international community, the United Nations and the European Union pertaining to the treatment of dalit women.[37]

The formation of the dalit women's bodies and the organising of the dalit women's meets have been emerging as critiques of the traditional dalit movements as well as the prevailing perspectives of Indian feminism.

Dalit feminists have been raising pertinent questions regarding the incomplete and exclusive character of Indian feminism and its genealogy emphasising the need for a rethinking in order to engage meaningfully with dalit women's "difference" from the ideal subjects of feminist discourse.

This emerging field of dalit feminism holds forth great potentials for strengthening the human rights of dalit women, as well as the dalit struggles for human rights as a whole. In this respect, the following points may be taken into account:

1. It is today urgently necessary that both dalit and feminist demands are rearticulated to incorporate the demands of dalit women in setting the agenda for struggles. The necessary pressure has to be built up by dalit feminists in this field and bodies such as NCDHR and NACDOR can play a steering role in this matter.

2. For developing its theoretical discourse, dalit feminism would have to draw from different strands of existing feminist discourse giving particular attention to Marxist Feminism, Eco-feminism and Black Feminism. Marxist Feminism could

help to develop insight into the nature of exploitation of dalit women in terms of production relations. Eco-feminism may be used to understand the intricate relationships between the environment and dalit women and the implications of the depletion of environmental resources for the lives of dalit women. In Black Feminist discourse dalit feminists could search for analogies in developing their own ideas.

3. It is imperative to highlight the traditional roots of women's exploitation as interwoven with caste identity and understand the dalit woman's social oppression in terms of the caste structure of society; to delve into the roots of brahminism and examine existing critiques of the system from a dalit feminist perspective.

4. Expanding the purview of dalit feminism would call for a focus on:
   (i) the life experiences of dalit women, their struggles in different fields and their perspectives; Sharmila Rege's work[38] can be viewed as a clear trend-setter in this respect;
   (ii) rewriting of history to bring in the contributions made by dalit women in different fields hitherto unrecorded; e.g., in areas as diverse as the freedom movement and the field of sports;
   (iii) highlight the contributions of people like Phule, Ambedkar and Periyar in not only critiquing the social system, but exposing the oppression of women and suggesting ways and means for women's emancipation and demand discussions of their ideas in feminist discourses.

5. Even as dalit feminists would have to develop a thorough critique of both Feminism and dalit movements and demand necessary reforms in both the discursive areas, to the extent possible they would have to develop necessary collaborative links with them, exploring their shared and tangled histories.[39]

6. New dalit women's leadership organisations would have to be established and existing ones strengthened with the aim of mobilising dalit women for:
   (i) economic uplift;
   (ii) educational development;
   (iii) cultural purposes;
   (iv) social awareness;
   (v) sharing of information and ideas; and
   (vi) political awareness and struggles.
7. Sensitising grass root level organisations like panchayat and municipal bodies to dalit women's concerns so that a dalit – feminist perspective may be introduced in course of time in the handling of all schemes to the extent that it is relevant.
8. Developing a body of literature including handbooks and directories to give information and guidance to dalit women regarding the resolution of their day-to-day needs and problems. These could include information regarding relevant laws, judicial decisions, government schemes that they may avail of, sources of funds, educational grants, names – addresses and contact numbers of government and nongovernment organisations to which they may turn to for different types of assistance, legal experts, names and contacts who may be willing to render free or cheap services to dalit women in distress.

Dalit organisations and human rights bodies could play a vital role in all the above-identified areas. NGOs could also play a catalytic role in bringing together dalit feminists, democratic individuals and social leadership organisations for the task of working out short-term tactical moves and long-term strategic policies, against the backdrop of the human rights discourse. This would have to be done keeping note of the new threats to which dalits and dalit women in particular have been exposed to because of the ongoing globalisation process.

Notes

1. Uma Chakravarti, *Gendering Caste: Through a Feminist Lens*, Stree, Kolkata, 2003, p. 36.
2. www.unhchr.ch/html/menu5/wchr.htm
3. *Toward Equality*, Report of the Committee on the Status of Women in India, Government of India, 1974.
4. By M. Swathy Margaret, "Dalit Feminism," Countercurrents.org, 03 June, 2005, www.countercurrents.org/feminism-margaret 030605.htm
5. Ibid.
6. Ibid.
7. Bela Malik, "Untouchability and Dalit Women's Oppression" in Anupama Rao, ed. *Gender and Caste,* Kali for Women and Women Unlimited, New Delhi, 2003, p. 102.
8. http://www.hrsolidarity.net/mainfile.php/2000vol10no04/398/
9. Leela Dube, "Caste and Women", Anupama Rao, ed., op. cit., p. 241.
10. Ibid.
11. Ibid.
12. Vidyut Bhagwat, "Marathi Literature as a Source of Contemporary Feminism", Maitrayee Chaudhuri ed., *Feminism in India*, Kali for Women & Women Unlimited, New Delhi, 2006, pp. 301–2.
13. Ibid., p. 309.
14. Ibid., pp. 308–9.
15. Sharmila Rege, "Dalit Women Talk Differently: A Critique of 'Difference' and Towards a Dalit Feminist Standpoint Position", Maitrayee Chaudhuri, op. cit., p. 215.
16. Ibid., p. 310.
17. Ibid.
18. Ibid., p. 308.
19. Ibid.

20. Uma Chakravarti, "Reconceptualising Gender: Phule, Brahmanism and Brahmanical Patriarchy", Anupama Rao, ed. op. cit., p. 173.
21. Eleanor Zelliot, "Dr Ambedkar and the Empowerment of Women", Anupama Rao, ed., op. cit., p. 205.
22. Ibid.
23. K.N. Kadam, compiled and edited, *Dr Babasaheb Ambedkar and the Significance of His Movement: A Chronology,* Popular Prakashan, Mumbai, 1991, pp. 68–9.
24. *Dr Babasaheb Ambedkar: Writings and Speeches*, ed. by Vasant Moon, Government of Maharashtra, Bombay, Vol. 14.
25. Ibid., p. 1324.
26. For a detailed discussion see V. Geetha, "Periyar, Women and an Ethic of Citizenship", Maitrayee Chaudhuri, ed., *Feminism in India*, op. cit., pp. 156–74.
27. V. Anaimuthu ed., *Periyar E.Ve Ra Sinthanaikal (Thoughts of Periyar*), Three Volumes, Sinthanaiyalar Kazhagam, Tiruchirapalli, 1974, cited in ibid.
28. *Kudi Arasu*, 6 March, 1932, cited in V. Geetha, ibid.
29. Gopal Guru, "Dalit Women Talk Differently", *Economic and Political Weekly*, 14–21 October 1995.
30. For details of the discussions at the Seminar see Sharmila Rege, "A Dalit Feminist Standpoint", Anupama Rao, ed. op. cit., pp. 95–8.
31. Dr Ruth Manorama has a Masters Degree in Social Work from Madras University and has been a leading activist in the area of dalit women's cause. She heads Women' Voice, an organisation working amongst poor women in the unorganised sector in urban areas of Bangalore. cf. Pramila Jayapal, "Low Caste Women to Protest at UN Racism Meeting: Protesting Bias in India", Adventure Divas, http://www.adventuredivas.com/despatches/india/tackling-caste-oppression
32. Anupama Rao, "Indian Feminism and the Patriarchy of Caste", *Himal*, February, 2003.

33. Pranjali Bandhu, "Dalit Women's Cry for Liberation: My Rights are Rising Like the Sun, Will you Deny this Sunrise?", in Anupama Rao, ed. op. cit., pp. 109–10.

34. Bela Malik, "Untouchability and Dalit Women's Oppression" in Anupama Rao, ed. op. cit., p. 102.

35. Sharmila Rege, "A Dalit Feminist Standpoint", Anupama Rao, ed. op. cit., p. 95.

36. Ibid.

37. http://www.franciscansinternational.org/news/article.php?id =1270

38. Sharmila Rege, *Writing Caste/Writing Gender: Reading Dalit Women's Testimonio's,* Zubaan, New Delhi, 2006.

39. Anupama Rao, ed., op. cit., p. 2.

Chapter 6

Religious Conversion and Human Rights

Dalit Converts as Victims of Caste Oppression

The link between caste oppression and the Hindu religion is clearly evident. Over a long period of history – from the ancient to the modern – a large number of scriptural texts of the Hindu brahminical order have elaborately laid down, defined and redefined the rules and regulations of the hierarchic society, the notions of purity and pollution, the status positions of people of different castes, their stipulated activities, their rights and absence of rights. Religion sanctified discrimination, social oppression and the violation of basic human rights of the low caste people.

In such a milieu, conversion has long been a language of protest. In different parts of the country dalits, as individuals or groups, have from ancient times sought solace in other religions. Sometimes they set up their own religious orders forming sects such as the *Ad Dharm* and *Motua Dharam;* at other times they turn to alternative institutionalised religious options like Christianity or Islam. However, to what extent such moves enable them to shed their stigmas and secure their basic human rights has remained debatable.

The major pre-existing institutionalised religions to which sizeable dalit conversion has taken place over the years happen to be Christianity, Islam and Buddhism. Chronologically speaking, such conversions appear to fall into three major periods – pre-British, British and post-independence. In the first mentioned period, conversions took place to Jainism and Buddhism from very early times; there were also conversions to Islam mediated through trading associations, Sufism and political linkages. During this time conversions to Christianity, too, took place in different parts of southern India such as Kerala and Goa. During the British period there were conversions to Christianity as also other religions such as Sikhism and Islam. It was a time when, on the one hand, traditional relations of production and distribution were getting undermined in the rural areas rendering the lowest castes more vulnerable. On the other hand, certain new opportunities were opening up in the form of acquiring new patrons and religious attachments. Thus, through conversions, attempts were made by the lowly castes to disengage themselves from the caste structures and renegotiate their social position. Post-independence saw some of the same dynamics of change. Conversion movements were linked to political movements and aspirations for social mobility and economic betterment.[1]

It was reported, for example, in the *Milli Gazette* of 28 October 2002 that "Over a hundred Dalits (low-caste Hindus) converted to Buddhism, Islam and Christianity on Sunday, October 27, in protest against the inequality in Hindu religion, which treats Dalits as sub-human, even less important than cattle".[2] Significantly, the new converts included families of five dalits lynched on October 15 for skinning a dead cow.[3] The same issue of the magazine reported, "Last August, 250 Dalits converted to Christianity in Tamil Nadu to escape oppression. Last year 1,500 similarly oppressed low caste Hindus embraced Christianity".[4] According to the BBC, 400 Dalits in Tamil Nadu were planning to convert to Islam "because of what they described as persistent unfair treatment by their higher caste Hindu neighbours".[5] A Delhi-based advocate, Rashid Salim Adil, a dalit convert to Islam, speaking to Yoginder Sikand on dalits, social liberation and Islam, stated, "Islam Gave Me Self Respect".[6]

At the inception of the Constitution, only dalit Hindus were recognised as fit for incorporation in the Scheduled Caste category. Six years later, in 1956 the order was amended to include the Sikhs. In 1990, the constitutional order was again amended, this time to include the dalit converts to Buddhism.

Buddhism: The Dalit Shelter

Buddhism had once been dominant throughout India. In fact, in terms of antiquity its presence goes back to a time when the caste structure was taking shape. It was at such a time that Buddhism offered a casteless, egalitarian religious option. As the noted historian Irfan Habib pointed out, the period between c. 550 to 200 BC was a very interesting period of change in Indian history and "the rise of Buddhism spearheaded an ideological revolt against brahminical dominance".[7] However, from the twelfth century onwards the influence of Buddhism began to decline and it was only in the nineteenth century that it was once again revived. Around this period, on the one hand, Buddhism was popularised amongst the caste Hindus through the Theosophical Society; on the other hand, amongst the untouchable castes its rendering as a tool of protest was undertaken first by Iyothee Thass and subsequently in the mid-twentieth century by Ambedkar.

Pandit Iyothee Thass was an untouchable Tamil who had converted to Buddhism in Ceylon and thereafter taken up a conversion drive amongst the local untouchables in Madras. His efforts led to the formation of the South Indian Buddhist Association. The Association came forth to prepare a civil rights agenda. It is significant to note that the members of the Association had made a presentation before the Montagu – Chelmsford panel studying legislative reform in 1917, together with other discriminated minorities seeking special facilities being accorded to the Muslims and the Christians, and suggested something like the present-day reservation policy.[8] A major conversion movement had taken place in Madras under the leadership of Thass around the turn of the century.[9]

The most publicised and prominent conversion movement amongst the dalits, however, undertaken in modern times was by Ambedkar. Committed to the cause of securing justice for the untouchable communities, Ambedkar had by the 1930s, become totally disillusioned with the Hindu religion and the Congress leadership whom he considered to be championing the cause of that religion. He realised that neither in the Congress nor in Hindu religion was there any place for the untouchables. They would have to stay away from both. Urging the untouchables to give up their Hindu connections, he passionately appealed to his fellow caste men, "you have nothing to lose except your religion". But, then, what was their alternative? Ambedkar was not in favour of an atheistic solution. He believed in the necessity of a religion. Under the circumstances, the question was, to which religion should the untouchables turn. It had to be a carefully thought out decision. After years of contemplation and assessment of the many pros and cons of converting to different religions, Ambedkar decided that Buddhism was the best option. He opted for Buddhism because it was "an indigenous Indian religion of equality; a religion which was anti-caste and anti-brahman".[10]

On 14 October 1956, Ambedkar renounced Hinduism along with an estimated half a million other dalits to embrace Buddhism. The ceremony was undertaken under the auspices of a Buddhist monk, Sri Chandramani at Nagpur. There were three stages to the ceremony. In the first stage, Chandramani initiated Ambedkar to the Buddhist faith, the *Pancha Shila*, i.e., the five precepts, namely abstention from killing, stealing, illicit sex, lying and taking intoxicants. This was followed by the *Tri Sarana* – taking refuge in the Buddha, the *Sangha* (Brotherhood of Monks) and the *Dharma*. The recitations were done in Pali, the language of the ancient Theravada literature. In the second stage, Ambedkar spoke in Marathi before the vast assembled crowd and committed himself to twenty-two oaths that he had formulated. Of these, the last dozen comprised of his dedication to Buddhism, including his own rendering of the *Pancha Shila*. The first ten, by contrast, were devoted to a careful set of rejections of brahminical Hinduism. In the third part of the ceremony, Ambedkar led the masses through the conversion process through a repetition of his twenty-two oaths. Here, too, the proceedings were in Marathi.[11] Ambedkar's decision to convert was a long thought out, calculated decision. As early as in 1927, at the time of the Mahad Satyagraha, Ambedkar had said that if the caste Hindus hampered the untouchables struggle, untouchables would have to look to some other religion for shelter.[12] By the mid-thirties, Ambedkar had decided, " I was born a Hindu, but I will not die one". After deep contemplation on the issue ranging over a span of almost two decades, he took the final decision of conversion as he realised that there would be no emancipation of dalits unless they left the religion (Hinduism) that allowed for such discriminatory treatment of the untouchables. Thus came the conversion ceremony months before his death.

By the time Ambedkar undertook the conversion he was thoroughly conversant with the Buddhist philosophy. According to his biographer, Dhananjay Keer, Ambedkar had started working on his magnum opus, The *Buddha and his Dhamma* from 1951.[13] In it, he spelt out the details of his path. Ambedkar's path of Buddhism was not the path of ancient or medieval Buddhism; it was neither Theravada, Mahayana or *Vajrayana* Buddhism. It was referred to as fourth path – *Navayana*. The path of *Navayana* Buddhism represented a revolutionary transformation of the Buddhist traditions in which it was rooted.

Ambedkar's death shortly after the conversion ceremony came as a blow to the converted *Mahars*. The *Mahars* who had embraced Buddhism found themselves in a difficult situation as the law offered reservations for only the Hindu *Mahars* and not the Buddhist *Mahars*. It took a special pact between one of Ambedkar's closest aides – Bhaurao alias Dadasaheb Gaikwad – from Nashik, and the Maharashtra government, to consider converted Buddhists on par with the Scheduled Castes. The problem was solved at the state level, but the Central Government was not willing to concede the claims. Job aspirants were told that if they wanted reservations, they would have to remain Hindu *Mahars*. This led to a piquant situation. Lakhs of *Mahars* who had converted to Buddhism and were seeking government help in education and employment chose to remain Hindu *Mahars* on record, while in their private lives they continued to follow Buddhism. In the census, they recorded themselves not as Buddhists, but as Hindu *Mahars*. The problem was solved only after V.P. Singh became the Prime Minister in 1989. A constitutional amendment ensured that dalits who had converted to Buddhism were granted Scheduled Caste status.[14] Thus, from 1990 they became eligible for the reservation facilities given to the Scheduled Castes.

Even though the Buddhist movement is largely confined to the *Mahars* in Maharashtra, a small number of Buddhists come from other castes as well. There are for example, some Buddhists to be found amongst the untouchable *Chamars* in Uttar Pradesh.[15] The impact of Ambedkar's Navayana Buddhism can be noted in Kanpur amongst the new dalit middle class elite comprising of bank employees, lecturers, teachers, clerical staff and doctors. Besides, a number of dalit IAS and IPS officers have become fervent supporters of *Navayana* Buddhism making financial donations and establishing Buddhist centres.[16]

The dalit Buddhist movement in Kanpur gained impetus with the arrival of Dipankar, a *Chamar bhikkhu,* in 1980. Dipankar had come to Kanpur on a Buddhist mission and his first public appearance was scheduled at a mass conversion drive in 1981. The event was organised by Rahulan Ambawadekar, an RPI dalit leader. In April 1981, Ambawadekar founded the Dalit Panthers (UP Branch) inspired by the Maharashtrian Dalit Panthers. The event met with severe criticism and opposition from Vishwa Hindu Parishad and was banned.[17]

In 2002, Kanshi Ram, the founder of the Bahujan Samaj Party, who hailed from a Sikh religious background, announced his intention to convert to Buddhism on October 14, 2006, the fiftieth anniversary of Ambedkar's conversion. Hundreds of his supporters were to convert at the same time. The special significance of this plan was that Ram's followers who were to convert would include not only untouchables, but persons from a variety of castes, who could significantly broaden Buddhism's support. Unfortunately, Kanshi Ram passed away on October 9, 2006. Nevertheless, he was cremated as per Buddhist rituals.[18]

The rift between the Buddhists and Hindu dalits has been noticeable, and not surprisingly, the division of dalits on religious lines have benefited organisations like the Shiv Sena. It has been recorded that Buddhists and Shiv Sainiks have fought many a pitched street battle, both in Mumbai and other parts of Maharashtra. [19]

Over the years the earlier radical edge of the conversion struggle got somewhat blunted. Many Buddhists went on to get a good education and hold high positions in government, and even in the private sector. Some of them, however, changed their surnames to escape being identified as dalits. But most neo-Buddhists today do not practise the basic tenets of Buddhism or follow the twenty-two oaths administered to them. In fact, many continue to visit the shrines of their traditional Hindu deities like *Khandoba*.[20]

It is pertinent to note that, even as there is amongst the Buddhist community widespread consciousness and bitter rejection of the brahminical notions, Buddhists apparently continue to practise untouchability against other untouchable castes. There exists perhaps as Timothy Fitzgerald observes, a "conflict within the minds of Buddhists when, for example, they simultaneously decry caste endogamy but in fact practise it".[21] There is also to be found a difference amongst the neo-Buddhists in terms of their emphasis or otherwise on the transcendental element. Whilst some emphasise the importance of *Vipassana* and view it as integral to Buddhism, others see it as alien to Ambedkar's revolutionary understanding of liberation and hence call for its rejection.

Whilst scholars like Wilkinson and Thomas[22] tend to suggest that conversion has not made any major difference in the social and occupational life of the converts to Buddhism, according to others, certain advantages have accrued to the dalits who converted to Buddhism. These neo-Buddhists as they are called, appear to have improved significantly over the Hindu dalits in terms of several parameters such as the sex ratio, literacy and work participation.[23]

In the Folds of Islam

Unlike Hinduism, Islamic ideology presents the vision of an egalitarian social order where all followers of Allah are to enjoy equal status position. Needless to say, to the downtrodden Hindus the possibility of emancipation through Islam has been clearly one of the several religious options. As a matter of fact, most Indian Muslims are descendants of untouchable and "low" caste converts.

Although the Quran is largely egalitarian in its social ethics, historians have opined that in medieval India Islam had made almost no impression on the caste system. With the marginal exception of Alberuni, Islam had produced no critique or condemnation of the system and caste had remained a prominent element of village life under the Islamic rulers.[24] The occupations set for castes like the *Chamars, Dhanuks* and *Dhirs* at the end of the Mughal rule was "working in the fields of *Zamindars* and peasants".[25] Upon conversion also, it was found that the converts tended to practise endogamy, although a greater degree of occupational and status mobility seems to have been tolerated amongst Muslims in general.[26] On the whole, as noted by the historian Irfan Habib, " it can, therefore, hardly be disputed that the caste structure of the village and its attending elements as formed in ancient India continued to function without recognisable change till the eighteenth century".[27]

Indian Muslim society is characterised by numerous caste like features, consisting of several caste like groups.[28] A sharp division exists between the *Ashraf* or nobles and non-*Ashraf* Muslims. The former claim foreign descent and therefrom a higher social status. It is believed that the *Ashrafs* are descendents of four categories of immigrant tribes. The first two claiming Arab origin, have the honorific titles of *Saiyyad* and Sheikh; the other two have ethnic names: Pathan (that is roughly Afghan) and Mughal.[29] The first corresponds more or less to the literate brahmins. The second is more numerous than the first, and it is believed that their ranks have expanded through influx from other categories. The Moghuls and Pathans largely correspond to the Hindu Kshatriyas. Even though the groups are not entirely closed groups, they are distinguished by status consciousness and marriage preferences.[30]

Amongst the non-*Ashraf,* three identifiable categories can be found. First, there are those who have converted from the higher castes, particularly the Rajputs. Secondly, a large number of professional groups corresponding to the Hindu artisan castes, mostly the weavers. Thirdly, there are the converted untouchables.[31] Descendants of indigenous converts are commonly referred to contemptuously as *ajlaf* or "base" or "lowly". As among the Hindus, the various *jatis* among the *Ajlaf* Muslims maintain a strong sense of *jati* identity. The dalit converts are referred to as the *Arzals.* They include the Muslim *Khatiks, Mehters, Bhangis, Lalbegis, Halakhors, Mochis, Mukris* and *Garudis*. Unlike their Hindu counterparts, even as they suffer from discrimination they are denied the Scheduled Caste status.[32] The Sachar Committee has observed that the Muslim society in India is socially stratified and "Arzals are the lowest in Muslim social structure. They comprise those having similar traditional occupations as their Hindu counterparts in the list of Scheduled Castes. It is widely believed that these communities are converts from the 'untouchables' among Hindus. Change in religion did not bring any change in their social or economic status. Because of the stigma attached to their traditional occupations, they suffer social exclusion. Despite this, they have been deprived of Scheduled Caste status available to their Hindu counterparts."[33]

The dominance of the elite Muslims over the resources and institutions of the community to the exclusion of the lower caste/class Muslims is amply evident from Table 1.

From the 1990s a few Muslim OBC organisations have surfaced on the national political scene challenging the social and political hegemony of the Muslim elite. Prominent among them are the All India Muslim OBC Organisation (largely confined to state of Maharashtra) led by Shabbir Ahmad Ansari and the Pasmanda Muslim Mahaz led by Ali Anwar (predominant in Bihar).[34] Apart from these, the All-India Backward Muslim Morcha (AIBMM) was set up in 1994 by Ejaz Ali, a young Muslim medical doctor from Patna, capital of the eastern state of Bihar, belonging to the *Kunjera* caste of Muslim vegetable sellers. In less than a decade of its founding, by early 2001 the AIBMM emerged as an umbrella group of over forty organisations claiming to represent different dalit Muslim castes. It now has branches in the states of Uttar Pradesh, Madhya Pradesh, West Bengal, Delhi, Rajasthan and Maharashtra, in addition to Bihar, where it has its headquarters.[35]

Table 1

Control of Resources and Institutions of Muslim Community

Name of the Institution	*Total Number of Members*	*Upper Class/Caste*	*Backward Class/Caste*
Office bearers of All India Muslim Personal Law Board (AIMPLB)	11	10	1
Executives of AIMPLB	39	36	3
Executives of All India Milli Council	48	44	4
Board of Directors of Imarat-i- Sharia (Bihar and Orissa)	21	19	2
Office bearers of Adara-i-Sharia, Patna	11	8	3

Source: Ali Anwar, *Masawat kee Jung: Pasemanjar: Bihar ka Pasmanda Musalman* (New Delhi, 2001) p. 136. For details, see pp. 235–259. cited in see Anwar Alam, "Democratisation of Indian Muslims: Some Reflections," *Economic and Political Weekly*, November 15, 2003, p. 4882.

The basic orientation of these OBC and dalit Muslim organisations is essentially Mandalite. Their primary concerns and demands being to include all backward communities among Muslims in the OBC and SC lists at the state and central levels. They also seeks to pressurise the mainstream political parties to give them more representation in their organisational structures, in ticket distribution at all levels of elections – municipal, assembly and parliament, in the council of ministers and in other state aided minority bodies.[36]

The emergence of caste politics is bringing about a radical change in the manner in which the sense of identity is being articulated. Aware of the importance of numbers in order to acquire political power and the economic benefits that accrue from it, the dalit movement has sought to establish a wider sense of dalit identity that transcends inter-caste and inter-religious divisions and differences among the "lower" caste majority. This wider dalit identity does not seek to deny individual *jati* identities. Rather, it takes them into account but seeks to subsume them within the wider collective dalit identity, based on a common history of suffering as well as the claims of common racial origins as indigenous people. This seems to have been a crucial factor in the emergence of a specific "dalit Muslim" identity that the AIBMM and similar organisations seek to articulate. "Lower" caste Muslim ideologues and activists are now trying to develop a new "dalit Muslim" identity, seeking to bring all the "lower" caste Muslims together, defined by their common identity as Muslim as well as dalit.

Christianity as Panacea

Historical records seem to indicate that entry of Christianity into India and conversions to the religion date back to around the sixteenth century. Christianity in Goa associated with the Portuguese entry and the Syrian Christian arrivals in Kerala set in motion significant conversions amongst the highest castes, including the brahmins.[37] In Tamil Nadu, however, the story was different. There, it was the dalits who were mainly converting to Christianity. In fact, it was the deliberate movement of the dalit communities away from their traditional religions.[38] Similarly, in Punjab, the *Chuhra* conversion movement (1873–1914) was a significant conversion movement of the dalits.[39]

Not surprisingly, apart from Buddhism and Islam, Christianity has remained one of the religious options for the dalits seeking to free themselves from the shackles of caste Hindu oppression, as Christianity like the other two mentioned religions does not recognise caste differences.

It is estimated that there are some sixteen million dalit Christians in India, comprising about 60 per cent of the country's total Christian population. But, even as converts, their dalit identity does not seem to leave them. They face discrimination from multiple sources, the most important being – upper caste lay Christians, upper caste Hindus, dalit Hindus, the state and government and the clerical authorities in the Church.[40]

Looking at facts, it is clearly evident that on the whole the occupational patterns of the dalit Christian are similar to that of the Hindu dalits. Glimpses of the picture become visible if we note that for most Punjabi Christians the context in which they converted did not change significantly following the conversion. They continued to be poor, landless rural labourers under the thumb of landlords and moneylenders even after conversion.[41] Equally significant is the fact that even in the Christian institutions, dalit Christian students are abysmally low.[42] A glance at the occupational patterns of the dalit Christians of the northwest of the country as also Tamil Nadu would be no less revealing. In northwest India, most of the dalit Christians are engaged in the unorganised sector and 11.48 per cent in manual scavenging. In Tamil Nadu, 54.75 per cent of the dalit Christians are agricultural labourers. The detailed occupational patterns are displayed in Tables 2 and 3 given below:

Table 2

Labour Pattern Among the Dalit Christians of Northwest India

Occupation	*Per cent*
Seasonal farm labour	14.08
Night soil labour	11.48
Bonded labour	05.09
Child labour	02.49
Casual labour	47.93
Migrant brick kiln labour	05.44
Public road construction labour	00.83
Grain market labour	04.85
Rural handicraft labour	01.66
Skilled labour	06.15

Source: Vidya Sagar Dogar, " Rural Christian Community in North West India", CISRS and ISPCK, New Delhi, 2000, cited in Prakash Louis, *Economic and Political Weekly*, 21 April, 2007, p. 1405.

Table 3
Occupations of Dalit Christians of Tamil Nadu

Occupation	*Per cent*
High administrative	0.62
Low administrative	2.68
Professional	0.68
Teaching	3.57
Clerical	1.73
Trade and commerce	0.75
Transport and public utility	1.72
Manufacturing, processing and service	2.26
Construction	2.80
Own cultivation	7.29
Agricultural labourers	54.75
Livestock, forestry	1.05
Menial	1.80
Others	18.74

Source: Anthony Raj, Discrimination Against Dalit Christians in Tamil Nadu, Ideas Centre, Madurai, 1992, p. 357, (unpublished document) cited in Prakash Louis, *Economic and Political Weekly*, 21 April, 2007, p. 1405.

Many a dalit Christian is disposed to believing that Jesus was a dalit in his own time. This line of thinking is particularly evident amongst the *Paraiyars* of South India. In this context, it is pertinent to note that even though Christians have one fixed book – the Bible, the scripture remains local, plural and dynamic in nature. And, amongst the not-so-literate dalit communities, it is the local and dynamic versions of oral scripture that hold sway.[43]

Discrimination and marginalisation have been evident within the frame of the Church in varying degrees. This has led to the emergence of the critical dalit response from within its parameters and has been referred to as dalit theology. Dalit theology began to take shape in the early 1980s when A.P. Nirmal, then a faculty member at the United Theological College, floated the idea of "*Shudra* theology". But now, dalit theology has come of age and it stands by its own uniqueness and creativity.[44] A.P. Nirmal, James Massey, M.E. Prabhakar, M. Azariah, K. Wilson, V. Devasahayam and F.J. Balasundaram are some of the prominent persons who figure in this theological movement. As theology predominantly became a vehicle to serve the elite interests, marginalising the dalits' faith, dalit theology manifested itself as a counter theology movement. Reformulation and revisioning were the objectives rather than reconstruction and deconstruction. Both the European missionary movement and the traditional Indian Christian theology of the twentieth century were rejected as metaphysical speculations having nothing to do directly with the history and existence of the marginalised majority within the Indian Church.[45] Archbishop George Zur, Apostolic Pro-Nuncio to India said while inaugurating the CBCI (Catholic Bishops Conference of India) in 1991: "Though dalit Christians make 65 per cent of the 10 million Christians in the South, less than 4 per cent of the parishes are entrusted to dalit priests. There are no dalits among the thirteen Catholic Bishops of Tamilnadu or among the Vicar-general and rectors of seminaries and directors of social assistance centres".[46] The attempt was to see Christ and Christianity from a dalit perspective, carving out their own space within the Church. Thus, while certain clerical authorities in the church have been thoughtless in this regard, certain other authorities in the church have from time to time raised their voices of appeal and condemned the denial of rights to dalits. These appeals, however, have not been pressed with enough vigour and constancy to produce tangible results. As a result, in many parts of the country, the dalit faithful continue to be the victims of this baseless and irrational practice at the hands of their fellow Christians.[47]

With the setting up of the Dalit Christian Liberation Movement (DCLM) in South India the struggles of the dalit Christians for equality and justice received a boost. In some of the northern states too efforts at bringing together the dalit Christians have been under way. [48] The DCLM submitted a manifesto to the Tamil Nadu Bishops' Conference that demanded inter alia that the

Church authorities should enact necessary laws to declare the practice of untouchability within the church as a punishable offence. It also demanded that the authority structure in the catholic church should be decentralised and democratised to incorporate dalit clergy and lay participation in the decision-making bodies such as parish councils, boards of trustees for education and multipurpose societies, etc.[49]

The bishops of Tamil Nadu, in 1990, acknowledged caste discrimination within the Church as violative of human rights. At the end of the meeting they issued a joint statement outlining certain measures for rectification of the situation. These included the following: that in places of worship and cemeteries, Catholic Scheduled Castes should be treated equally; that in admissions to Catholic educational institutions, preference should be given to Catholic Scheduled Castes; in jobs in schools run by the dioceses and religious congregations Scheduled Castes Catholics should be given preference; and, funds mobilised through the joint action of Tamil Nadu bishops and religious congregations for the higher education of eligible Scheduled Castes Catholics. Further, continuous efforts were to be made to secure the rights of the Christian Scheduled Castes from the central and state governments.[50]

A National Conference on Human Rights was organised by the National Coordination Committee for Dalit Christians at YMCA in New Delhi on 27 November 1997. Bishops, members of parliament, government officials, commission secretaries, directors of various organisations, theologians, priests, religious, media persons, etc. participated in the meeting. On 3 October 1998, 7,000 people staged a rally in Delhi, the national capital, demanding the introduction of the long pending bill for constitutional rights for dalit Christians. The rally was attended by around 3,000 young people sporting black bands. They came from every corner of India. The rally was inaugurated at the Sacred Heart Cathedral by the Most Rev. Dr Alan de Lastic, Archbishop of Delhi, President of the CBCI. Also present were religious superiors and Christian dalit leaders. The delegates to the rally were welcomed by Bishop Chinnappa, Chairman Catholic Bishop's Conference of India (CBCI) Commission for SC/ST/BC. In his speech, he criticised the government for delaying the extension of equal rights despite being fully aware of the inhuman conditions in which the dalit Christians subsist. Loudly voicing their slogans in demand of change, the rally proceeded to parliament but they were blocked in front of the parliament street police station.[51]

The Poor Christian Liberation Movement (PCLM) was established in 1990 and registered in March, 2000 under Indian Public Trust Act, 1920, as a non-political, non-partisan and non-profit making organisation. The source of inspiration was stated to be Jesus Christ, Ambedkar and Mahatma Gandhi.[52] Interestingly, PCLM submitted a memorandum to Prime Minister Manmohan Singh on 27 August 2004 demanding that instead of meeting the demand of the Church leadership of including the converted Christians in the Scheduled Castes category, a Dalit Christians Finance and Development Board be constituted for the concerted welfare and development of converted dalit Christians all over the country. They felt that inclusion of the dalit Christians in the category of Scheduled Castes is not going to make any difference.[53] This, however, seems to be a minority viewpoint amongst the dalit Christians, as the more vocal opinion appears to be in favour of their demand for Scheduled Caste status.

Nonetheless, repeated appeals for recognition of their Scheduled Caste status seems to fall to deaf ears as the dalit Christians remain denied of reservation facilities on the ground of their being Christians. Here, religion, rather than their socioeconomic condition, becomes decisive.

Postscript

Like their Hindu counterparts, dalit converts to other religions are frequent victims of human rights violations. Economic marginalisation, social exclusion and humiliation continue to chase them. That is, neither have they been able to totally escape from the trappings of their earlier identity, nor could they find the anticipated human dignity within the new milieu. On the whole it seems that in many cases conversion to the otherwise egalitarian religions have failed to assure the measure of social justice that the dalit converts had expected. Here, of course, the responses to conversion have not been uniform in all instances. Sometimes, discrimination is more overt than at other times. But, the humiliation and pinch remains, not to be overlooked or ignored. The non-dalit Buddhists look down on the neo-Buddhists as an inferior lot; the *Ashraf* and even *Ajlaf* Muslims do not consider the *Arzals* as their equals; and, the dalit Christians face constant humiliation at the hands of the non-dalit Christians.

Marginalised as they are, the dalit converts to other religions have persistently been struggling for their rights. The struggles have been essentially on two fronts. One, in terms of the wider social surroundings. The other is in terms of the non-dalits within their own religious folds. Struggles of the dalit converts thus revolve around different issues. Most importantly, they demand social justice and human rights in society at large, within their community and the necessary support from the state. It is here that the question of reservation has repeatedly come up; and, for the converts, barring the neo-Buddhists, the state response has so far been negative. Even as the struggles amongst the dalit Christians and Muslims gain momentum, the hurdles remain to be crossed. In this respect it is pertinent to note that at a seminar held in New Delhi in March 2005, which addressed freedom of faith for dalits in India, dalit movements of various faiths expressed support for the Christian and Muslim dalits who have been demanding equal rights. [54]

The Justice Ranganath Mishra Commission on religious and linguistic minorities, set up in March 2005, recommended a sub quota for the religious minorities within the 27 per cent reservation in jobs for OBCs. Headed by the former Chief Justice of India, the panel was to suggest measures for economic and educational welfare of religious and linguistic minorities and was also asked to determine the criteria for identifying socially and economically backward sections among these minorities[55]. The Commission was of the opinion that the Scheduled Caste status should be extended to dalit Muslims and dalit Christians along with similar deprived sections, if any, among Jains and Parsis. It observed that:

> Para 3 of the Constitution (Scheduled Castes) Order, 1950 – which originally restricted the Scheduled Caste net to the Hindus and later opened it to Sikhs and Buddhists, thus still excluding from its purview the Muslims, Christians, Jains and Parsis, etc. – should be wholly deleted by appropriate action so as to completely de-link the Scheduled Caste status from religion.[56]

An independent research study was commissioned by the National Commission for Minorities in April 2007. It was conducted by Professor Satish Deshpande of the Sociology Department of Delhi School of Economics, Delhi University over a period of eight months. The National Sample Survey's 61st Round survey data (2004–05) was the basis of the data source. It was found that the Muslim dalits are generally worse off among all dalits in terms of most economic and educational criteria. However, Christian dalits, too, were found to be far behind non-dalits and especially upper caste Christians. It was noted in the Study that, "there is no room for disputing the fact that they are invariably regarded as 'socially inferior' communities by their coreligionists."[57] They are dalits first and then Muslims and Christians. As such, the study felt that there is a strong case for offering dalit Muslims and dalit Christians the same constitutional safeguard as were available to the Hindu, Sikh and Buddhist dalits.[58]

Whilst it is important to understand the limitations of conversion as a way of attainment of social justice and the problems generated by the difficulties that the convertees have faced in gaining recognition of their Scheduled Caste status, it is perhaps true to say that, "the prospect of religious conversion … does not lie only with the present but also in an anticipatory future".[59] Through conversion, the dalit communities are able to construe a different world vision, which even if not concretely experienced, have utopian consequences.[60]

Notes

1. Rowena Robinson and Sathianathan Clarke, "Introduction: The Many Meanings of Religious Conversion on the Indian Sub-continent", in Rowena Robinson and Sathianathan Clarke,

ed., *Religious Conversion in India: Modes, Motivations and Meanings*, Oxford University Press, New Delhi, 2007, pp. 16–17.

2. http://www.milligazette.com/dailyupdate/20021028.htm
3. Ibid.
4. Ibid.
5. news.bbc.co.uk/2/low/south_asia/2344445.htm
6. By Rashid Salim Adil and Yoginder Sikand, "Politics Of Conversion,"countercurrents.org, http://www.countercurrents.org/dalit-sikander030404.htm
7. Irfan Habib, *Essays in Indian History: Towards a Marxist Perception*, Tulika, New Delhi, 2000, p. 65.
8. See G. Aloysius, *Religion as Emancipatory Identity, A Buddhist Movement Among the Tamils Under Colonialism*, New Age International Publishers, Delhi, 1998, p. 50.
9. Ibid.
10. J.R. Kamble, *Rise and Awakening of Depressed Classes in India*, National, Delhi, 1979; Owen Lynch, "Dr B.R. Ambedkar: Myth and Charisma", Michael Mahar, ed., *The Untouchables in Contemporary India*, The University of Arizona Press, Tucson, 1972.
11. Gary Tartakov, "B.R. Ambedkar and the Navayana Diksha", Rowena Robinson and Sathianathan Clarke, ed., *Religious Conversion in India: Modes, Motivations, and Meanings*, Oxford University Press, New Delhi, 2007, pp. 192–3.
12. Dhananjay Keer, *Dr Ambedkar, Life and Mission*, Popular Prakashan, Bombay, 1990, p. 92
13. Ibid.
14. http://www.indianexpress.com/printerFriendly/14524.html
15. Timothy Fitzgerald, "Ambedkar, Buddhism and the Concept of Religion", S.M. Michael, ed., *Dalits in Modern India*, Vistaar Publications, New Delhi, 1999, pp. 132–3.
16. Maren Bellwinkel-Schempp, "From Bhakti to Buddhism: Ravidas and Ambedkar", *Economic and Political Weekly*, June 9, 2007, p. 2181.

17. http://en.wikipedia.org/wiki/Main_Page#cite_note-maren_roots-4
18. *The Hindu*, 10 October, 2006.
19. http://www.indianexpress.com/printerFriendly/14524.html
20. http://www.indianexpress.com/printerFriendly/14524.html
21. Timothy Fitzgerald, op. cit., p. 132.
22. T.S. Wilkinson and M.N. Thomas, eds., *Ambedkar and the Neo-Buddhist Movement*, The Christian Literature Society, Madras, 1972.
23. Dr Shura Darapuri, "Dalit Budhists Far Ahead of Hinduised Dalits", *Dalit Voice*, June 1–15, 2008, p. 12.
24. Irfan Habib, op. cit., p. 142.
25. Ibid., p. 143.
26. Ibid., p. 142.
27. Ibid., p. 144.
28. See Anwar Alam, "Democratisation of Indian Muslims: Some Reflections," *Economic and Political Weekly*, November 15, 2003, p. 4881.
29. Louis Dumont, *Homo Hierarchicus: The Caste System and its Implications*, Oxford University Press, New Delhi, 1999, pp. 206–7.
30. Ibid.
31. Ibid., p. 208.
32. *The Hindu*, 27 January, 2008.
33. Quoted in Iqbal A. Ansari, "Reservation for All Dalits Irrespective of Faith", *Muslim India*, 288, June 2008, p. 26. The Sachar Committee was a high-level committee appointed by the Prime Minister under the Chairmanship of Justice Rajindar Sachar, retired Chief Justice of the Delhi High Court, to study the "Social, Economic and Educational Status of the Muslim Community of India". The Sachar Committee prepared its report in November 2006 and presented it to the parliament on 30th November 2006.
34. See Anwar Alam, "Democratisation of Indian Muslims: Some Reflections," *Economic and Political Weekly*, November 15, 2003, p. 4885.

35. http://www.thesouthasian.org/archives/2004/the_dalit_muslims_and_the_alli.html
36. See Anwar Alam, "Democratisation of Indian Muslims: Some Reflections", *Economic and Political Weekly,* November 15, 2003, p. 4885.
37. Rowena Robinson, "Sixteenth Century Conversions to Christianity in Goa", Rowena Robinson and Sathianathan Clarke, ed., *Religious Conversion in India: Modes, Motivations and Meanings,* Oxford University Press, New Delhi, 2007, pp. 290–315.
38. For a detailed discussion see Sathianathan Clarke, "Conversion to Christianity in Tamil Nadu: Conscious and Constitutive Community Mobilization Towards a Different Symbolic World Vision", in Rowena Robinson and Sathianathan Clarke, ed., op. cit., pp. 322–349.
39. See John C.B. Webster, "Christian Conversion in the Punjab: What has Changed?", Rowena Robinson and Sathianathan Clarke, ed., op. cit., pp. 350–375.
40. http://www.dalitchristians.com/Html/Discrimination.htm
41. Prakash Louis, "Dalit Christians: Betrayed By State and Church", *Economic and Political Weekly,* 21 April, 2007, p. 1404
42. Ibid., p. 1405.
43. Sathianathan Clarke, *Dalits and Christianity: Subaltern Religion and Liberation Theology in India,* Oxford University Press, Delhi, 1998, p. 30.
44. George Oommen, "The Emerging Dalit Theology: A Historical Appraisal",http://www.religion-online.org/showarticle.asp?title=1121
45. Ibid.
46. quoted in ibid.
47. Ibid.
48. Prakash Louis, *Economic and Political Weekly,* 21 April 2007, p. 1406.
49. Anthony Raj, *Betraying the Hope of the Poor,* DCLM Publication, Madurai, pp. 4–5, cited ibid., pp. 1406–07.

50. Cited in Prakash Louis, *Economic and Political Weekly*, 21 April 2007, p. 1407.
51. http://www.dalitchristians.com/Html/demonstration.htm
52. http://www.dalitchristian.org/about.htm
53. http://www.dalitchristian.org/news.htm
54. http://www.christianpost.com/article/20050317/1308_Religious_"Untouchables"_in_India_Unite_for_Affirmative_Action.htm
55. *The Telegraph*, Calcutta, Tuesday, May 22 2007.
56. Ibid.
57. *The Hindu*, Saturday, Apr 05 2008
58. "Reservation for Dalit Muslims etc.: NMC Press Release, April 3, 2008", *Muslim India*, 290, August 2008, p. 15.
59. Sathianathan Clarke, "Conversion to Christianity", Rowena Robinson and Sathianathan Clarke, ed., op. cit., p. 288.
60. Ibid.

Chapter 7

Dalits, Displacement and Human Rights

Upper Caste Violence and Dalit Displacement

Of the many woes of the dalits, displacement has been a major one. Dalits, over the years, have suffered displacement on many different counts. Many a time, upper caste violence has forced dalit individuals and families to flee their villages, leaving behind what little they possess. It should be remembered that dalits are particularly vulnerable to forced displacement in the aftermath of episodes of caste violence. In a report submitted by the Centre for Human Rights and Global Justice and Human Rights Watch in February 2007 to the UN Committee on the Elimination of Racial Discrimination (CERD), it is argued that the typical scenario is one where dalit villages are attacked and looted by neighbouring upper caste villagers, forcing them to settle for months in temporary homes on government property. The perpetrators largely enjoy full impunity and little is done to help the displaced dalits return home or to prosecute those responsible for the attacks.[1]

This has remained a pretty common phenomenon across the country. But, that has not been the only cause of dalit displacement. There have, no doubt, been other causes that have led to widespread exodus of dalits from their places of habitation – all under threat of violence. Loot, arson, rape and murder have underlined such forced displacement. Examples are almost unending.

One of the many spine-chilling incidents leading to the displacement of dalit people was the Karamchedu dalit massacre in 1985. Karamchedu is in Prakasham District, close to Krishna District of Andhra Pradesh. In 1985, the atrocious dalit massacre took place under the leadership of the local landlord Chenchu Ramaiah, who was father of Venkateswara Rao, N.T.Rama Rao's elder son-in-law. Venkateswar Rao was also the then Health Minister in the N.T.Rama Rao Government in the State. Following the massacre, the entire dalit population of the region fled from Karamchedu and lived for years in makeshift tents at Chirala town, eight kilometres away from their native village.[2]

As recently as in 2008, *The Hindu,* carried a Report wherein it was stated regarding the state of Gujarat:

> Over 100 members of 19 dalit families are spending their days in makeshift camps in front of the Banaskantha District Collector's office in Palanpur for the last seven months because they have nowhere to go. They have been forced to migrate from their native village, Bukna in Vav taluka, after a dalit was murdered following a quarrel with some caste Hindus of the village over a passage through the dalit's household plot to their fields.[3]

Manjula Pradeep, executive director of the Navsarjan Trust, a voluntary organisation working for the dalits in the State, drew attention to the fact that, twenty-two members of five families in Kasumbad village in Borsad taluka of Anand district of Gujarat were also living in unsafe conditions and would be forced to migrate to some other villages if the authorities did not provide them security. The events leading up to the situation were as follows: The head of the family, Ramanbhai Makwana, was murdered in this village by caste Hindus after a quarrel over flying kites on the "*Utran* festival" day on 14 January 2006. The caste Hindus wanted the dalit families to withdraw the police complaint on the murder and threatened them with dire consequences if they did not. The murder took place in the presence of the police and yet no step was taken to book the culprit. The dalit families were refused protection if they went out of their homes to earn their livelihood.[4]

These are just a few of the many instances that occur across the country – some of which get recorded, others do not.

The Partition of India and Dalit Displacement

Perhaps, the largest involuntary movement of the dalit population in India resulted in the wake of the partition of the country. The partition of India affected large sections of the dalit population forcing them to move out of their homesteads in undivided Bengal in search of refuge elsewhere. While the Indian refugee problem has been a pet area of research, few have investigated the plight of the dalit refugees per se. In fact, not surprisingly, the few scholars who have demonstrated interest in the matter have been dalits themselves.

The historic partition of India when it took place in 1947, had not only truncated the country, but displaced hundreds of people of whom a sizeable portion comprised of the dalit communities. It also set in motion a massive refugee flow that was to continue for years to come.

It may be noted that, in 1947 at the time of the partition of India and soon thereafter, more than 2,58,000 refugees came to India. They mostly belonged to the upper caste Hindu categories. Even as the initial refugee flow did not stop altogether, it subsided in course of time, only to be revived in 1950. Communal disturbances in East Pakistan in 1949 led to a massive exodus in 1950. By official records, another 1,82,000 refugees entered West Bengal, while the total entering Assam, Tripura and West Bengal worked out to be 15,82,000. These refugees, however, were different from the earlier lot in that they were almost 100 per cent dalits – belonging mostly to the *Namasudra* community.[5]

They were welcome neither by the state machinery already burdened with the refugee problem, nor by the caste Hindus. Under the circumstances, their miseries were boundless. Needless to say, that while all displaced persons were undoubtedly traumatised by their displacement, the dalits were worse off. Their worst tragedies went down in history with the sorrowful events of Marichjhapi.

Recalling the events of Marichjhapi. There had been a heavy influx of refugees from East Pakistan into India between 1963–64. it was estimated that more than two lakh people had come. They were all dalits and adivasis. Of them, about one lakh came to West Bengal, the rest went to Assam and Tripura. As West Bengal was already overburdened with the refugee problem, the State and the Central Governments agreed to rehabilitate the newcomers at places other than West Bengal. accordingly, arrangements were made. They were to be settled at Dandakaranya and other camps. However, conditions there were hardly congenial and discontent amongst the refugees mounted over time. Ultimately, in 1978 many of the refugees decided to desert their respective rehabilitation sites and move to the Sundarbans where they hoped they would be able to make a living. Accordingly, they moved to Marichjhapi in hundreds and set up their homes at the place. The government, however, was determined to push them back to their allotted places. The conflict that followed left many wounded and fifteen dead; hundreds were arrested and many others are said to have died of starvation and disease. A sad tale of human rights violations.[6]

Today, the dalits still bear the legacy of the partition as many suffer inadequate rehabilitation support, fail to obtain citizenship rights and are denied caste certificates necessary for access to the special support schemes in the fields of education and employment assured to members of the Scheduled Castes.

Dalits as Victims of Development

Independent India's development strategy too has had its toll. Massive displacement has resulted from various development projects. Of the displaced, dalits and tribals have been the worst affected.

It is estimated that some five lakh persons are displaced every year as a direct consequence of administrative land acquisition.[7] These figures of the displaced shoot up as we include along with them those displaced by other causes such as non-plan projects, acquisition for urban growth, pollution, soil degradation, etc., as well as secondary displacement.[8] The Land Acquisition Act, 1894, which provides the basis for such ongoing displacement has proved to be a powerful weapon in the hands of power holders, a tool that they can use with ease for depriving dalits or oppressed, the tribals, backwards and the peasants, of their legitimate rights. After independence, approximately three crore of people were displaced for setting up the power plants, irrigation projects, mining companies, steel industries and many more development projects in the country. Among them, 40 per cent displaced people are tribals and 20 per cent are dalits, which means the 60 per cent displaced people are from the marginalised communities, who sacrificed everything for the sake of the "development" but they are still untouched of the development.[9]

It is today amply evident that the economic development strategy in India is largely nurtured at the cost of the dalits, a large section of the victims being tribals and the lower castes. The costs of many of the large infrastructural development projects, both in material and human terms, have to be primarily borne by them in terms of loss of land, displacement, social disruption and psychological shock. People are often forcibly moved out of their habitats, long established residential communities are disorganised, kinship groups and family systems scattered and social networks that frequently serve as insurance against a variety of crises situations, are torn apart. They are alienated from their traditional symbolic markers such as ancestral shrines, holy rivers, mountains, forests, traditional places of worship and much more. The lopsided euphoria of nation building has submerged their cries of destitution, translating their woes into perceived "sacrifices for national interest". What is not voiced is that these sacrifices are most frequently being extracted and are not made voluntarily.

Despite widespread criticisms, successive Indian governments have demonstrated their determination to proceed with such controversial development projects, which lead to extensive devastation in and around the project areas. The big dam projects and mining areas in different parts of the country hold out numerous examples of large-scale displacement of population whereby the project affected people (PAPs) are rendered homeless and traumatised. Equally traumatising have been the effects of many of India's defence development exercises. A conservative estimate of the numbers displaced may be obtained from Table 1.

Table 1
A Conservative Estimate of Persons Displaced by Various Categories of Projects

Type of Projects	*Number Displaced*	*Number Rehabilitated*	*Backing*
Coal and Other Mines	17,00,000	4,550,000	12,50,000
Dam and Canals	1,10,00,000	27,50,000	82,50,000
Industries	10,00,000	3,00,000	7,00,000
Sanctuaries and Parks	6,00,000	1,50,000	4,50,000
Others	12,00,000	3,00,000	9,00,000
Total	1,65,00,000	39,50,000	1,15,00,000

Source: Walter Fernandes et al., *Displacement and Rehabilitation: An Estimate of Extent and Prospects*, Indian Social Institute, New Delhi, 1989.

The largest numbers of those displaced are the victims of the hydroelectric and irrigation projects. Mining takes the second position, while other factors follow.

What befalls the poor tribals and low caste oustees can vividly be described in the words of the noted litterateur and activist struggling against the Sardar Sarovar and Maheshwar Dams, Arundhati Roy:

> What has happened to these millions of people? Where are they now? How do they earn a living? Nobody really knows. When history is written, they won't be in it, not even as statistics. When it comes to resettlement, the government's priorities are clear. *India does not have a National Resettlement Policy*. Displaced people are only entitled to a meagre cash compensation. The poorest of them, Dalits and Adivasis, who are either landless or have no formal title to their lands, but whose livelihoods depend entirely on the river – get nothing. Some of the displaced have been subsequently displaced three and four times – a dam, an artillery proof range, another dam, a uranium mine. Once they start rolling there's no resting place. The great majority is eventually absorbed into slums on the periphery of our great cities, where it coalesces into an immense pool of cheap labour (that builds more projects that displaces more people) ... and still the nightmare doesn't end.[10]

The displacement of the dalit population in and around various project sites and the overall backwardness of such population in educational and economic terms form a continuum.

For the displaced the problems are manifold. As is clearly evident from the experiences of the Sardar Sarobar Project, there is lack of planning on the part of the several states involved (in this case the states involved are Madhya Pradesh, Maharashtra and Gujarat), gross underestimation of the number of people to be displaced, insufficient resettlement land and different policies regarding entitlement to compensation in the case of different categories of oustees.[11] Their lack of skills and experience in coping with the complexities of the modern market economy make them particularly susceptible to getting entangled in fraudulent transactions and losing out on the little cash compensation that, if fortunate enough, they may have been able to lay hands upon.

Interesting insight into the problem could be obtained by looking into statistics relating to the occupational classifications of the Scheduled Castes and Scheduled Tribes over the span of 1961 to 1991 (see Table 2):

Table 2

Occupational Classification of Main Workers From 1961 to 1991 Census (in percentage)

Category of Workers	*1961* Gen. S.C. S.T.	*1971* Gen S.C. S.T.	*1981* Gen. S.C. S.T.	*1991* Gen. S.C. S.T.
Cultivators	52.78 37.76; 68.18	43.38 27.87; 57.56	41.53 28.17; 54.43	39.74 25.44; 54.50
Agricultural Labourers	16.71 34.48; 19.71	26.32 51.74; 33.04	25.16 48.22; 32.67	19.66 49.06; 32.69
Household Industry	6.38 6.56; 2.47	3.55 3.33; 1.03	3.99 3.31; 1.42	2.56 2.41; 1.04
Other Workers	24.13 21.20; 9.64	26.75 17.06; 8.37	29.32 20.30; 11.84	38.04 23.08;11.76

Source: National Commission for Scheduled Castes and Scheduled Tribes, Annual Report, 1993–94, New Delhi, pp. 59–60.

It is clearly evident from Table 2 that between 1961 and 1991 the percentage of Scheduled Caste and Scheduled Tribe workers engaged in cultivation has declined on the one hand, and on the other hand there has been, during the same period, a marked rise in the proportion of agricultural labourers, bearing out the fact that over the years these sections of the population have been steadily losing whatever land they had.[12]

Globalisation, Displacement and Human Rights

Structural adjustment and globalisation, sweeping the country from the late 1990s, have threatened these weaker sections of Indian society as never before. Capitalism's immense appetite for newer pastures and the setting up of large industries without regard for the fallout on the one hand, combined with the rollback of welfare allotments of the state on the other, adversely affect the poor project affected peoples in a dual sense. The gigantic industrial mega projects, many of which are foreign funded, swallow their homes and shelter as well as their traditional sources of livelihood.

In March 1993 a New National Mineral Policy was announced by the government with much fanfare aimed at attracting private and multinational investors for large-scale expansion of mineral exploitation in the country. It may be noted in this context that India is a major mineral producer and the world's fourth largest producer of hard coal and bauxite and fifth in terms of iron ore. And, most of these minerals are mined in the Jharkhand region.[13]

Major mining companies of the world, including the White Industries of Australia and the Canadian Met-Chem Company, have been showing great interest in the Jharkhand region.

The UK-based RTZ Corporation, one of the largest mining conglomerates in the world and notorious for various human rights violations, too, has, inter alia, been revealing an interest in the mining of iron ore in the area. It is significant to note that international environmental pressure groups and human rights bodies such as Minewatch and Partizans (both based in London) have documented RTZ's involvement in the violation of indigenous peoples rights, the alleged contribution of the corporation to the war in Papua New Guinea, environmental destruction in South America and South East Asia and the export of toxic wastes. The company had been fined in 1988 and 1990 for breaches of health and safety regulations.[14]

The Coal India policy is being constantly propelled by the World Bank. Many of the 25 new mines in the Upper Karanpura (Damodar) valley in the Jharkhand region, which are likely to displace more than a lakh of people, mostly tribals and low castes, are Bank funded.

Post-globalisation, the scenario is all the more grim as encouraging the processes of liberalisation and privatisation, massive land acquisition across the country for setting up Special Economic Zones (SEZs) as per the SEZ Act of 2005 that came into force in 2006, is on the agenda. The process has already begun. More than 500 SEZs will be established in India of which 237 are already approved by the central government in 19 states, 63 are being notified and 23 are operational. Total land needed in order to establish 500 SEZs is nearly 150,000 hectares.[15] The displacements that are likely to take place over the coming years, it is feared, will be massive. Estimates show that close to 114,000 farming households (each household on an average comprising five members) and an additional 82,000 farm worker families who are dependent upon these farms for their livelihoods, will be displaced. In other words, at least 10 lakh people who primarily depend upon agriculture for their survival will face eviction.[16] The voices of protests can already be heard nationwide. The worst off of the displaced are and will continue to be, as usual, the poor, the tribals, minorities and the dalits.

More land than in the past is now required and massive acquisition is likely to be pushed ahead in the context of liberalisation. Alongside this, a concern for rehabilitation of the displaced is officially on display, under pressure from world bodies, probably in order to check the mounting opposition to such acquisitions, rather than out of love for the displaced.[17]

The Displaced and the Indian Governmental Policies

In 1951, the Convention Relating to the Status of Refugees, often referred to as the Refugee Convention, was adopted. It had restricted geographical and temporal applicability with its focus on post-War Europe. In 1967, in an effort to give the Convention universal application, a Protocol relating to the Status of Refugees (1967 Protocol) that removed the restrictions of the Convention was added. Together, these two key legal documents provide the basic framework for refugee protection across the world. However, despite her major refugee problem, India has repeatedly declined to join either the 1951 Refugee Convention or its 1967 Protocol. Also, India has all along resisted the demands for national legislation to govern the protection of refugees. Needless to say, under the circumstances, the handling of the refugee situation has hardly been systematic, and have suffered from inadequacies and uncertainties. Under the circumstances, and keeping in mind the general cultural ethos of brahminism, it is not difficult to understand the hardships to which the dalit refugees were subjected over the different phases of their influx and thereafter. Repeated pressures from the international community and civil rights organisations have so far failed to make a dent.

The handling of the problems of the project affected people too have been clumsy to say the least. Even as the central and state governments seek to attract large investors on the "Special Economic Zones", "Private-Public Partnerships" and "Build-Operate-and-Transfer" policies, the governments are yet to accept their full responsibilities to resettle and rehabilitate the displaced population groups. The Land Acquisition Act, which still forms the basis of acquisitions, when applied to large-scale acquisitions have most frequently resulted in displacement and deprivation of means of livelihood for the affected people, but did not give them the right to resettlement or rehabilitation. It is only recently that the government has moved to introduce in Parliament the Rehabilitation and Resettlement Bill 2007, to fill in some of the lacunae. In fact, two significant pieces of legislations – the Land Acquisition (Amendment) Bill 2007 and the Rehabilitation and Resettlement Bill, 2007 – were introduced in the Lok Sabha last year and are now before a parliamentary standing committee.[18] The Rehabilitation and Resettlement (RR) Bill was introduced in response to popular opposition in different parts of the country to the takeover of land for the creation of Special Economic Zones (SEZs).[19]

Concluding Observations

It must be understood that displacement is not just shifting people from one place to another, but it is the destruction of their livelihood resources, culture and the identity that they nourished and developed through the ages. Only a fraction of the displaced get relocated through official efforts. The others are, at most, left with the promises of rehabilitation. Cash compensation, as and when available, hardly compensates the losses. Almost invariably, the displaced is worse off on displacement than previously.

For any democratic paradigm to be viable, three basic rights need to be reaffirmed. First, people should have the right to be informed. Secondly, they should have the right to articulate their interests. Thirdly, they should have the right to seek representation of their interests. The second and the third mentioned rights rest on the premise of the first as no sensible articulation or representation of interests is possible without information. Where, as in the case of displacement, the very essence of survival is under threat, it is all the more important to highlight these rights.

It is imperative to understand the links between various forms of exploitation to which the dalits and other weaker sections of Indian society are being constantly subject. Their overall backwardness – educational, economic and political – and their relative inexperience in aptly utilising the modern idioms of politics have made them particularly susceptible to marginalisation. For aggregation and representation of their perceived interests they have had to depend on political parties and NGOs. Thus, what they can or cannot lay claims to is frequently dependent upon what one or the other political *"dada"* or NGO thinks suitable for them.

In any process of development induced population displacement and resettlement process several key social actors may be identified. First, there is the government. It not only initiates, supports and conducts public sector development programmes, but also permits private sector undertakings to pursue or not pursue one or the other industrial scheme. Secondly, there are the policy makers in the private sector undertakings, operating as important social actors in the context of those projects, which they initiate and finance. Thirdly, there are the agencies that plan and execute/or execute the development programmes. Fourthly, those sections of the population who benefit from the schemes. Fifthly, the public groups, including the NGOs and advocacy groups, who take an interest in the socio-economic and environmental implications of the policies. And, finally, there is that section of the population, which bears the main costs of development in so far as they are displaced and stand threatened materially and emotionally.[20]

There is ample statistical data to demonstrate that amongst the social actors mentioned above, representatives of the last category are hardly present in the government, or as policy makers in the private sector, or in the agencies that plan and execute the schemes, or in the leadership positions in the public concern groups. They (that is, the members of the last category) are thus grossly under-represented in virtually all the forums involved in determining their fate. Others purportedly speak for them, or bypass them altogether while taking crucial policy decisions affecting their conditions. Instead of appreciating that a conscious, articulate and rational population is a great national asset, which is essential for democracy to take root in any society, the administration often treats dissent as defiance and assertion as insurrection.

Protection of the interests of the dalits demand that:

1. In programmes initiated and carried out by the private sector, the government's role as an important actor must be maintained. In relation to questions of displacement and resettlement and rehabilitation the government's control on the one hand and accountability on the other must be duly recognised and legally ensured.

2. Those who are displaced or affected by the development projects must be called upon to participate in the execution of

the policies and must get a significant share of the benefits of the project. As things stand today, those who stand to lose from a project and those who stand to gain form two distinct categories. It is imperative that these two categories be merged, with the traditional losers sharing in the gains and the traditional gainers sharing the burdens of the projects.

3. At least 50 per cent representation should be given to persons likely to be affected by a project, on all bodies involved in decision-making pertaining to the project.

4. As dalits are the most adversely affected by the development projects, at least 50 per cent representation should be ensured to them on all policy-making bodies at the national level, including the highest level bodies, so that they are in a position to meaningfully influence policy decisions.

5. These dalit representatives should enjoy absolute veto in relation to all projects where massive displacement is calculated to occur.

6. No scheme, as a result of which displacement is expected to occur, should be sanctioned without an accompanying detailed plan for resettlement and rehabilitation. Such a plan, once it is announced, should not be liable to change in a manner that could adversely affect the interests of the displaced or other project affected people.

7. The resettlement and rehabilitation plan should specify the time limit within which those to be displaced would be resettled and rehabilitated. Under all circumstances, the resettlement should take place before any actual physical displacement takes place. In the event of a failure to resettle and rehabilitate the people within the stipulated period, the project affected people should be entitled to additional compensation fixed at a monthly rate and calculated on the basis of the total months of delay. The compensation amount should be determined on the basis of average daily material loss and mental trauma associated with delay in resettlement.

8. Finally, it needs to be noted, that without overall distributive justice being ensured to the dalits, the problem of displacement cannot be remedied. Developmental priorities need to be redefined and in those redefined priorities the dalits must count as beneficiaries. Where they do not count in such capacities, developmental policies have to be reconsidered.

   In conclusion it can be said that displacement is not simply a loss of land or homestead. It involves a total loss of identity; an identity that has evolved through generations in close relationship with the surrounding environment including the land, the forests, the trees, and the animals and the water bodies, not to speak of the folk who comprise the community or the extended family of the victims. In a word, displacement demeans the human dignity. Only, where in a society human dignity receives its due respect can the trauma of displacement be truly appreciated, steps taken to remedy the damage and prevent its recurrence as far as possible.

Notes

1. Centre for Human Rights and Global Justice & Human Rights Watch, February 2007, pp. 45–46; *AHRC,* January 2007, p. 2.
2. http://www.ambedkar.org/News/SiliconValley.htm
3. Manas Dasgupta, "These Dalits Have Nowhere to Go", *The Hindu*, 19 April, 2008.
4. Ibid.
5. Dilip Kumar Halder, "Dalits are the Worst Victims of Partition of Bengal: A Human Rights Question", Biswajit Chatterjee and Debi Chatterjee ed., *Dalit Lives and Dalit Visions in Eastern India*, Centre for Rural Resources, Kolkata, 2007, p. 55.
6. For a detailed discussion see ibid., pp. 48–70.
7. See Smitu Kothari, "Who's Nation? The Displaced as Victims of Development", *Economic and Political Weekly,* 15 June, 1996, p.1476.
8. Ibid., pp. 1476–7.

9. *Tehelka,* 29 August, 2008.
10. Arundhati Roy, "The Cost of Living", *Frontline,* Volume 17, Issue 3, Feb.5–8, 2000.
11. H. Jack Ruitenbeek and Cynthia M. Cartier, "Evaluation of Narmada Projects: An Ecological Economics Perspective", *Economic and Political Weekly,* 26th August, 1995, pp.2138–9.
12. National Commission ..., op. cit., pp. 59–60.
13. Ibid.
14. Mathew Areeparampil, op. cit.,p.1528.
15. http://www.merinews.com/catFull.jsp?articleID=130932
16. Ibid.
17. Walter Fernandes, "Land Acquisition (Amendment) Bill, 1998: Rights of Project Affected People Ignored", *Economic and Political Weekly,* October 17–24, 1998, p. 2704.
18. Rema Nagarajan, "Will Changing Land Laws Ensure Peace?", *The Times of India,* 31 Aug, 2008,
19. Ibid.
20. See Michael M. Cernea, "Public Policy Responses to Development Induced Population Displacements", *Economic and Political Weekly,* June 15, 1996, p. 1515.

Chapter 8

Dalit Struggles for Social Justice

A Historical Overview

The Early Protests against Brahminism

The roots of dalit protest go back to ancient India's materialist, *Lokayata* tradition wherein there was no place for the supernatural, the philosophy of *Karma,* the notion of transmigration of the soul or the brokerage of the brahmin priesthood. The focus was on the gross; on life as it was at any given point of time in the contemporary world. Despite the obscurity of that heritage, its historicity is beyond doubt.[1]

This apart, even as the brahminical order had been crystallising, two heterodox sects rooted in the *Sramanic* tradition came to reflect the growing discontent of the lesser castes. They were the Buddhists and the Jains. Both these faiths denied the efficacy of the vedic rites and the preeminence of the priestly caste. Both spoke in the language of the lay folk and displayed an essentially democratic approach towards religious and social organisation. For a time, both these religions posed formidable threats to the brahminical order. Buddhism, under the reign of Emperor Ashoka, enjoying his steadfast support, had risen to the position of being a leading religion in India. Jainism, by the end of the fourth century BC had spread to the southern part of the region and notwithstanding internal dissensions, established itself as one of the important religions. Ample evidence of the influence of these two non-brahminical sects can be found in a variety of inscriptions, literature and architectural creations of the pre-Gupta period.[2]

With the brahminical revival under the Guptas, however, decline of these two powerful sects had set in. Land grants, which were typical during the period, gave rise to feudal conditions wherein the priestly caste and the royalty developed a highly symbiotic relationship. Under the marriage of convenience, the kings laboured to protect the rules expounded in the *Dharmasastras* while the priests in return urged the people to perform their caste assigned duties and render obedience to the king.[3] The earlier laxity of the vedic religion came to be replaced, in course of time, by a greater clarity and cohesiveness of the Hindu brahminical philosophy. And, as its corollary, there came about a progressive marginalisation of the heterodox sects.[4] Both Buddhism and Jainism succumbed to that fate.

As the earlier sects were subject to processes of pressure and assimilation, in course of time, however, new protestant groups began to appear. Some were breakaway radical elements of the older groups that were going through the assimilative process; some others grew clearly from the Hindu genetic line and took on postures of protest in search of greater egalitarianism. Here, the impact of certain extraneous ideological systems could easily be discerned. The history of most of these sects however reveal that their initial radicalism was in course of time diluted in face of the continuous onslaught from brahminical Hinduism. Step by step, they too moved into the orbit of the latter just as many other protestant groups had done before them.

From the earliest days, protest against caste and its sustaining brahminical ideology had operated at the religious plane, attempting to build up for the individual a more egalitarian alternative. Such moves almost invariably demanded a widening of the participatory base of the religious order and denial of caste and other distinctions based on birth. There were socioeconomic compulsions behind these movements, but they were not socio-economic movements as such, nor did they raise socioeconomic and political demands in any direct fashion. Vis-à-vis the brahminical order they were by and large non-aggressive in the sense that they did not seek to crush the caste system altogether.

Rather, they were inclined towards laying down norms for observance by their own sect or group members. [5]

In fact, protesting the exclusion perpetrated by the brahminical tradition, many of the low caste groups developed their own alternative religious space without altogether dissociating from the Hindu fold. Such religious tradition in certain cases tended to reveal an admixture of elements of orthodox Hinduism and survivals of animism and nature worship. And, from ancient times till today in villages across the length and breadth of the country, we come across such folk expression of protest articulated in their own language and in their own style and manifest widely in the worshipping of village deities. In front of the village gods, all are equal, there being no caste discrimination or untouchability. The priests too have been found to hail from low caste categories. In Bengal, the worship of the goddess of serpents, Manasa Devi throughout the monsoon month of *Sravan* (July–August) or the boat worshipping by the rejoicing untouchable *Chandals* in what is called the *Chandal Kudni* are but a few examples of that mood.

Protests in Medieval India

Medieval India witnessed varied forms of religious protests against the dominant brahminical order of society. There was the emergence of the *Sants* who placed an overwhelming emphasis on love as the characteristic emotion of true religion. The *Sant* tradition emerged from the *Bhakti* stream of thought. While some scholars choose to incorporate the *Sants* within the general *Bhakti* category, others regard it as a separate line.

The *Sants'* philosophy involved the total rejection of all Hindu brahminical ceremonies, the scriptures, incantations, food taboos and caste distinctions. Most of these *Sants* were drawn from the low castes and spoke the language of the folk. One of the most popular of the *Sants* to oppose the caste system was Kabir. Through his verses or *Dohas* he uncompromisingly exposed the bigotry of ritualistic religion and the falsehood of the brahminical claim of superiority. Criticising caste, Kabir set forth the logic of his arguments thus,

In the womb there is no sign of family or caste because everyone is born of the divine drop.

Speak, O Pundit, from whence have you become a Brahmin?
Do not waste your life by calling yourself a Brahmin.
If you are a Brahmin, born of a Brahmin mother,
Why did you not choose a different way of coming to this world?
In what way are you a Brahmin and am I a Sudra?
How am I made of dirty blood and you of (pure) milk?[6]

Kabir's warning to the common man was clear,

O friend, Pandas are adroit butchers –
Most holy and high-born are they deemed,
they demand reverence and homage from all;
men beg to be initiated by such priests – this makes me laugh, O brother.
They narrate stories from holy books
Which once listened to, they claim,
Will grant the remission of sins;
But they oblige men to do heinous deeds.
Says Kabir, listen O friends,
These priests of the Iron Age
Are thoroughly depraved.[7]

Strictly speaking, Kabir was not a philosopher. Neither was he a social revolutionary. He did not partake of elaborate philosophical discourses, nor did he collect around himself a band of students for systematic instructions on any particular philosophical line. Yet, he undoubtedly had a philosophy and that philosophy permeated the entire range of his creations. Based on his ideas, the *Kabir Panth* came into existence and in course of time spread to different parts of northern India.[8]

The influence of the *Bhakti* movement in medieval India was widespread. In eastern India the *Chaitanya* movement drew a large following from the laity across vast stretches of Bengal and Orissa. In Bengal, *Chaitanya* turned the tide of *vaisnavism* towards *Bhakti*. The essence of his teachings and his style of functioning were antithetical to caste philosophy. On the one hand it aimed at striking at the roots of the vested interests of the priestly class and liberating the common man from that tyranny. On the other hand, he sought to bring together the numerous low caste Hindus and Muslims onto the platform of *Krisna Bhakti*.

It is on record that long before the advent of *Caitanya* on the scene, certain low castes like the *banias* and the *valajikas* (Baruis) were adherents of the *vaisnava* faith and *vaisnavism* in the form of the *Radha-Krisna* cult had come to establish a measure of influence amongst the low castes of Bengal.[9] *Caitanya's* own emotional commitment and charismatic personality furthered the process of extending *vaisnava* influence amongst the oppressed castes at least in Bengal. By turning to the *vaisnava* faith as espoused by *Caitanya*, low caste Hindus could remain Hindus by faith and at the same time shed their caste humiliation in the company of their *vaisnava* coreligionists. Thus, to them, it was like a breath of fresh air.

Protests of the Nineteenth and Early Twentieth Centuries

From the eighteenth century onwards, the struggle against caste and the brahminical ideology became by and large more secularised. It remained neither confined to mere debates and discussions on religious philosophy, nor to the search for shelter under professedly more egalitarian theosophical promises. Even as the religious arena of struggle was not abandoned, struggles were increasingly channelised in socioeconomic and political directions. Increasingly the low castes began to articulate their grievances in material terms and make demands on the state authorities for their redressal. It is pertinent to note in this respect that democratic awakening of the low castes and their emergent consciousness pertaining to their basic rights came about as part of the general national awakening of the Indians during the British rule, and evolved as its continuum. Exposed to and faced by the compulsions of the situation, the traditionally oppressed castes who till then had largely internalised the brahminical values, felt impelled to question them.

The demand for education came up as one of the main demands of these subordinate castes in the struggle against brahminism. Over centuries, brahmins had maintained strict monopoly over education and the right to knowledge. The system of oral transmission of vedic knowledge had been retained for long even after the mechanism of writing had come into use, as part of that scheme. Selectively, only brahmins were imparted the vedic knowledge through oral transmission by the guru or master. Others, i.e., the non-brahmins, depending on their caste status were either entitled to no education or limited education. The British government in India secularised education and structured it along liberal, democratic lines. Liberty, equality, the worth of the individual and representative institutions came into focus. Even as initially that "new" education was only within reach of a limited upper caste Indian elite, in course of time its benefits did trickle down to the lesser privileged sections of society. Amongst those who did come across such exposures to western education were men like Jotirao Phule[10] and B.R. Ambedkar.

Jotirao Phule was born in a low caste *Kshatriya Mali, Kunbi* sub-caste family in Maharashtra in 1827. In course of time he emerged as the pioneer of the non-brahmin movement in Maharashtra. He was extremely critical of the brahminical scriptures and the caste system, holding them to be responsible for the plight of the low castes. While he himself had limited education in the formal sense of the term, through his early contacts with missionaries he was able to appreciate the immense importance of education in the struggle for emancipation of the downtrodden. Thus, in his pioneering work amongst the *Sudras,* he maintained his focus on the question of their educational uplift. Phule stressed on education and organisation as tools for countering the brahminical ideology. His establishment of the first school for the untouchables and for women significantly contributed towards generating low caste consciousness and mobility.[11]

Around the same time that Phule was building up his struggle, Sri Narayana Guru – who was born in an *Ezhava,* middle class agricultural family in Chempazhanthi near Trivandrum in 1855 – was extolling the untouchable *Ezhavas* in Kerala to pay heed to education in extricating themselves from their age-old social stigma. It may be noted that, in Kerala, the *Ezhavas,* who were amongst the most backward and oppressed section of the Hindu population comprising in 1891, of 16.20 per cent of the region's population were the first to lead bitter struggles for social emancipation that were later emulated by other low castes including the *Pulayas.*

Sri Narayana Guru concentrated on setting up temples for the low caste *Ezhavas.* The first such temple dedicated to Lord Siva was set up in 1887 at Aruvippuram and, being consecrated by a member of the untouchable community, came as a direct challenge to the brahminical order. After the initial success, he set up several other temples and in course of time emerged as a popular leader of the poor, low castes in the region. In 1898–99 Narayana Guru registered a *Yogam* (association) to manage the affairs of the temples. In 1903 at a special session of the *Yogam* it was decided to transform the *Yogam* into the Sri Narayana Guru Dharma Paripalana Yogam (SNDP) with the aims and objects of developing spiritual and secular education and helping in the economic advancement of the *Ezhavas.* It is not surprising that as the temple entry movement gained momentum, Sri Narayana Guru emerged as one of its earliest pioneers. He was at one and the same time a spiritual leader and a social reformer. As a result of the Narayana Guru movement the *Ezhavas* developed a sense of their own worth that transformed them from passive underlings into a community that after the nineteenth century, took the lead in various radical movements for the emancipation of the downtrodden. The SNDP movement had an overall liberating influence on Kerala's society of the period. Its success, moral and social legitimacy and principles of equity, some of which were rooted in or sanctioned by Sri Narayana Guru's teachings, were carried over to the field of radical politics and contributed to the process of radicalisation of politics in the region.[12]

Apart from raising the social consciousness of the *Ezhavas,* the SNDP movement served to create a sense of solidarity in the *Ezhava* masses from the Cape in the south to the border of Karnataka in the north. Many major battles for social reform in the region were led by the SNDP during the first half of the twentieth century. It was largely in response to their agitational representation that in Travancore, the government schools were for the first time in 1905 opened to the low caste students.[13] In 1910, government girls' schools were opened to Christian and *Ezhava* girls.[14] In course of time, Sri Narayana Guru extended his reform movement to the Malabar region as well.[15] The combination of the Guru, the efficient organiser Palpu and the hardworking Kumaran Asan made the *Yogam* well-known throughout Kerala within a short span of time.[16]

In an altogether different part of the country, around about the same time, another popular protest movement of several untouchable castes was developing. It was the *Motua* movement that emerged around the middle of the nineteenth century in Bengal. Whilst its main base was amongst the *Namasudra* community, it was popular amongst the *Poundras, Goalas, Malos* and *Muchis.* Initially launched by Harichand Thakur who was born in a *Namasudra* family of Faridpur in 1812, the movement was expanded and popularised by his son Guruchand Thakur who, after the death of his father in 1878, took up the lead of the movement.

Apparently the movement was of a religious nature, organised around the name of "Hari" with an emphasis on collective singing and dancing of the devotees in demonstration of spiritual ecstasy. However, beyond that religiosity the thrust of the movement was secular with its primary targets being to (i) establish ways and means of attaining perfect peace of mind within the parameters of family life, and (ii) eradicate social inequality and ensure uplift of the downtrodden. In 1881, under the initiative of Guruchand Thakur the first *Namasudra Mahasammelan,* attended by an estimated five-thousand devotees, was held at Dattadanga at Khulna. There, in his presidential address he emphasised education, decency of behaviour, cleanliness, health and strength of character as prerequisites of advancement. Guruchand can well be described as the father of the *Namasudra* renaissance. He took the initiative in the establishment of educational institutions for the weaker castes and gave an overall leadership to the *Namasudra* movement for change of their earlier derogatory nomenclature of *"Chandal"* to that of *"Namasudra"*.

The first half of the twentieth century witnessed the emergence of a major mobilisation of untouchable castes in north-western India under the fold of a newly established religious movement initiated by Mangoo Ram – the *Ad Dharm* movement. Mangoo Ram Mugowalia, who was to become a virtual cult figure in course of time, was born at Mugowal, a village in the district of Hoshiarpur, on 14 January 1886.[17] He was initially associated with the *Gadr* Movement. However, by the twenties, he came to realise the utmost need for a social revolution and hence moved from the political to the social arena of struggle. The *Ad Dharm* movement drew its inspiration from the *Bhakti* movement, especially from Kabir, Ravidass and Namdev. It aimed at securing a respectable place for the untouchable castes through cultural transformation and political assertion, rather than seeking patronage from above. The movement aimed at carving out a distinct identity for the untouchables, independent of the Hindus, Sikhs and Muslims.

The impact of this movement that was launched in 1924, is noticeably evident from the observations of the Punjab Census Report of 1931:

> The most notable feature of the present census from the stand-point of return of religion has been the adoption of the term 'Ad-Dharmi' by numerous Chamars and Chuhras and other untouchables. A new instruction to the religion was given this year, namely, 'Persons returning themselves as Ad-Dharmis should be recorded as such.[18]

Even though the movement weakened after independence the roots of recent dalit assertions in Punjab can be traced back to it.

It may be noted that as the low caste members across the country took up their own cause and stepped forth to challenge the caste order, protest forms became more militantly activist. Such trends were visible in protests organised around temple entry, the use of tanks, wells and roads. Protesting brahminical chauvinism was not confined to the untouchable castes. The touchable *Sudra* castes, too, came forward to register their grievances and protest.[19]

Sudra protests took on a particularly organised and radical form in southern India under the leadership of E.V.Ramasami. E.V.Ramasami, better known as EVR or Periyar (The Great One) was born in Erode in southern India in 1879. He considered the brahmins and their Sanskritic culture to be responsible for the social, economic, political and cultural backwardness of the non-brahmins in Tamilnadu. As such, he sought to smash the edifice of that culture and root it out lock, stock and barrel; to replace indignity with dignity, inegalitarianism with egalitarianism.

EVR structured his alternative in terms of the Self-Respect Movement. He raised the slogan of *Cuya Mariyadai* (Self-Respect). The Tamil weekly, *Kudi Arasu* became the principal organ of the movement. EVRs passionate speeches delivered in simple straight forward fashion succeeded in drawing a sizeable following for the Self-Respect Movement. The first Self-Respect Conference was held at Chengalpattu in 1929.

Amongst the most sustained struggles that came to be launched by EVR and the Self-Respect Movement were those in relation to temple entry, access to public spaces and institutions, gender equality, abolition of untouchability, brahminism, caste, and religion. EVR was an atheist who chose to be extremely outspoken in his atheistic beliefs. He strongly expressed his rejection of the idea of god, as well as idol worship; and, used sharp language and agitational methods for expressing that opposition. Periyar's and the Self-Respecter's views on religion revolved around critiques of the brahmin priest and brahminism, the scriptures, religion as a world view, religious practices, festivals and rituals.

As it is, from the 1920s leftism had made its debut in India; socialist ideas were becoming popular and the working class movement was fast expanding. In such a milieu, "class and class struggle" were becoming familiar concepts. The growth of the new consciousness was further stimulated by the great depression of the late twenties. Even as it adversely affected the Indian economy, it propelled the masses towards an unprecedented degree of political activism. They put up stiff resistence against the increasingly stiffling measures that the colonial power was keen on imposing. Mass upsurges took place in different parts of the country. In terms of involvement, these uprisings broke the bounds of elitism, caste wise as well as class wise.

In short, alongside the widening of the educational base, national political rumblings and the manifold domestic ramifications of international developments created the environment for radical thinking. Such radicalism found expression, on the one hand, in the communist sponsored class struggles and, on the other hand in the highly politicised caste movements of the day spearheaded by leaders like Ambedkar and Periyar.

Towards the close of the colonial period, the untouchables had, through their struggles and the astute leadership of Ambedkar, earned a recognition of sorts in their identity as "Depressed Classes" and then "Scheduled Castes". On the eve of independence they feared that, following British withdrawal power would pass into the hands of the caste Hindus who, in comparison to the British, would be more adversely inclined towards those who were low in the caste hierarchy. Propelled by such apprehensions, Ambedkar strove to articulate and win for the Depressed Classes their demands for the incorporation of special safeguards in the Constitution. In front of the Simon Commission (1928), at the three Round Table Conferences in London (1930–32) and in the Constituent Assembly, Ambedkar consistently presented the untouchables demands for social justice. The greatest concession that he succeeded in winning for the Depressed Classes through such struggles was the constitutional guarantees of certain compensatory discriminatory measures. He managed to bring the problem of untouchability into focus and ensured the conditions under which a large number of Scheduled Castes representatives in the legislatures were to underline in the days to come, the necessity of improving the socioeconomic and educational conditions of such peoples.

Through a sustained process of political mobilisation on the one hand and hard political bargaining on the other, Ambedkar succeeded in establishing the untouchables as Scheduled Castes and as a politically relevant category both to themselves and to others, thus bringing the untouchables from invisibility to visibility, from silence to articulated protest. Under his leadership, the untouchables learnt to effectively articulate and aggregate their interests in political terms. They acquired a sense of self-esteem and consciousness that was indeed unique and over the years reached a level comparable perhaps to the Black Consciousness Movement of the Negroes.

Post-Independence Dalit Struggles for Rights

Not surprisingly, after independence, politicisation of the oppressed castes and their mobilisation around material demands proceeded at an unprecedented pace. They came under the banners of various caste organisations, political parties, and several extremist left groups.

Introduction of parliamentary democratic institutions failed to end deprivation. However, tolerance of the same was clearly diminishing. As universal adult suffrage established the importance of numbers, political mobilisation along caste lines received a boost. Growth of caste-based political parties, caste lobbying and vying of political parties with each other for control of different caste vote banks proved to be some of the major aspects of the new political milieu. Within a short span of time, the importance of the vote bank became all too clear to the dalits themselves as also to others.

The post-independence dalit movement has been greatly influenced by the Ambedkar legacy. On his death, Ambedkar left behind a legacy comprising of a large body of writings; a political party for the oppressed – the Republican Party; a nascent Buddhist conversion movement; a system of higher education begun with Siddharth College in Bombay and which was spreading to other cities; a host of reserved places for Scheduled Castes in education, administration and legislative bodies; and a critical mass of awakened ex-untouchables.[20]

In the early 1970s, the Dalit Panthers emerged in Maharashtra as part of the countrywide wave of radical politics. Relying on the teachings of both Marx and Ambedkar and drawing inspiration from the Black Panther Movement in the USA, young dalit writers including Namdeo Dhasal, Arjun Dangle and J.V. Pawar took the initiative in trying to build up a grand war against the *varna-jati* system. Their tools were both political and cultural. However, the long-lasting impact of the Panthers in the field of dalit culture was perhaps more than in the field of politics. Through their efforts there emerged an altogether new genre of protest literature. Dalits associated with and inspired by the movement articulated their interests through a wide range of creations – stories, novels, poetry, music and drama. In fact, it would not be an overstatement to say that since the seventies Marathi literature virtually underwent a revolution. Forceful writings came from poets like Daya Pawar, Waman Nimbalkar, Arjun Dangle, Namdeo Dhasal and J.V. Pawar, as also short story writers like Tarachandra Khandekar, Yogiraj Waghmare, Avinash Dolas Yogendra Meshram and others. Their passionate demand for human rights finds reflection in the following lines of Sharankumar Limbale's poem titled *White Paper*:

> "I do not ask
> for the sun and moon from your sky
> your farm, your land,
> your high houses or your mansions
> I do not ask for gods or rituals,
> Castes or sects
> Or even for your mother, sisters, daughters.
> I ask for
> my rights as a man.
> Each breath from my lungs
> Sets off a violent trembling
> In your texts and traditions
> Your hells and heavens
> Fearing pollution.
> ... .
> I'll uproot the scriptures like railway tracks.
> Burn like a city bus your lawless laws
> My friends !
> My rights are rising like the sun.
> Will you deny this sunrise?"[21]

Even as with the birth of the Dalit Panthers there came about a major paradigm shift in the hitherto structured language of dalit politics, differences within the Panthers surfaced by the 1980s and splits began to take place. In course of time, most factions joined or allied with the Congress.[22] Some Panther leaders such as Namdeo Dhasal even moved towards the RSS.[23]

In southern India, the *Sudra* struggle against brahminism, the roots of which go back to the pre-independence period and, which at a point of time linked up with Tamil nationalism in the Tamil land, acquired an unparalleled strength over the years giving birth to the Dravidian forces – the Dravida Kazhagham (DK), the Dravida Munnetra Kazhagham (DMK) and the All India Dravida Munnetra Kazhagham (AIDMK). While in course of time, the movement lost much of its political edge, it remained the core of an emergent non-brahmin ideology and the rallying slogan for the non-brahmin forces.

At the national level, the rise of the Bahujan Samaj Party in UP was clearly symbolic of the self-assertion of the dalits. While in the mid-1980s, during the early years of its formation, the social base of the BSP was narrow and confined to the upwardly mobile, educated and mainly government employees, by the 1990s it had broadened to include the poorer sections of the community. As it stands today, capturing political power appears to be its main agenda with most of its activities revolving around the maneuverings of electoral politics. Notwithstanding the many limitations of the party, its rise has undoubtedly marked the possibilities of the emergence of new equations in national politics and has brought forth an overall attention to the dalit agenda in Indian politics hitherto unheard of.

The central demands around which political mobilisation and bargaining of dalits have tended to revolve, in post-independence India, primarily relate to:

(i) effective implementation of the existing constitutional and legal provisions for safeguarding the interests of the listed classes;

(ii) incorporation of new castes in the lists of beneficiaries;

(iii) extension of scheduled status to those non-Hindus who had prior to conversion occupied low status in the Hindu caste hierarchy and were deemed to be untouchables; and

(iv) widening of the range of available facilities through necessary legal amendments and enactments, administrative and judicial initiatives.

Parliamentary politics, affirmative action in favour of dalits, the influence of socialist ideas and the overall impact of the Mandal Commission Report have resulted in the perceptible rise of a dalit elite in India. This new elite comprises of people who have had formal education, government jobs, a resultant measure of economic stability and a sharp consciousness of their rights. It is an elite which can visualise their position differently, compared to their forefathers. And, it is a section of this elite, faced with newer challenges thrown up by the intricate and myriad links between the traditional caste order and the forces of globalisation, that seeks to address dalit concerns from a human rights perspective.

Notes

1. For an exhaustive description of that tradition see Debiprasad Chattopadhyaya, *Lokayata: A Study in Ancient Indian Materialism,* Peoples Publishing House, New Delhi, 1992.
2. Ram Sharan Sharma, *Aspects of Political Ideas and Institutions in Ancient India,* Motilal Banarsidass, Delhi, 1991.
3. Ibid.
4. See Max Weber, *The Religion of India, The Sociology of Hinduism and Buddhism,* translated by Hans H. Gerth and Don Martindale, The Free Press, Illinois, 1960, pp. 18–9.
5. For a detailed discussion see Debi Chatterjee, *Ideas and Movements Against Caste in India: Ancient to Modern Times,* Print-o-Graph, Calcutta, 1998.
6. Ram Kumar Varma, *Kabir, Biography and Philosophy,* Prints India, New Delhi, 1989, p. 66.

7. V.K. Sethi, *Kabir: The Weaver of God's Name,* Radha Soami Satsang Beas, New Delhi, 1984, p. 268.
8. See Muhammad Hedayetullah, *Kabir, The Apostle of Hindu Muslim Unity,* Motilal Banarsidass, Delhi, 1977, p. 218.
9. A.K. Majumdar, *Caitanya: His Life and Doctrine, A Study in Vaisnavism*, Bharatiya Vidya Bhavan, Bombay, 1969, p. 78.
10. For a detailed biographical outline see Dhananjay Keer, *Mahatma Jotirao Phule, Father of the Indian Social Revolution,* Popular Prakashan, Bombay, 1974.
11. See Debi Chatterjee "Dalit Liberation Struggles", Immanuel Ness ed., *International Encyclopedia of Revolution and Protest,* Blackwell Publishing, 2009, pp. 954–961.
12. See P.S. Velayudhan, "Sree Narayana Epoch of Religious Movement in Modern Kerala", S.P. Sen ed., *Social Contents of Indian Religious Reform Movements*, Institute of Historical Studies, Calcutta, 1978.
13. See A.M. Abraham Ayrookuzhiel, *Swami Anand Tirth, Untouchabilty, Gandhian Solution on Trial,* Christian Institute for the Study of Religion and Society, Bangalore, 1987, p. 15.
14. Ibid.
15. Ibid.
16. Ibid.
17. Ronki Ram, "Dalits and the Ad Dharm Movement in Punjab", http://www.bhagwanvalmiki.com/ronki1.htm
18. http://www.bhagwanvalmiki.com/mangoo-ram.htm
19. For a detailed discussion of dalit struggles see Debi Chatterjee "Dalit Liberation Struggles", Immanuel Ness ed., *International Encyclopedia of Revolution and Protest,* Blackwell Publishing, 2009, pp. 954–961.
20. Eleanor Zelliot, "The Dalit Movement", *Dalit International Newsletter* 1(1): 1 and 4, 1996, cited in S.M. Michael, op. cit., p. 111.
21. Sharankumar Limbale, "White Paper", Arjun Dangle, ed., *Poisoned Bread: Translations from Modern Marathi Dalit Liter-*

ature, Orient Longman, Bombay, 1992, pp. 64–5. The poem has been translated by Priya Adarkar.

22. Bipan Chandra, Mridula Mukherjee and Aditya Mukherjee, *India After Independence: 1947–2000,* Penguin, Kolkata, 2000, p. 446.

23. In 2006, he publicly joined the Rashtriya Swayamsevak Sangh's call for "Hindu brotherhood". http://en.wikipedia.org/wiki/Namdeo_Dhasal

Chapter 9

Dalit Struggles for Human Rights at the International Fora

When other human rights activists and institutions in India were planning to celebrate the completion of the fiftieth year of the promulgation of Universal Declaration of Human Rights (UDHR) as a response to the call of the United Nations, 78 dalit activists and human rights activists from across the country, concerned about the frequent atrocities and the blatant lack of implementation of the SC/ST (Prevention of Atrocities) Act of 1989, met in Bangalore to discuss a programme of action, deliberated and resolved to make use of this opportunity to "highlight the issue of caste and untouchability" among the international community, international organisations including the UN bodies and especially in UNCHR. This paved the way for the formation of the National Campaign on Dalit Human Rights (NCDHR), which gathered massive support from various dalit activists, including dalit intellectuals, academics, bureaucrats, NGOs, dalit organisations/movements, dalit trade unions, writers and journalists, etc. The inauguration of the campaign took place on 10 December 1998 with the submission of 50,000 signatures and the campaign memorandum to the President of India. This was followed by the drafting of an inaugural folder with a Charter of Dalit Human Rights.

Setting up of the National Campaign on Dalit Human Rights

The National Campaign on Dalit Human Rights (NCDHR) was officially launched in India in December 1998. The purpose was to promote solidarity, cooperation, and collective action at the national level for the promotion of dalit human rights. Its efforts were largely directed towards demonstrating the link between dalit issues and human rights issues. The move came against the backdrop of worldwide activities centring around the completion of fifty years of the Universal Declaration of Human Rights (UDHR).

The campaign brought together dalit activists from different states and union territories in India and focussed on raising awareness amongst dalits, government institutions, civil society and the press that violation of dalit rights are in fact violation of human rights. It launched signature campaigns, organised national public hearings, held press conferences, issued press releases and undertook the release of campaign literature. It also met dignitaries including the President, the Prime Minister of India, National Human Rights and Women's Commission Members to impress upon them the urgency of the matter. Its efforts were not confined within India. Outside the country's borders, the NCDHR stepped up efforts to mobilise opinion on the dalit question.

The NCDHR was involved in a variety of events such as the World Conference Against Racism at Durban in 2001, all World Social Forums, the 40-days dalit *Swadhikar* rally across India in 2004, the first-ever public hearing on "The Situation of the Dalits in India" at the European Parliament in Brussels (December, 2006), and the first International Conference on the Human Rights of Dalit Women at The Hague (November 2006).[1]

It may be noted that the NCDHR was not set up as an attempt to subsume, replace or negate ongoing efforts of the dalits and others in various mass organisations, peoples organisations, labour unions, etc. Rather, its aim was to galvanise the movements into a representative body that would collectively organise, educate, agitate and demand an end to untouchability and casteism once and for all in both the government and civil society.

The main professed objectives of the NCDHR are to:

- create awareness and support for dalit human rights by highlighting the issues of dalit human rights in civil society;

- strengthen the unity and solidarity of dalits and dalit movements across the nation and the world;
- prepare status reports on dalits covering the areas of livelihood, education, land and labour, gender equity for dalit women, life and security, and reservation and employment;
- pressurise central and state governments and state and national level statutory bodies to give top priority to dalit rights;
- pressurise statutory bodies of the UN and other international organisations to give top priority to dalit issues; and
- highlight the culture and contribution of dalit communities to society.

Thus the ultimate aims are to ensure:

- That India and the international community recognise and uphold that dalit rights are human rights and decide to abolish effectively untouchability; and
- To cast out caste so as to build a new, just social order.[2]

Formation of the NACDOR

The National Conference of Dalit Organisations, NACDOR-I was organised between 8 and 10 December 2001. In NACDOR-I, we saw the participation of about 150 dalit organisations from 15 states. Since then, many other dalit organisations approached and joined NACDOR. In less than five years, National Conference of Dalit Organisations (NACDOR) emerged as a powerful assertion of the dalits. NACDOR on the occasion of India Social Forum in New Delhi, ensured the participation of more than 300 partner dalit organisations.[3]

Shortly after NACDOR-I, a conference of dalit intellectuals and activists was held at Bhopal in Madhya Pradesh on 12 and 13 January 2002, to deliberate on issues pertaining to the welfare and justice of the dalit population and chart out a new course of action for dalits for the twenty-first century. A declaration was unanimously adopted at the Conference incorporating a 21-Point Action Agenda. This came to be known as the Bhopal Declaration. It outlined the delegates' faith in Ambedkar's teachings as well as in the UN's human rights discourse, making special mention of the Universal Declaration of Human Rights. It highlighted, inter alia, the need to "make reservation mandatory in the private and corporate sector in the same proportion as in the public sector … ." And "develop the capacities and skills of dalits to help them cope up with the demands of these different sectors". It also emphasised the need for the dalits to make common cause with other liberation and human rights movements in and outside the country.[4]

The process of organising NACDOR-II, *Vision and Voices of New Dalit*, was launched on 13 November 2006 in New Delhi. Digvijay Singh, former Chief Minister of Madhya Pradesh, Sharad Yadav, former minister in the Central Government and President of Janata Dal (U), Sanjay Paswan, former Central Minister, Ram Das Athavale, MP, industrialist and founder of Amity University, Ashok K. Chauhan, Arjun Dangle, renowned dalit writer, Jean Dreze, reputed economist, Kiran Sharma, Programme Director of Poorest Areas Civil Society Programme participated in the deliberations.[5] In the Golden Jubilee Year of *Dhamma Chakka Pravartan* Day by Baba Saheb Ambedkar, Ashok Bharti, convener of NACDOR proposed *Panchsheela* for the overall empowerment of the dalits. It was unanimously adopted by a voice vote. The adopted principles of NACDOR-II are: (i) struggle for land and natural resources, (ii) education, (iii) health, (iv) employment and entrepreneurship, and (v) dignity – leadership, caste annihilation, justice, etc.[6]

The Dalit Diaspora Steps In

Till the 1990s, people living outside India, dalits and non-dalits alike, had shown limited interest in matters relating to caste discrimination and struggles of dalits in India. From the 1990s the scenario changed significantly and we find the dalit diaspora demonstrating active interest in bettering the conditions of dalits in India. The role played by the NCDHR in generating this interest was significant. The efforts were however facilitated by the fact that the communication revolution had made interaction across borders remarkably easy, speedy as well as cheap; as a result of e-communication, sharing ideas, mobilising and disseminating information became possible at a level that had earlier been unimaginable.

It is important here to put in a word about the composition of the dalit diaspora. It can broadly be classified into two categories. The "old" and the "new". Whilst the former is made up of the indentured labourers and assisted labourers who had been taken by the colonial powers and contractors to different countries of South Asia and Africa, the "new" dalit diaspora comprises of semiliterate and professionally trained dalits who emigrated especially to London and the USA as industrial labourers, technicians, other professionals and students – mostly after the 1960s.[7] It is this latter stream, which is politically more conscious, though it has succeeded in influencing to an extent the "old" diaspora as well.[8]

It may be noted that members of the dalit diaspora were, not infrequently, subject to caste discrimination from the non-dalit Indians in the countries of their residence. The new dalits, reacted to it and set about to form their own organisations. In the UK, from the late 1960s, the dalits established Buddha Vihars. A Buddhist Council – as a federation of seven Ambedkarite organisations – was set up in 1985. The FABO or the Federation of Ambedkarite and Buddhist Organisations and the VODI or the Voice of Dalits International are also working in the UK. In 1975, literate NRI dalits in the USA formed VISION – Volunteers in Service to India's Oppressed and Neglected. The 90s saw a new stimulation of interests.

Dalit Solidarity Networks: Forging the Links

From the late 1990s, Dalit Solidarity Networks were set up in different countries to promote the cause of dalit human rights. Dalit Solidarity Networks have formed in the US, Germany, the UK, the

Netherlands, France, Denmark and Sweden. They have brought under their folds individuals as well as concerned groups. Besides, they have linked up with international human rights organisations like Amnesty International and Human Rights Watch for the purpose. Seminars and workshops are organised, websites put up, signature campaigns and petitioning are undertaken.

In March 2000, the International Dalit Solidarity Network (IDSN) was formed. It is a network of national solidarity networks, groups from affected countries and international bodies concerned about caste discrimination. It aims at linking grassroot priorities with international mechanisms and institutions to establish "dalit rights" as "human rights". Its work involves encouraging the UN, EU and other bodies to recognise the fact that caste-based discrimination must be treated as a central human rights concern.[9] In relation to the UN, its lobbying is directed mainly at the Human Rights Commission, the Sub-Commission for Civil and Political Rights and the UN Committee on the Elimination of Racial Discrimination (CERD) among others.[10]

An appeal was made on the occasion of Ambedkar Day by the Dalit Solidarity Network of UK to the Indian government to eliminate manual scavenging by 2009–10. Manual scavenging is an inhuman practice where dalits are employed to remove human excrement from dry toilets and sewers using basic tools. Though this practice was abolished by law in 1993, it is estimated by the Indian Government that 1.3 million dalits, mostly women are still employed as manual scavengers across India. The call marks the beginning of an international campaign initiated by Safai Karmachari Andolan – *"the Liberation Movement of those employed as scavengers"* – to end manual scavenging before the Commonwealth Games in Delhi in 2010. Similar calls have been made by the Dalit Network, the Netherlands, and the Rafto Foundation in Norway.[11]

Dalit Conferences at the International Level

The First World Dalit Convention was held in Kuala Lumpur, Malaysia on 10 and 11 October 1998. It was organised by the Dalit

International Organisation and sponsored by the Indian Progressive Front, Malaysia. [12]

In the resolutions adopted at the Convention, it was unanimously resolved to "urge the United Nations to immediately appoint 'Special Rapporteurs' to commence investigation into this Human Rights violation and also take appropriate measures to effect the implementation of fundamental 'Human Rights' instrument for dalits in India and other parts of the world" (Resolution No 1).[13]

The delegates came out in strong criticism against the Government of India and condemned vociferously the atrocities against the dalits. They urged the central and state governments to:

"... safeguard all the rights provided for in the Constitution especially the Reservation Quotas to SC/ST people at all levels including Police, Armed Forces, Judiciary and also immediately fill up all vacant places without any further delay." And also to "supervise the strict implementation of the Reservation Rights at Local, State and Federal level including Police and Armed Forces and also give judicial and punitive powers to the National Commission for the welfare of SC/ST communities so that commission can play a meaningful and effective role" (Resolution No 2).[14]

The year 2000 saw the organising of The International Conference on Dalit Human Rights by the Voice of Dalits International (VODI) in London, in association with the Dalit Solidarity Network, UK, and the communities of Shri Guru Ravidass Sabha, Bhagwan Valmiki Welfare Trust and the Ambedkarite organisations in UK between 16–17 September 2000. Ramdas Athawale inaugurated the Conference. The Conference participants appealed to the United Nations and Government of India to take steps to stop atrocities against dalits (the untouchables) in India. The Conference also appealed to the international community to intervene immediately to stop all kinds of Human Rights violations particularly those faced by dalits in India.[15]

In 2003, an International Dalit Conference was held at Vancouver. The assembled delegates pointed out that "the caste problem is not the problem of dalits alone, but also of the entire nation" and, "without the annihilation of caste and the elimination of primordial loyalties, India will not be able to realise its full socioeconomic potential and claim its rightful place among the community of nations". An eleven-point charter of demands was put forward. It highlighted the dalits' claim for a rightful share in India's national institutions, wealth and capital, and called on private corporations and MNCs to accept their responsibilities. The conference participants even called on international funding agencies to exert necessary pressure on the Indian government to protect the interests of the dalits.[16]

The International Dalit Solidarity Network (IDSN) and the Dalit NGO Federation of Nepal organised an International Consultation on Caste-Based Discrimination: Establishing Dalit Rights in the Contemporary World; the Role of Governments, the United Nations and the Private Sector in Kathmandu from 29 November to 1 December 2004.

The Consultation brought together dalit activists from several South Asian countries, representatives of other communities suffering similar forms of discrimination (such as the *Burakumin* of Japan), UN human rights experts, United Nations agencies, representatives of bilateral and multilateral agencies, Nepalese NGOs and government officials, national human rights institutions, IDSN members and associates as well as private sector representatives. The Consultation's aim was to explore measures to promote implementation of relevant laws, regulations, policies and recommendations to end caste-based discrimination as a key human rights responsibility of governments, civil society and the international community.

In the course of the Consultation, four thematic areas were covered, i.e., implementation of General Recommendation XXIX on "descent-based discrimination", adopted by the Committee on the Elimination of Racial Discrimination' (CERD) in August 2002; effective use of United Nations mechanisms in eliminating caste-based discrimination; the role of the private sector and transnational corporations; and mainstreaming of dalit rights in development programmes. The Consultation contributed significantly towards identifying new strategies to challenge non-implementation of existing measures, and providing a forum for brainstorming on new measures at relevant levels.

The Kathmandu Dalit Declaration was launched on 1 December 2004, at the end of Consultation. The Declaration is seen as a challenge to decision-makers in governments, the EU, UN and donor agencies, civil society, the private sector and financial institutions to take action to end caste discrimination. The Kathmandu Declaration suggests concrete steps and measures to address injustices against dalits at various levels.[17]

Dalits and Dalit Issues at the UN

From the 1990s, the dalit struggle moved to the international arena. For the first time, the caste question was discussed at the World Conference on Human Rights at Vienna in 1993. Subsequently, it was raised at the World Summit on Social Development held at Copenhagen in 1995. However, caste-based discrimination in other countries was generally little discussed at the international or national levels. For the first time, a detailed critical examination of the system by the UN took place in 1996. Thereafter, the debate continued in different treaty based bodies.[18]

An important effort to bring the issue of violation of dalit's human rights into the agenda of the UN was attempted in the context of the Durban Conference on Racism, 2001. The World Conference Against Racism was held from 31 August to 7 September 2001 in Durban, South Africa. It was the Third World Conference on this issue. The previous world conferences had been held in 1978 and 1983 and had primarily focused on ending apartheid in South Africa.

At the Third World Conference in 2001, the member-states of the UN focused on the causes and consequences of various manifestations of racism, strengthening existing human rights mechanisms and UN conventions (such as Convention on the Elimination of All Forms of Racial Discrimination), and developing practical, action-oriented measures and strategies to combat contemporary forms of racism and intolerance. From the dalit perspective, the WCAR was a rare opportunity to raise the visibility of India's "hidden apartheid" at the international level. It was a crucial opportunity for dalit groups to come together on a common platform and make a united stand against caste discrimination before the international community and the UN. Through one voice, a common strategy, joint lobbying and advocacy, and the mutual support of other communities and organisations from across the globe, dalits sought to influence the content of the final resolutions adopted by the member-states so that they reflect dalit realities. WCAR consisted of both an Inter-Governmental (IG) Conference and a parallel NGO Forum. In the former, the governments of the UN member-states were the decision-makers, while the NGOs primarily participated as lobbyists, observers and information providers. Although NGOs did not have the right to vote at the IG conference, they had a variety of opportunities to influence the agenda, direction and outcome of the conference.[19] At the conference, dalit groups from across the world with support from several international human rights organisations fought a tough battle for the inclusion of caste in the official charter on race as a form of descent-based discrimination. Their efforts, however, were thwarted by the resistance of the Government of India. The Government of India argued that caste discrimination was not an issue relevant to the assessment of its performance vis-à-vis the human rights conventions to which it was a party. The arguments rested on three premises. First, caste is not race; secondly, internal mechanisms were adequate to promote the welfare of the untouchable castes and protect the human rights of the dalits and as such there was no need to invoke international human rights mechanisms; thirdly, change is a slow process and all that was necessary was being done.[20]

Even though the dalit contingent lost the battle in face of the hostility of the Indian government, they did succeed in making their point. [21] As a matter of fact, the dalit contingent of more than 160 activists was one of the largest and best organised non-governmental delegations present, and drew strong international support from governments, UN officials, and India's own National Human Rights Commission.

The declaration produced by the parallel NGO conference affirmed the conclusions of the Committee on the Elimination of Racial Discrimination and the United Nations Sub-Commission on the Promotion and Protection of Human Rights that untouchability, bonded labour, manual scavenging and other caste-based abuses are repugnant and insidious forms of racial discrimination.

On December 23, 2002, the United Nations Committee on the Elimination of Racial Discrimination in concluding its discussions on descent-based discrimination, strongly condemned caste practices as violative of the International Convention on Elimination of All Forms of Racial Discrimination. It noted that "fresh efforts, as well as intensification of existing efforts, need to be made at the level of domestic law and practice, in order to eliminate the scourge of descent-based discrimination and empower communities affected by it". Among the recommendations of the Committee on Elimination of Racial Discrimination are the following: (i) to resolutely implement legislation and other measures already in force; (ii) to formulate and put into action a comprehensive national strategy with the participation of members of the affected communities, including special measures in accordance with Articles 1 and 2 of the Convention, in order to eliminate discrimination against members of descent-based groups; (iii) to educate the general public on the importance of affirmative action programmes designed to address the situation of victims of descent-based discrimination; (iv) to ensure where relevant, that judicial decisions and official actions take the prohibition of descent-based discrimination fully into account; and (v) to take substantial and effective measures to eradicate poverty among descent-based communities, and combat their social exclusion or marginalisation.[22]

On 19 April 2005, the UN Commission on Human Rights adopted by consensus a decision to appoint two Special Rapporteurs to tackle the entrenched problem of caste-based discrimination. The Commission was endorsing an earlier decision taken by its Sub-Commission on the Promotion and Protection of Human Rights to conduct a comprehensive analysis of the problem and find solutions for its eradication. This was the first time a political body of the UN referred directly to the problem. The Sub-Commission will now undertake a three year study, led by two experts given the title of "Special Rapporteurs", and will draft a set of Principles and Guidelines to eliminate this form of discrimination.

The decision of the Commission came in the wake of an International Consultation held in Kathmandu in 2004 on how to address the problem. The Consultation adopted what is known as the Kathmandu Dalit Declaration, which provides concrete proposals for not only governments, the UN and development agencies, but also the private sector, trade unions and international financial institutions. One of the proposals has now been fulfiled in the form of the appointment of the Special Rapporteurs.

The efforts to internationalise the issue of caste-based discrimination against dalits in South Asia that had been undertaken in 2001 at the United Nations World Conference Against Racism (WCAR) in Durban, suffered a serious setback at the Durban Review Conference held between 20–24 April, 2009 in Geneva. While in 2001, WCAR had at least discussed caste euphemistically as "discrimination based on work and descent", in line with terminology devised by the UN's Committee on the Elimination of Racial Discrimination (CERD), the outcome document of the Durban Review Conference (DRC) evaded even an allusion to caste.[23]

International Human Rights Organisations and NGOs: Taking up the Dalit Cause

In the wake of the overall activism surrounding the UN Durban Conference on Racism a large number of NGOs in the West revealed a dynamic interest in the dalit problem. These included, inter alia, Anti-Slavery International, Lutheran World Federation, Asian Human Rights Commission, India Committee of the Netherlands, Minority Rights Group, Christian Aid, Oxfam, Amnesty International, Holdeen India Programme and Commonwealth Human Rights Initiative. A couple of examples given below will demonstrate the nature of concern as it was expressed on the issue by some of these organisations.

On 21 March 2001, marking the International Day for the Elimination of Racial Discrimination, Human Rights Watch called for an end to caste-based discrimination around the world. Human Rights Watch saw the World Conference Against Racism, Racial Discrimination, Xenophobia and Related Intolerance that was to take place in South Africa from 31 August to 7 September 2001 as a significant opportunity for the international community to address the situation of South Asia's 240 million dalits. The organisation was extremely critical of the attitude of the Government of India and decried its attempts to sabotage the efforts of Indian NGOs to raise awareness of the caste struggle at preparatory meetings in the lead up to the Conference.[24]

Human Rights Watch, in its recommendations at Durban noted, inter alia, that "nationally, concerned governments must act to uphold their own constitutional principles and international treaty obligations and work toward the full enjoyment of rights by all citizens, regardless of caste or descent. Globally, the international community must take advantage of the opportunity this World Conference represents to make progress on one of the world's most severe and forgotten abuses". It also stated specifically, "All governments, and in particular those of countries whose citizens suffer from caste or descent-based discrimination and abuse, should ratify and fully implement the International Convention on the Elimination of All Forms of Racial Discrimination".

These apart, Human Rights Watch opined that:

- All governments should support efforts to implement the resolution on discrimination based on work and descent adopted by the UN Sub-Commission on the Promotion and Protection of Human Rights in August 2000.
- Concerned governments should extend invitations to the special rapporteur on racism to investigate caste-based discrimination and other forms of discrimination based on descent in their respective countries.
- All governments should ensure that caste-based and similar discrimination against marginalised populations is explicitly addressed in the declaration and programme of action of the WCAR, and any followup plan of action thereafter.

- Dalits in South Asia, *Buraku* people in Japan, and other populations in similar situations should be explicitly acknowledged as groups of people who have been subject to perennial and persistent forms of discrimination and abuse on the basis of their descent.[25]

Moreover, Human Rights Watch felt that concerned governments should:

(i) Establish a program and timetable to enforce the abolition of "untouchability", segregation, or similar practices.

(ii) Enact and fully enforce laws aimed at ending abuses associated with caste, such as child labour, bonded labour, land reform, manual collection of human waste, and forced prostitution or similar practices.

(iii) Monitor and publicise the extent to which existing laws to end caste discrimination have been implemented.

(iv) Allocate adequate funds for programs for the socioeconomic and educational support of communities that have faced discrimination on the basis of caste or descent.

(v) Ensure greater participation by the affected communities in civil administration, especially the administration of justice, including in key institutions such as the police and judiciary.

(vi) Ensure that all necessary constitutional, legislative, and administrative measures, including appropriate forms of affirmative action, are in place to prohibit and redress discrimination on the basis of caste, and that such measures – including those already instituted in Japan and India – are continued until discrimination is eliminated.

(vii) Launch nationwide public awareness campaigns regarding legal prohibitions on discrimination on the basis of caste or descent. This campaign should explain in simple terms what actions are legally prohibited and what recourse is available to victims of discrimination and abuse.

(viii) Provide political and financial support for programs of the United Nations and regional bodies to assist countries seeking to eradicate caste discrimination.

(ix) United Nations development agencies should pay particular attention to caste violence and caste discrimination, assess the impact of their existing programs with regard to caste, and develop programs and strategies designed to curb abuse and encourage accountability.[26]

The cooperation between Human Rights Watch (HRW), with its good international advocacy knowledge, and the Indian NGO, National Campaign on Dalit Human Rights (NCDHR) was indeed significant. Human Rights Watch launched a programme of work on dalits in India in 1997 with financial support from the Ford Foundation. Keen to support further development of domestic advocacy on caste issues, the Ford Foundation promised to fund continuing work provided that Human Rights Watch could assist dalit NGOs to forge a common organisational platform. This was achieved in 1998, when following a national meeting in India, the NCDHR was set up. By 1999, the NCDHR was working closely with its domestic partners and Human Rights Watch to launch a national campaign in line with the HRW publication of *Broken People: Caste Violence Against India's "Untouchables"*. They rallied for grassroots support, collected some 2.5 million signatures demanding greater action to eradicate the effects of caste-based discrimination, which they presented to the then Indian Prime Minister, A.B. Vajpayee in December 1999, and called upon the UN to take action in support of dalits. The NCDHR now has offices in several Indian states and is the most prominent dalit NGO in India within the transnational advocacy network on caste issues.[27]

The Asian Human Rights Commission, too, was no less sympathetic to the dalit cause at Durban. Adopting an extremely critical stand on of the Indian government's role, in a statement issued in the wake of the developments at Durban, the Asian Human Rights Commission observed:

> The World Conference against Racism, Racial Discrimination, Xenophobia and Related Intolerance (WCAR), held in Durban, South Africa, from Aug. 31 to Sept. 7, 2001, has brought into sharp focus several extreme forms of discrimination. Among these is the issue of caste – more specifically, the issue of the Dalits – for caste became a highly visible issue during the international debate on racial discrimination.

> It became obvious during the conference that Indian diplomats, in their extreme activism to keep caste out of the final declaration of this world gathering and its work programme, not only brought the Indian government into high disrepute, but also brought down the moral standing of India before the eyes of the world. India also lost any possibility of claiming to be a world leader in the promotion and protection of human rights until it changes its public position on the caste issue. The international conscience, which is being awakened to one of the cruelest forms of discrimination after many centuries of neglect, is naturally questioning the Indian stand and is asking, "What kind of nation is this?"[28]

NGOs did a magnificent job organising the strategy sessions of the dalits at the NGO (Non-Government Organisation) Forum, which precede the UN World Conference Against Racism (WCAR). The dalit campaign leadership arrived at the world conference against racism with some 1,200 black vests. On the back of each, in bright orange was the legend "Include Caste in WCAR". They arrived with about the same number of white headbands with "dalit rights are human rights" written on them. The vests and headbands were everywhere; increasing the pressure for a fair hearing.

Notes

1. http://www.ncdhr.org.in/ncdhr/aboutncdhr/
2. www.ncdhr.org
3. www.nacdor.org/TEXT FILES/ what we do. htm
4. www.pucl.org/Topics/Dalit_tribal/2002/bhopal.htm
5. Ibid.
6. Indian organisations launch NACDOR–II, 2006/11/21, http://editor.ekduniya.in/Action/news/gcapnews.2007–04–19.61556 36170
7. Vivek Kumar, "Understanding Dalit Diaspora", epw.org.in at http://www.chetna.net/articles/dalit_diaspora.htm
8. Ibid.

9. IDSN Annual Number Report 2004 at http://www.idsn.org/index.htm
10. Ibid.
11. *www.dsnuk.org/news_events.htm*
12. For a detailed discussion of the conferences see Debi Chatterjee, "Dalit Situation in India Since the 1990s: An Examination of Certain Issues and Trends", *Socialist Perspective,* Vol. 33, No. 1–2, June–September 2005.
13. Ibid.
14. Ibid.
15. Ibid.
16. Ibid.
17. www.nepaldalitinfo.20m.com
18. Ambrose Pinto, "Caste Discrimination and UN", *Economic and Political Weekly,* 28 September 2002, p. 3989.
19. See http://www.Dalits.org/WCAR.htm
20. http:/doccentre.net/docsweb/CasteRace/
21. See http://www.dalits.org/WCAR.htm
22. Ambrose Pinto, op. cit.
23. *The Hindu,* 24 May, 2009.
24. http://www.hrw.org/reports/2001/globalcaste/
25. Ibid.
26. Ibid.
27. Corinne Lennox,, Ethnicity and Democratic Governance Project Immigration, Minorities and Multiculturalism in Democracies http://cache.search.yahoo-ht2.akadns.net/search/cache?ei=UTF-8&p=dalit+human+rights%2C+conference%2C+1998%2C+kuala+lumpur&fr=slv1-frz6&u=www.edg-gde.ca/7-DLennoxpaper.pdf&w=dalit+human+rights+conference+1998+kuala+lumpur&d=QCsVGpzfQvMu&icp=1&.intl=us
28. http://www.ahrchk.net/statements/mainfile.php/2001statement/29/

Chapter 10

Concluding Observations

Human rights is today a matter of global concern. Over the years, through various debates and intersections of ideas and opinions, a plethora of human rights documents have emerged largely under the aegis of the UN, to give shape to the international human rights discourse.

India has remained a strong votary of human rights. It is a signatory to several important human rights declarations and conventions. It has incorporated the guarantees of basic human rights in its Constitution on the whole in line with the provisions of the Universal Declaration of Human Rights. It has set up various commissions of relevance over the years aiming at the protection of human rights, particularly of the vulnerable sections; of these, special reference may be made of the national and state commissions on human rights, the women's commissions at the national and state levels, the commissions for the Scheduled Castes and Scheduled Tribes and the Backward Classes Commissions. Over the years, India has adopted a host of statutory enactments and government orders to promote and protect human rights. At the international level, India has repeatedly expressed its concern for human rights violations at different points of time, in different parts of the world. Yet, the chink in the armour is all too visible as India's inability to secure the human rights of the weaker sections of the population, particularly the dalits, more than half a century after independence, remains a festering wound on its body politic.

The Contemporary Indian State and Dalit Human Rights

From ancient times, in India, the identity of the individual has remained submerged in the identity of the community to which he belongs. His religion, caste and sub-caste identifications have been decisive in determining his social position, status, the rights assured to him or the wrongs to be inflicted on him. Human rights seen in terms of the inalienable rights of the individual were thus unknown formulations. "Rights", socially speaking, were perceived in terms of group rights, not individual rights. The rights of the group, and only through it the group members', varied according to social standing in terms of the brahminical hierarchy.

Brahminism still remains an overarching reality in Indian society. It continues to sustain the ideological basis of the hierarchic stratification of society. Traditionally, the "sacred" was identified as the repository of power, status and authority to the exclusion of large sections of the population. The connivance of different types of vested interests were legitimised in the name of the supernatural. That stratified societal structuring is all but abolished.

There is ample evidence to prove that historically, in ancient India, the state was openly partial to the maintenance of the caste order. The temporal and the royal authorities colluded with each other in this respect as protecting *Varnashrama Dharma* became the responsibility of the state – the *Raj Dharma.*

Through the medieval period as well as during the British rule, the open sanctification of the caste order, came to be replaced by a more veiled support for the system, in a language that was different from the earlier times. Under the veil of neutrality, patronage was extended to the brahmin in different forms.

The official position of the contemporary state vis-à-vis dalit human rights has remained ambiguous. On the one hand, a professed commitment to the dalit cause has come to permeate most, if not all of mainstream political discourse. The language of modern democratic politics has necessitated it, just as the commitment to human rights expressed through the support extended to the many international treaties and conventions has necessitated. The Constitution of independent India assures equality and justice to its citizens irrespective of caste differences. The obnoxious practice of untouchability is legally forbidden. A host of laws have added to India's statutory commitments in this respect. Yet, the realities continue to be far removed from the legal constitutional discourse. Successive reports of the Commissioner for Scheduled Castes and Scheduled Tribes and the reports of the National Commission for Scheduled Castes and Scheduled Tribes have highlighted the persistent marginalisation of these people as also the mechanisms perpetrating such marginalisation. Whilst government correctives have been operative, the remedies applied to the problem have been essentially piecemeal and inadequate. What comes is very often "too little, too late". Equally questionable is India's reluctance in accepting the discussions of dalit human rights at the international fora. The fact that successive Indian governments have resisted the discussion of caste-based discrimination within the ambit of descent-based discrimination appears to reflect brahminical overtones, to say the least. The reasons behind the ambiguity of the state position can only be understood by taking note of the social and historical realities.

The worst victims of societal stratification in India are the untouchables or the dalits. Doomed to a debased existence, segregated from the rest of the society, marginalised in varied senses, they are denied the very basics of human rights. Even today, many do not have the resources to meet the bare needs of life. The denial of the individual is based not on his or her identity as a person – the plank on which the dominant human rights discourse rests, but on the person's belonging or not belonging to a group. What matters immensely, and unfortunately, is being a "dalit" and not being a "brahmin" or at least a member of a "clean caste". That defines life. That defines the premises of human rights violations. And, that defines the difficulties in gaining redressal of rights violations.

It has to be conceded that the practice of untouchability is far from extinct. Discriminatory mechanisms continue to operate at the social level and perpetrate the marginalisation and overall exclusion of the dalit population from the structures of power, decision-making and the goods and services made available by the state. Under-representation in the higher echelons of government services and near absence in the private sector managerial/administrative levels, high incidence of poverty, marginal or no land holdings or capital resources, and low educational levels in formal terms, combine to perpetrate their vulnerability.

The brahminical social stigma and the overall entrenched marginality encourage the easy stereotyping of the dalits as people of inferior caliber, having a "low" culture or "no" culture at all and unworthy of equal treatment. The utter scientific fallacy of such stereotyping and its gross negation of human rights is hardly taken note of. The propagation of these ideas is partly the result of the internalisation of the brahminical values that structure the subconscious orientation of large sections of the population and partly the result of the carefully planned social engineering undertaken by vested interests with an eye to maintaining the "exploitable" pool of marginalised people.

Dalit women and children are specially vulnerable. Even as India claims to be fully committed to the implementation of the Beijing Platform for Action and has adopted a rights-based approach to promoting equality of women, has evolved a multifaceted strategy aimed at their empowerment through awareness raising, political participation, economic independence, education, health, and legal standards with the objective of enabling women to overcome the disadvantages that they face and to enable them to play an effective and equal role in society, the horrors faced by dalit women in their day-to-day lives remain largely unaddressed. They remain easy prey to the vulgar demonstrations of power by the powerful. The rape and assault of dalit women at the hands of upper caste men are common incidents that are almost legitimised. Family members and kinsfolk can rarely stand up to the violence for fear of reprisal.

For the dalit children, childhood remains an elusive dream – lost in the quagmire of poverty, illiteracy and child labour. Endemic poverty, low literacy levels, high drop out rates at schools and the widespread prevalence of child labour form a vicious circle. For many a child born in a dalit family, childhood is lost in the trappings of trafficking and prostitution. All this happens despite the fact that India adopted a National Charter for Children in 2003 to reiterate her commitment to the cause of the child in order to see that no child remains hungry, illiterate or sick; and has undertaken several initiatives, including the setting up of a National Commission for Protection of Child's Rights and has adopted measures towards the eradication of child labour.

Conversion – one of the earliest tools used by dalits seeking to escape brahminical onslaught – has hardly helped the converts to secure their basic human rights. In most cases the converted have remained extremely vulnerable to attacks from within the folds of their newly opted religious order as also from casteist Hindus from whose pressures they had sought to dissociate themselves through conversion. This is evident on examination of the plight of dalit converts to Christianity, Islam, Buddhism and Sikhism. The violence unleashed on dalit Christians at Kandhamal in Orissa in 2007 by Hindu fundamentalists and the half-hearted response of the state remains a sad statement of contemporary dalit history. No less shocking is the shooting of two Ravidasi Dalit Sikh leaders of the religious sect, Dera Sachkhand in Vienna in May 2009 and its subsequent fallouts in Punjab and Haryana bringing to the surface the contempt of the Jat Sikhs for the dalits.

Globalisation has increased the overall vulnerability of the dalits. The state support that they had enjoyed till the 1990s in the form of reservations, grants and subsidies were, post-90s, getting progressively reduced either directly or indirectly. The state's structural adjustments, emphasis on privatisation and curtailment of the public sector have clearly left the dalits worse off.

With the flourishing of the big industrial projects, massive displacement comes as an inevitable corollary and, as already noted, the Scheduled Castes and Scheduled Tribes are the most susceptible. Once thus displaced, they are almost invariably worse off – suffering a greater degree of marginality. Bound to a policy of pushing ahead with reforms, the state fails to undertake the necessary correctives. Commitment to market-friendly reforms gain priority over dalit friendly reforms for obvious reasons.

Evolving Patterns in Dalit Struggles

The struggles for human rights of the dalits, with the long historical antecedents of socio-religious and economic protests have, in recent years, proceeded largely along two distinct courses.

One operates at the national level and revolves mainly around electoral politics. Ambedkar's efforts had probably been the most potent single factor in the early development of that process. Subsequently, the struggles were carried ahead along several different channels by the different strands of the Republican Party, the Bahujan Samaj Party and a host of smaller Ambedkarite groups and lobbies operating at the different levels of the socioeconomic space.

The major achievements of these struggles appear to be,

(i) to gain recognition of the importance of dalit issues at the level of political negotiations;

(ii) to extract promises at the national level from different political parties – the incorporation in their programmes, manifestoes and speeches of commitments to look into dalit human rights violations and adopt corrective measures; and

(iii) the rise of the BSP, a dalit party, as a major political force in national level politics.

The second line of struggle is the struggle waged in terms of the international human rights discourse, with a focus on mobilising world opinion against caste and getting UN support for the same. This line of struggle has been headed by dalit intellectuals, NGOs and rights bodies in India and abroad. It is far removed from electoral politics. Rather, it operates at the level of the civil society organisations. Here, the demands are located differently, articulated in a different style and are addressed to a different set of target people. Issues like human dignity and private sector reservations figure prominently in the lists of demands; the mastery of modern technology becomes evident in the significant departure from earlier modes of struggles – many of which had been focussed on street protests and the like. The prime intended audience here is not the Indian voter – rather, it is the international community, the dalit diaspora and the Indian dalit elite.

And, it is in the context of this mobilisation that passionate debates on locating or not locating caste in terms of race have been raging. Much of these debates have revolved around the Durban Conference of 2001, though they have not remained confined to it.

Durban Conference and the Caste-Race Interface

The developments centring around the Durban Conference in 2001 brought into focus a debate area that was by no means new. It was the debate on whether caste and race could be equated.

Through the 1930s and 1940s quite a few community studies had been undertaken by the US sociologists seeking to get an insight into the pattern of racial segregation as it existed in the deep South of the USA. To them, "caste" appeared to be a convenient analytical concept in understanding ideas relating to the nature of racial divisions. It is difficult to pinpoint exactly when the word first came in for such use, but it gained a general currency, largely due to the influence of W. Lloyd Warner, who was an anthropologist by training.[1] Such perspectives, however, tended to view caste in a sort of detatched sense failing to reckon with its integral connection with Hindu social philosophy.

This dissociation of caste from its Indian Hindu roots, however, stood challenged in the writings of the well-known Black sociologist, Oliver Cromwell Cox. His book *Caste, Class and Race* was first published in 1948. In its pages it was clearly evident that Cox was unwilling to accept the equation between caste and race. To him, caste in India was essentially systemic, involving an ordering of groups in society, based on the Hindu culture.[2]

None of the early protagonists in the caste-race debate seemed to have had any firsthand knowledge about Indian society. It was Berreman, an anthropologist by training, who entered the debate at a relatively late point of time, who had undertaken some field work in a north Indian village – Sirkanda. He came out in agreement with Warner and Davis that caste and race were comparable.[3] But, then, he emphasised the fact that caste was like race in constituting a pathological violation of human dignity and, like the racial divide in the USA, it depended on force and repression.[4]

Durban virtually resurrected the debate. All over again people started to talk of the caste-race links. Whether or not the two could be equated. This time, however, the question was being discussed at a different level, from a different angle. It was not in order to understand race, but in order to define the nature of caste and the caste system that the two were being taken up for comparison. Both before and after Durban dalit groups and their supporters inside and outside India came forth to assert, "casteism is racism and worse". The idea was to see that within the wider frame of UN activism against racism, India's caste system and the practice of untouchability were taken up. The aim was to mobilise international support in favour of dalit human rights and strengthen the struggle against caste-based social exclusion.

There were academicians and activists on both sides of the debate. Much was written and much more said on the matter. Andre Beteille, a leading Indian sociologist argued against the inclusion of caste in Durban.[5] He said, " I am now convinced that identifying the races in the population of India will be an exercise in futility".[6] He went on to say, " we cannot throw out the concept of race by the front door when it is being misused for asserting social superiority and bring it again through the back door to misuse it in the cause of the oppressed".[7]

Andre Beteille's views however were passionately contested by others. For example, Kalpana Kannabiran in her article titled *Race and Caste: A Response to A. Beteille,* argued that "The analogy between race and caste, I would argue does not date back to Ashley Montague or to Franz Boas, as Beteille argues, but more than a couple of centuries earlier to the original application of the term *casta* itself, a term that recognised the kinship between race and caste".[8] She went on to add that, "The debates on race with reference to the Indian subcontinent that Beteille speaks about are predicated on an unquestioned acceptance of caste as a social group".[9] She was not the only one to challenge the views of Beteille. There were many others countering his arguments from different perspectives. While some argued for inclusion of caste in the Durban agenda from the historical angle, some took up a sociological stand, and still others addressed the issue from the perspective of social activism.[10]

The opposition to the inclusion of caste in the WCAR agenda revolved around the logic that,

(i) caste and race are not synonymous,

(ii) its inclusion in the Durban agenda would dilute the real thrust of the Conference,

(iii) caste-based discrimination in India is a domestic problem internationalisation of the issue would embarrass India, and

(iv) India has suitable constitutional and other arrangements to handle the issue.[11]

The main arguments that were put forward to justify the demand for inclusion of caste in the Durban agenda were as follows:

(i) caste and race discrimination are both cunning social constructs of socially dominant forces,

(ii) both involve hierarchic ordering of social groups, supported by social institutions,

(iii) in both, birth defines position and inequality is inter-generationally transmitted,

(iv) both lead to similar forms of discrimination,

(v) in both caste and race, the lowest in the hierarchy are not merely discriminated against but are compelled to perform menial tasks,

(vi) even if technically speaking, caste and race are different, hairsplitting arguments over definitions should be avoided and, given the urgency of the need for international attention, caste should be discussed at Durban, and

(vii) after all, caste-based discrimination is a form of descent-based discrimination and the International Convention against Racial Discrimination prohibits descent-based discrimination.[12]

Post-Durban Trends and Perspectives for the Future

Specificities of the gains and losses apart, it has to be conceded that developments in and around Durban brought about an international awareness of the problem of untouchability viewed from a human rights perspective. It was discussed and debated at different levels and at different fora. The mobilisation of dalit and human rights bodies as well as the publicity given to the matter were undoubtedly enormous.

Post-Durban, caste and caste-based discriminations became issues that could no longer be ignored by the UN. This is evident from the fact that on 23 December 2002, the United Nations Committee on the Elimination of Racial Discrimination in concluding its discussions on descent-based discrimination, strongly condemned the practices as violative of the International Convention on Elimination of All Forms of Racial Discrimination and in 2005, the UN Commission on Human Rights adopted by consensus a decision to appoint two special Rapporteuers to tackle the entrenched problem of caste-based discrimination.

Clearly, the "rights" perspective that had dominated the dalit discourse for years was now being extended and transformed to incorporate the "human rights perspective", and the "local" nature of the struggles were, in certain respects, becoming "supra local".

Today, post-90s, the concern for human rights is globally centerstage. At such a juncture, the structuring of the dalit discourse in terms of the human rights paradigm is tactically sound and bound to draw widespread attention, as is already evident. It is bound to create much greater pressure on the Indian government and cause greater discomfort than what fragmented domestic pressures alone could create. With the focusing on "human rights" of the dalits a holistic approach comes to the fore bringing up the question of human dignity rather than mere fragmented rights.

The post-90s has witnessed the coming up of the demands such as private sector reservations, emphasis on the social responsibilities of the multinational corporations, the demands for UN interventions in favour of dalit human rights and concerns of dalit women. These are new ideas, concerning new perspectives – widening the existing paradigms of dalit discourse. Much of this diversification is in the context of the altered realities of the globalising world. For example, one of the important issue areas to come into prominence is the private sector where marginalisation was already extensive. With the expansion of the private sector, the woes of the dalits are likely to increase manifold, hence to provide them with a legitimate entry point into the private sector, the demand for "private sector reservation" is rightly being raised.

Ghanshyam Shah identifies two positive changes that appear to have taken place as far as the dalits are concerned. The first is that crude and blatant forms of social discrimination at least in the public sphere are today practised far less frequently than in the past, though they have by no means disappeared. Secondly, a middle class within the community has emerged. The factors that he considers responsible for these developments are as follows:

(i) overall acceptance of equality as a desirable norm as a result of the permeation of liberal and radical philosophical discourse;

(ii) capitalist development, though sluggish, has weakened the traditional functioning of the caste system;

(iii) protective discrimination through reservations in government jobs and admissions to educational institutions has paved the way for dalits to enter the middle class; and

(iv) competitive politics within the parliamentary framework, within the provisions of reservation of seats, has created political consciousness among the dalits on an unprecedented scale.[13]

Notwithstanding certain positive achievements, the tasks confronting the dalit leadership in independent India are indeed complex and difficult. First, they face the problem of educating and mobilising the fragmented, poor, largely illiterate or minimally literate, stigmatised dalit masses; a task that no doubt continues to be extremely difficult. Second, is the need to face the constant and varied forms of pressures coming from the brahminical forces.

Efforts to stand up for dalit human rights are frequently met by boycotts, arson and other crimes. Third, remains the task of trying to make the government protect dalit human rights.[14]

Despite the new trends in mobilisation in the wake of the changing scenario, the dalit movement in India has till now remained largely fragmented with major differences around questions of targets, leadership, coordination, "graded inequality", lack of awareness and understanding of the complexities of the issues, widespread illiteracy, the rural-urban divide, political fragmentation, differences along religious lines and on attitudes towards religion, class differences and lack of coordination of movements across regions as some of the visible hurdles. Even as significant advances are noticeable in the field of global networking for dalit human rights, effective networking amongst dalit groups has hardly developed at the grassroot level within the country. At the grassroot level, dalit struggles are still waged largely along earlier lines focussing on questions of reservations, education, land rights, displacement, and citizenship rights (where relevant, as in West Bengal). What appears to be in focus at such a level is a fragmented rights approach rather than a holistic human rights perspective. This is, by and large, the general observable pattern so far as the functioning of the dalit political parties, pressure lobbies – SC/ST cells in government offices, Ambedkarites movements are concerned. To go beyond such styles of functioning and emphasise a holistic, integrated human rights perspective in handling the dalit question remains the urgent need of the hour. The global attention that has already been generated will no doubt go a long way in helping to forge the links between people, organisations and issues in this context.

Locating the dalit problem in a wider societal context that takes into account the nature of production relations and power structures, continues to be one of the weakest points of the dalit movement. Unfortunately, this thwarts the process of development of class consciousness amongst the dalit population and dims the chances of building up durable and meaningful connections with other oppressed sections of society who, like them, have been victims of ruthless human rights violations perpetrated on them for surplus extraction below value.

The elements of continuity and change in the nature of dalit exploitation prior to the 1990s and thereafter, need careful understanding, as globalisation, with its emphasis on privatisation and the open market has increased the vulnerability of the dalits in varied respects. Confronting it will be immensely difficult for dalit activists in the days to come. The State, straddled with obligations of structural adjustment, would not be able to adopt a pro dalit economic programme beyond a point even if it wished to. Thus, merely pressurising the state would not suffice. Globalisation itself would have to be critiqued from a dalit perspective and carefully planned strategies evolved to resist its onslaught.

The internationalisation of the dalit question in the context of Durban must be understood as having varied implications. In the positive sense, it has undoubtedly strengthened the dalit cause through the coverage of wider issue areas, a more integrated approach, greater and more diverse levels of mobilisation, involvement of the diaspora and the international community. On the other hand, the complicating factors are as follows. The initiative and leadership here rests with the apolitical NGO sector; a sector that relies heavily on externally generated support in multiple senses of the term. Its inability to, or disinterest in tying up with the political has meant the inability to build extensive grassroot networking as also the inability to develop a holistic approach in terms of moving towards a solution. Moreover, the vulnerability in terms of external pressures can hardly be overstated. It is also important to assess how far, and along what lines the involvement of the international community should be encouraged. It is true that mobilised world opinion against caste and caste-based discrimination is needed. And, here the UN could surely play a vital role. However, in internationalising the dalit issue, caution has clearly to be advised. Identifying friends and foes could be crucial. The issue should not become a stick in the hands of US-led capitalist forces to beat India with. We have seen how "democracy" and "human rights" have been usurped in the globalising world legitimising neo-imperialist expansion. Afghanistan and Iraq provide glaring examples. The sword of Damocles appears to hang over several other states as they get castigated as "rogue states". Under the circumstances, it is imperative to differentiate between the call for genuine human rights and US-led pedagogy ! Whilst the former has to be nurtured, the latter fought off. The strength necessary for doing this can come only with a convergence of the "political" and "apolitical" strands of the struggles, a genuine commitment to human rights and the building up of a strong democratic ethos capable of firmly combating all forms of social exclusion and challenging the brahminical order.

Notes

1. cf. Ursula Sharma, *Caste,* Viva Books, New Delhi, 2005, p. 15.
2. Ibid., p. 17.
3. Ibid., p. 19.
4. Ibid.
5. "Race and Caste", *The Hindu,* March 10, 2001.
6. Ibid.
7. Ibid.
8. PUCL Bulletin, http:/www.pucl.org/reports/National/2001/beteille.htm
9. *http:/doccentre.net/docsweb/CasteRace/*
10. See the arguments presented by Gail Omvedt, "The UN, Racism and Caste I and II", *The Hindu*, April 10, 2001; "Caste, Race and Sociologists I and II", *The Hindu*, October 18 and19, 2001.
11. For an exposition of the different arguments for and against inclusion of caste in the Durban agenda, see "Caste and Race", p. 6, http:/doccentre.net/docsweb/CasteRace/
12. Ibid., pp. 5–6.
13. Ghanshyam Shah, ed., *Dalit Identity and Politics,* Sage, New Delhi, 2001, p. 39.
14. S.M. Michael, "Dalit Vision of a Just Society in India", S.M. Michael ed., *Dalits in Modern India: Vision and Values,* Vistaar, New Delhi, 1999, p. 111.

Appendices

APPENDIX 1

International Conference on Dalit Human Rights, London, 2000

International Conference on Dalit Human Rights organised by VOD International at Shri Guru Ravidass Community Centre at 28 Carlyle Road, Manor Park, London, in association with the Dalit Solidarity Network, UK and the communities of Shri Guru Ravidass Sabha, Bhagwan Valmiki Welfare Trust and the Ambedkarite organisations in UK, has appealed to the United Nations and Government of India to take steps to stop atrocities against dalits (the untouchables) in India. The Conference has appealed to the international community to intervene immediately to stop all kinds of Human Rights violations particularly those faced by dalits in India. To this effect, the Conference has adopted a declaration called "London Declaration", which forms part of this short report.

Ramdas Athawale, Member of Parliament, inaugurated the two-day conference. He drew the attention of the participants to the deplorable plight of the dalits in India even after 53 years of independence. He called for concerted efforts by the dalit communities abroad, particularly in the UK for creating awareness in the West and building up pressure on the Government of India to implement the laws and safeguard the interest of the dalits. Giving the keynote address, Rev. David Haslam, the Chair of the Dalit Solidarity Network, UK, narrated the numerous instances of human right violations in India and India's efforts to oppose the move to include Caste in the agenda of the forthcoming UN Commission on Race in 2001. He equated Caste with Race. Speaking in the opening session, Balchandra L. Mungekar, the Vice Chancellor of the University of Bombay, highlighted the importance of Dalit Human Rights, explaining the social and economic context of the dalits in India. He appealed to the dalit communities in the UK to think positively for planning and supporting programmes for the economic and social development of their less fortunate brethren in India. N.C. Naithani, the representative from the Indian High Commission, focussed on the need for more measures for uplifting the dalit communities. Welcoming the delegates and participants, Irene Beckett, Chairman of VOD International, called for unity amongst dalits worldwide. She endorsed the belief of Ambedkar in liberty, equality and fraternity and said everyone has a moral obligation to examine the caste system and the effects on the dalits.

The Conference was fruitful with deliberations of various aspects and issues pertaining to the dalits in India, in its various sessions. It started with a session on dalits and Human Rights. Yogesh Varhade, the president, Ambedkar Centre for Justice and Peace, USA and Canada, pointed out the violations of basic human rights of dalits in India, despite all the UN resolutions, and the laws in India. He further said that the practice of untouchability is still prevalent in different forms in India and the existence of caste system accentuates the practice and consequent atrocities against the dalits. Chairing the session, V.T. Hireker, President, Ambedkar Centre for Justice and Peace, UK called for immediate attention of UN and the International Agencies to the genocide taking place in India in the name of caste system and untouchability.

Speaking on Constitution and dalits, Sreenivasan, President, Federation of Ambedkarite and Buddhist Organisations, UK said that India has a good constitution and set of laws and rules, but the lack of implementation of these laws and rules is the basic problem faced by the dalits. He called for the pressure from international community on the Government of India for the proper implementation of its own laws and rules. Chairing the session,

M.S. Padda, Secretary General, Bhagwan Valmiki Trust, UK, expressed the concern about the plan for constitutional review in India, which is against the interest of dalits and the denial of their constitutional rights established by the efforts of Baba Sahib Ambedkar, the all time leader of dalits in India.

The plenary session was chaired by Lawerncia Kwark, Project Officer, CCFD, France, who stressed the importance of the affected community to stand together at the India level and the international level. Mungekar presented a paper on educational situation of dalits. He emphasised the need for special attention on the educational progress of the dalits as a means for safeguarding their basic human rights. Speaking on the occasion, Satpal Muman, General Secretary, Ambedkar International Mission, pointed out the prevalence of caste system amongst the Indian communities in UK and called for the attention of the authorities concerned to stop such practices, treating it as racism. J. Muthumary, Professor and Head of the Department of Botany, University of Madras, who spoke next explained how the women face double atrocities and humiliations in India under the caste system. The situation of dalit women are more alarming and deserving very serious attention. Vaman Nimbalkar explained the work of the National Campaign on Dalit Human Rights (NCDHR) in India and sought the support of the international community in its struggle for basic human rights of dalits.

The second day started with the paper on the role of Overseas Dalit Organisations. M.S. Bahal, General Secretary, Ambedkar International Institution, reminded the representatives of different dalit organisations to think and plan to help their brethren in India so as to enable them to capture political power. Presiding over the session, P.C. Sondhi of Ambedkar International Mission, requested the various dalit groups, such, as Ravidassias, Valmikies, Ambedkarites and Christian dalits to come together on a common platform to support the struggle of dalits in India. V. Anand spoke on racism and the perceptive of Ambedkar.

Northern Aid Agencies and dalits, which was altogether a new subject, was handled by Leo Bashyam, Head, Asia Desk, Christian Aid, UK. He suggested the need for a body that will coordinate, network, communicate and share information with the various advocacy groups working on dalit issues in the north. Agencies in the north, taking into account of the peculiarities of dalits should design appropriate strategies to support the struggle of dalits for social and economic development. Chairing the session, Catherine Gaudard, Freres des Hommes, France, explained her experience of working with dalit and stressed the need for increased attention of donor agencies to the problem of dalits.

M.C. Raj, Director, REDS, India, presented the Plan for the Millennium for the dalits in India. He explained the process of globalisation and brahminisation. In this context he elaborated the various sub plans of dalitisation for the socioeconomic, religious, cultural and political development of the dalits. Chairing the session, Eugene Culas of VOD International stressed on the need for specific and concrete programmes from all the dalit communities and their organisations in UK and abroad for their brethren in India.

The conference has discussed the Plan for the Millennium by dividing into four groups. Several suggestions emerged out of it, including the need for united action in the future by all the UK-based dalit groups – in the form of a secular organisation called VODI-UK under VOD International, to coordinate the efforts of all the dalit organisations in UK for the cause of the promotion of dalits in India.

Addressing the concluding session of the conference, G.S. Chambers, President, Supreme Council of Ravidass Sabha in UK and Abroad, called for the unity among the dalit organisations in UK for tackling the problems faced by dalits. He has also stressed the need for international efforts as well as pressure building from within to stop violation of human rights of dalits. Jeremy Corbyn MP presided over the concluding session. He explained some of his efforts to take the issue to the UN Commission on Race. He wanted the Government to implement the provisions of all the international covenants to which India is a party and thereby stop all atrocities against dalits. In the valedictory address, Ramdas Athawale MP from India wanted the unity among the dalit movements and organisations in India for which he requested the help of all the Indians in UK. Balchandra L. Mungekar, the Vice Chancellor of University of Bombay spoke on the social and economic repercussions of globalisation on the life of dalits. He compared the caste system to capitalism, which denies the rights and privileges of the lower class to the benefit of the upper class, (which are synonymous to lower castes and upper castes in India). In the context of the present situation of increasing exploitation of dalits, he called for immediate and integrated attempts from international community to consider the problems of dalits with topmost priority.

Source: http://www.ambedkar.org/Worldwide_Dalits/Report.htm

APPENDIX 2

Excepts from WCAR NGO Forum Declaration, 3rd September 2001

Caste and Discrimination Based on Work and Descent

84. Work and descent-based discrimination, including caste discrimination and untouchability, being a historically entrenched, false ideological construct sanctioned by religion and culture, which is hereditary in nature and affects over 300 million people in the Asia Pacific and African regions at the personal, social and structural levels, irrespective of their religious affiliation.

85. The practice of untouchability, rooted in the caste system, stigmatises 260 million dalits in South Asia as "polluted" or "impure", thereby denying them entry into places of religious worship, participation in religious festivals, assigning them menial and degrading work including cleaning toilets, skinning and disposal of dead animals, digging graves and sweeping, and the forced prostitution of dalit women and girls through the traditional system of temple prostitution (*Devadasi*).

86. The system of "hidden apartheid" based on caste practices of distinction, exclusion and restrictions denies dalits' enjoyment of their economic, social, political, cultural and religious rights, exposing them to all forms of violence and manifests itself in the segregation of housing settlements and cemeteries, segregation in tea stalls ("two-cup" system), denial of access to

common drinking water, restaurants, places of worship, restrictions on marriage and other insidious measures all of which inhibit their development as equals.

87. Caste discrimination and "untouchability" practised against generations of dalits for centuries together amounts to systemic "generational and cultural Daliticide", which is the mass scale destruction of their individual and collective identity, dignity and self-respect for generations through cultural methods and practices.

88. Any action or even any sign of an attempt to act by dalits either individually or collectively to assert their rights is met with extreme measures of violence such as burning or destruction of their homes, property and crops, social boycott, rape or gang-rape of dalit women and murder by dominant caste individuals or groups, police or the bureaucracy, and that in such instances the State often acts with impunity and in connivance with these perpetrators.

89. Work and descent-based discrimination against the *Buraku* people of Japan has existed for over 400 years and continues to be experienced today by over 3 million people in relation to marriage, employment and education, with new forms of discrimination emerging such as discriminatory propaganda and incitement to discrimination against them, especially on the Internet.

90. The vulnerability of the victims of work and descent-based discrimination, including caste discrimination and untouchability, is aggravated by legal systems and law enforcement machinery that fail to protect them and hence are responsible for the continued perpetuation of discrimination, and by States that are themselves often the law-breakers.

Source: Excepts from WCAR NGO Forum Declaration, 03 September 2001. The document is the outcome of an international process before and during the NGO Forum of the WCAR held in Durban, South Africa 28 August – 1 September 2001.
http://www.eyeontheun.org/assets/attachments/documents/durban_ngo_declaration_2001.pdf

APPENDIX 3

Vancouver Declaration: International Dalit Conference, 2003

Adopted unanimously by The International Dalit Conference Vancouver, BC, Canada,

16–18 May 2003

We, the dalits, from all over the globe having assembled at the International Dalit Conference, to deliberate the issues concerning the 250 million Dalits (Scheduled Castes and Scheduled Tribes) of India and their future in the 21st century,

Inspired by that great thinker and philosopher of the oppressed, Babasaheb B. R. Ambedkar,

Rededicate ourselves to his mission to bring about a democratic and peaceful transformation of India whereby all its citizens, irrespective of their gender, caste, creed, language and region, will enjoy the fruits of equality and justice,

Whereas the world has entered the third millennium and is progressing towards accomplishing the goals of Liberty, Equality and Fraternity, and whereas India has failed to eradicate untouchability and caste and descent-based discrimination and is yet to achieve basic fundamental human rights,

Call upon the dalits of the world to unite in their activism in the true spirit of interfaith and multiculturalism, and resolve to work tirelessly for the upliftment of the community,

Affirm that every human being has the inherent right to life and dignity and that Black is Beautiful and Dalit is Dignified,

Mindful of the fact that the dalits and tribals, accounting for a fourth of India's one billion population, continue to be the victims of manifold discriminations and violence,

Mindful also that women belonging to these sections are the victims of gender caste discrimination,

Sincerely believe that the caste problem is not the problem of dalits alone but also of the entire nation and without the annihilation of caste and the elimination of other primordial identities,

India will not be able to realise its full socioeconomic potential and claim its rightful place among the community of nations,

Uphold our unwavering belief in the Indian Constitution as well as the unity and integrity of India,

Take cognizance of the universal ideals enshrined in several international and national covenants and treaties – from the Universal Declaration of the Human Rights to the Bhopal Declaration – and

Endorse wholeheartedly the Bhopal Declaration in letter and spirit,

Affirm our mission to support the struggles of oppressed people worldwide and muster all possible support from anywhere for the advancement of the dalit cause,

Resolve to propagate knowledge of Babasaheb as a philosopher of emancipation to all the oppressed anywhere in the world, and to fulfil the pledge,

Resolve also to build our own educational, cultural and other institutions for the advancement of the community, we

Rededicate ourselves to institutionalise the process started in the Conference through constant coordination and by setting up a formal institutional structure for better networking among the resident and non-resident Indian dalit community as well as to make use of international institutions and processes to sensitise the world about the plight of the dalits and tribals in India,

We therefore demand,

1. The rightful and proportionate share of dalits and tribals in India's national institutions, wealth and capital must be recognised. Economic exclusion hitherto practised in the name of caste must be done away with. The community should have equitable access to means of production and economic empowerment.

2. Since no development is possible without gender justice, women of these groups must be given priority in all developmental activities. They must have formal, legally sanctioned rights on par with men.

3. Private Corporations and Multinational Corporations operating in India must recognise and accept their social responsibilities.
4. The United Nations and its affiliates, and nongovernmental agencies concerned with human rights, social and economic development, must recognise that the dalits are a special group and create separate dalit divisions managed by the dalits themselves. Their programmes and projects should have special dalit components as well as special focus in their reports.
5. Dalit studies must be included in Indian and international educational and research institutions, especially in North America and Europe, and universities should recognise the need to admit dalit students on priority.
6. The World Bank and other International Financial Institutions should attach conditional special component clause and must ensure the rightful share of the dalits in the funds they lend to India for socioeconomic and sustainable development.
7. The international governmental and nongovernmental development aid agencies should focus on dalit development and empowerment with initiatives to be inbuilt in their system and adopted in the funding programmes.
8. Sustained efforts must be made at the United Nations to expedite the process of formally equating caste-based discrimination with racial discrimination.
9. Untouchability is practised in many countries such as Bangladesh, Nepal, Pakistan and Sri Lanka. No effort must be spared to address the problem by the world community.
10. Reorganise the National and State Commissions for SCs and STs as the SC and ST Vigilance Commissions and the decisions of these Commissions should be binding.
11. All laws, rules and regulations meant for protecting the rights of the dalits must be included in the Ninth Schedule of the Constitution of India, to prevent unjust and lengthy litigation process which always goes against the community.

Source: http://www.ambedkar.org/News/VancouverDeclaration.htm

APPENDIX 4

The Hague Declaration on the Human Rights and Dignity of Dalit Women

Hague Conference on Dalit Women,

20–21 Nov 2006

The Netherlands

We, the participants of the Hague Conference on Dalit Women's Rights, held in The Hague on 20 and 21 November 2006, after deliberating upon the issues of discrimination, violence and impunity against dalit women, adopt this Declaration on the Human Rights and Dignity of Dalit Women.

In South Asia – that is, India, Nepal, Pakistan, Bangladesh and Sri Lanka – dalits have endured discrimination based on work and descent for centuries, and this discrimination continues today. The dalits – known as "untouchables" or outcastes – number around 260 million people in South Asia. On account of their caste, they experience discrimination, social exclusion and violence on a daily basis. Although economic growth in the region has been strong over the past decade, caste disparities remain and are in fact increasing. The situation of dalit women in these countries needs urgent and special attention. They constitute one of the largest socially segregated groups anywhere in the world and face systemic and structural discrimination thrice over: as dalits, as women, and as poor.

Systemic Discrimination, Violence and Impunity

The caste system declares dalit women to be intrinsically impure and "untouchable", therefore socially excluded. In class terms, the vast majority of dalit women are poor; many are landless daily wage labourers who are systematically denied access to resources. As women, they are subjugated by patriarchal structures. Due to this intersectional discrimination, dalit women are specifically targeted for daily, egregious acts of violence, in particular for sexual violence, including the *Devadasi* system of forced and ritualised prostitution. On account of their "impure" caste and poverty, dalit women comprise the majority of manual scavengers, that is, labourers who clean human excrement from dry toilets. When they assert fundamental rights, dalit women are targeted for punitive violence by dominant castes. Due to patriarchal notions of community honour residing in women, dominant caste violence against dalit women functions to punish the entire dalit community and teach dalits a lesson of obedience to caste norms. Moreover, dalit women are discriminated against not only by dominant castes on account of their caste, class and gender, but also by their own communities on account of their gender. Dalit women have less power within the dalit community in general.

When considering discrimination and violence against dalit women, one can state that impunity is the key problem dalit women face today – not only while seeking legal and judicial redress for violence, but also while attempting to access and enjoy their fundamental rights and freedoms. Perpetrators enjoy virtual immunity from prosecution for violence against dalit women, as the police, who themselves often harbour caste prejudices, wilfuly neglect to enforce the law. Not only the police, but perpetrators and their communities use their political, social and economic power to silence dalit women, thereby denying them access to justice. The nature of collusion between state and dominant caste actors is such that the modern rule of law has no place in the hierarchical order of socioeconomic and political power relationships, as caste-based power supersedes state derived executive authority.

Assertion by Dalit Women

Dalit women today are not simply passive victims; the current mood is not one of mere acceptance, but one of determination to "transform their pain into power". In fact, they have been active throughout history, though often this has not been recognised and recorded. They have been actively involved in the anti caste and anti untouchability movements. Today they are the strongholds of the dalit movements in thousands of South Asian villages, and are often at the forefront of struggles for basic human rights. They continue to play a critical role in the movements for land and livelihood rights and against untouchability, pointing to the potential for their self-emancipation, given adequate support. They are making their mark as independent thinkers and writers in the literary world by critiquing dominant caste ideologies. They participate today as visionary leaders in the local governance institution by asserting their rights. While they continue to struggle against structural discrimination and exclusion, violence and impunity are systematically unleashed by dominant castes to keep them in their place.

While recognising the gendered nature of caste discrimination for dalit women, these women have turned their "suffering" into one of "resistance", actively participating shoulder to shoulder with men in their communities in the anti caste and anti untouchability movements. They have simultaneously contributed to the welfare of their families, sustained their communities given their labour for producing food and wealth for their countries. In this regard, dalit women build their identities on a culture of resistance against the hegemonic culture of the caste system, expressing their defiance and revolt against the caste, class and gender discrimination that oppresses them. This assertion of distinct identity and simultaneous forging of a collective identity in multiple struggles marks the dalit women's movement in various ways.

Human Rights of Dalit Women

The countries where caste discrimination persists are party to most of the relevant human rights instruments: the Universal Declaration on Human Rights and treaties such as the International Covenant on Civil and Political Rights (ICCPR), the International Covenant on Economic, Social and Cultural Rights (ICESCR) and the International Convention on the Elimination of All Forms of Racial Discrimination (ICERD). These treaties provide equal rights for men and women. As these countries are also party to the Convention on the Elimination of All Forms of Discrimination Against Women (CEDAW), governments have a specific obligation to make sure that women can realise their human rights. It is generally accepted in international legal standards that governments have to do more than just pass laws to protect human rights. Governments have an obligation to take all measures, including policy and budgetary measures, to make sure that women can fulfil and enjoy their fundamental rights. Equally importantly, governments must implement these laws, policy measures and programmes to fully discharge their obligations under international law. This includes an obligation to exercise due diligence in punishing those who engage in caste-based discrimination and violence.

Millennium Development Goals and Dalit Women

In 2000, a total of 189 countries accepted the Millennium Declaration and agreed to take the necessary action in order to attain eight specific goals: the Millennium Development Goals (MDGs)[1]. The realisation of human rights of dalit women will have a substantial positive effect on the realisation of the MDGs. This is because dalit women are extremely poor, and make up 2 per cent of the world's population. In India, for example, 60 million children do not attend primary school; a disproportionate number of these children are dalit girls.

International Conference on Dalit Women's Rights

Over the years dalit women's organisations and movements have increasingly voiced their specific concerns and asserted their separate identity, calling for solidarity from the International Community. The Fourth World Conference on Women in Beijing in 1995 saw for the first time international recognition given to the discrimination faced by dalit women. Dalit women also played a crucial role in the World Conference Against Racism in South Africa in 2001, where dalit issues were brought to the fore of the international attention. Following the National Conference on Violence against Dalit Women in Delhi on 7 and 8 March 2006, Justitia et Pax Netherlands, Cordaid, and CMC as members of the Dalit Network Netherlands (DNN), in collaboration with the National Campaign on Dalit Human Rights (NCDHR) and other dalit and dalit women's organisations, responded to the request of dalit women and organised the International Conference on the Human Rights of Dalit Women on 20 and 21 November 2006 in The Hague, The Netherlands.

Focus of International Conference

Caste, class and gender discrimination prevents dalit women from enjoying their basic human rights, particularly to dignity, equality and development. Atrocities and violence against dalit women are both a means of sustaining systemic discrimination, as well as a reaction when particularly untouchability practices and caste norms are challenged or not adhered to. Impunity for this discrimination and violence is then used as a means to preserve the existing caste and gender disparities. Before dalit women can enjoy their human rights, and before the Millennium Development Goals can be achieved, discrimination, violence and impunity must stop.

Therefore we, the participants of The Hague Conference on Dalit Women's Rights, call upon the respective governments in Nepal, India, Pakistan, Bangladesh and Sri Lanka to take seriously the voices of dalit women as they explain their specific situation, to support them in asserting their rights and to ensure dalit women and girls are brought on par with the general population in terms of overall development (e.g., poverty reduction) within a period of five years. We call upon the international community to undertake and support every possible measure to fight the widespread discrimination, violence and impunity committed against dalit women.

Recommendations

Recommendations to the respective governments of Nepal, India, Pakistan, Bangladesh and Sri Lanka:

- Disaggregate all criminal, economic, social and political data on the grounds of gender and caste.
- Evolve and implement a comprehensive strategy to address impunity and ensure criminal justice for dalit women.

- Grant powers to make legally binding recommendations to relevant National Human Rights Institutions to establish an independent complaints and monitoring mechanism to address the discrimination and violence against dalit women.
- Enact domestic violence (prevention and protection) laws that acknowledge the unique vulnerability of dalit women, allocate adequate resources and ensure a comprehensive monitoring mechanism with representation of dalit women for effective implementation of these laws.
- Provide support to establish informal organisations for dalit women to freely discuss the social, domestic and development issues in their own community and to strengthen leadership within local governance structures.
- Mandate proportional representation of dalit women elected into parliaments, legislatures and local governance systems, including equal distribution of other minority groups, such as *Jogins/Badis* (India/Nepal) irrespective of their faith, and provide adequate budget allocations in this regard.
- Restore lands earmarked by governments for dalits and register them in the name of dalit women or jointly with men, and also acquire and distribute surplus lands by implementing reform acts and distribute lands to dalits in proportion to their populations in each country.
- Issue legal title to lands possessed and enjoyed by dalit women and men, in the name of dalit women or jointly with men; grant each dalit family five acres of land registered in the name of dalit women; allocate and distribute sufficient budget for the purchase of land and distribute to dalit women; ensure payment of equal and living wage to dalit women without discrimination.
- Ensure dalit women enjoy equal access to and share of common property resources, in particular water resources, and provide budgetary support to create common property for their own.
- Enact appropriate legislation to prevent displacement of dalits and alienation of their lands in the name of

development projects and schemes in the context of economic globalisation.

- Eradicate the practice of manual scavenging and the *jogini* system and enforce rehabilitation policies and programmes for their alternative livelihood and sustenance.
- Implement laws that prohibit bonded or forced labour.
- Allocate sufficient budget for full primary and secondary level education of all dalit girls, including funds for staff in schools and infrastructure, and vocational institutions
- Ensure reduction of prenatal mortality, infant mortality and maternal mortality among dalit women on a time bound basis.
- Provide assistance to launch a national campaign of caste sensitisation and elimination of caste, class and gender discrimination.

Recommendations to the International Community, to the United Nations and the European Union:

Recalling the Universal Declaration of Human Rights;

Having regard to the UN Convention on the Elimination of All Forms of Discrimination Against Women and all other relevant UN Conventions;

Having regard to General Recommendation XXIX of the UN Committee on the Elimination of Racial Discrimination, in particular to Paragraphs 11–13;

Having regard to and reinforcing the urgency of the ongoing UN study on "Discrimination Based on Work and Descent" and the development of Principles and Guidelines for the effective elimination of this form of discrimination, we call upon:

- The international community to ensure that the large gap is closed, at the latest by 2015, by achieving targets of the Millennium Development Goals for the population in general and dalit women and girls in particular, through providing additional measures for dalit women and girls to realise their right to development on par with others.

- The United Nations Human Rights bodies and mechanisms, the United Nations organisations, intergovernmental institutions and organisations, the European Union, bilateral aid agencies and international nongovernmental organisations to give full recognition and effect to the content and the recommendations of The Hague Conference on the Rights of Dalit Women.
- The international community to express its outrage against the caste induced, systematic practice of untouchability and atrocities against dalits in South Asia in general and against dalit women in particular.
- These institutions and bodies to raise the issues and concerns of dalit women at all levels and to involve and introduce all necessary measures, and to support and secure the implementation of the recommendations of this Declaration with a sense of great urgency.
- The Human Rights Council to address the issue of untouchability and violence against dalit women and men and the impunity related to caste practices and discrimination.
- The ILO in its annual Global Reports on fundamental labour rights (no child and no forced labour, non-discrimination in employment and the right to association and collective bargaining) to highlight and propose measures to fight the systematic violation of these fundamental rights as far as dalit women and girls are concerned.

1. The MDGs are: (i) reduction of extreme poverty and hunger by half; (ii) primary education for all boys and girls; (iii) gender equality and empowerment of women; (iv) reduction of child mortality by two-thirds; (v) reduction of maternal mortality by three-quarters; (vi) combat HIV/aids, malaria and other diseases; (vii) clean drinking water and 100 million slum dwellers above the poverty line; (viii) more aid, fair trade, less debt.

Source: http://www.franciscansinternational.org/docs/statement.php?id=478

APPENDIX 5

Representation of Scheduled Castes and Scheduled Tribes in Public Sector Undertakings

Group	*S.C. %*	*S.T. %*
A	7.37	1.88
B	9.12	3.28
C	18.71	8.42
D(Excluding Sweepers)	21.90	9.76
Total	17.74	7.77
Group D (Sweepers)	85.19	3.16
Grand Total	18.55	7.71

Source: Annual Report, National Commission For Scheduled Castes And Scheduled Tribes, 1993–94, New Delhi, 1996, p. 99.

APPENDIX 6

Land Acquisition Rules

To date, India has no national resettlement and rehabilitation policy. Only three states, Maharashtra, Madhya Pradesh and Punjab, have statewide resettlement and rehabilitation (R&R) policies. The Maharashtra Project Affected People's Rehabilitation Act of 1976, amended in 1986, is the most comprehensive. Other states have issued Government Orders or Resolutions, sometimes sectorwide but more often for specific projects. Two national parastatal companies, the National Thermal Power Corporation (NTPC) and Coal India Limited (CIL) have completed and issued R&R policies … . Many organisations in India have lobbied for a national rehabilitation policy.

Land acquisition in India is covered by a national law, the 1894 Land Acquisition Act (LAA) and its subsequent amendments. The LAA allows for land acquisition in the national interest for water reservoirs, canals, plants, fly ash ponds, transmission lines and highways to be carried out by the respective States, in accordance with its provisions. Under the LAA, compensation is in cash for the loss of land, other productive assets (such as standing crops and fruit and fodder trees), house plots and residences. A separate law, the Coal-Bearing Act of 1957 (CBA), covers land acquisition of coal bearing land. Restoration of community and household productive assets, or of standard or quality of life, is not covered by the LAA but becomes a policy question determined on a project by project basis, unless a state or parastatal company policy applies.

The Land Acquisition Act of 1894 is summarised below. This summary is adapted from a Draft Report by the World Bank on Resettlement and Rehabilitation in India (April 1994):

- Land identified for the purpose of a project is placed under Section 4 of the LAA. This constitutes notification. Objections must be made within 50 days to the Collector (highest administrative officer) of the concerned District. The CBA requires 30 days for objections;
- The land is then placed under Section 6 of the LAA (or Section 7 of the CBA). This is a declaration that the Government intends to acquire the land. The Collector is directed to take steps for the acquisition, and the land is placed under Section 9. Interested parties are then invited to state their interest in the land and the price. Under Section 11, the Collector shall make an award within two years of the date of publication of the declarations. Otherwise, the acquisition proceedings shall lapse;
- In case of disagreement on the price awarded, within 6 weeks of the award the parties (under Section 18) can request the Collector to refer the matter to the Courts to make a final ruling on the amount of compensation;
- Once the land has been placed under Section 4, no further sales or transfers are allowed. However, since the time lag between Sections 4 and the others following it is about three years, land transfers are not uncommon;
- Compensation for land and improvements (such as houses, wells, trees, etc.) is paid in cash by the project authorities to the State government, which in turn compensates landowners. In the case of acquisition for coal projects, the coal companies make direct payments to landowners;
- The price to be paid for the acquisition of agricultural land is based on sale prices recorded in the District Registrar's

office averaged over the three years preceding notification under Section 4. The compensation is paid after the area is acquired, actual payment by the State taking about two or three years. An additional 30 per cent is added to the award as well as an escalation of 12 per cent per year from the date of notification to the final placement under Section 9. For delayed payments, after placement under Section 9, an additional 9 per cent per annum is paid for the first year and 15 per cent for subsequent years.

APPENDIX 7

PUCL Bulletin, December 2001

All India Conviction Rate Under PCR Act and SC/ST Prevention of Atrocities Act During 1991 to 1998

Year/Crime Head	*Conviction Rate*
PCR Act.	
1991	26.2
1992	29.4
1993	33.0
1994	21.4
1995	35.5
1996	23.9
1997	27.2
1998	22.6
SC/ST Prevention of Atrocities Act	
1995	39.2
1996	38.1
1997	31.4
1998	32.2

Notes

1. Prior figures of SC/ST Prevention Act are not available.
2. 1995 figure exclude data of Bihar, Gujarat, Meghalaya, and Daman & Diu on SC/ST Prevention of Atrocities Act. due to its non-availability.

Source: http://www.pucl.org/reports/TamilNadu/2001/casteism-tab3.htm

APPENDIX 8

Crime Against Dalits

Year	*Total No. of Crimes*	*Murder*	*Rape*	*Arson*	*Civil Rights Protection*	*Total of Col. 3 to 6*
1	2	3	4	5	6	7
1990	15250	463	672	260	2788	4183
1991	18368	523	655	323	2944	4445
1992	24922	616	849	406	2900	4771
1993	24973	510	798	369	2531	4208
1994	33910	546	992	533	1731	3802
1995	32996	571	872	500	1528	3471
1996	31440	543	949	464	1417	3373
1997	27944	513	1037	389	1216	3155
1998	25638	516	923	346	724	2509
1999	21469	445	879	303	575	2202
Total	256910	5246	8626	3893	17779	36119

Source: http://www.pucl.org/reports/TamilNadu/2001/casteism-tab1.htm

APPENDIX 9

The Scheduled Castes and Scheduled Tribes (Prevention of Atrocities) Act, 1989, No. 33 of 1989

(11th September, 1989)

An Act to prevent the commission of offences of atrocities against the members of the Scheduled Castes and the Scheduled Tribes, to provide for Special Courts for the trial of such offences and for the relief and rehabilitation of the victims of such offences and for matters connected therewith or incidental thereto.

Be it enacted by Parliament in the Fortieth Year of the Republic of India as follows:

Chapter I
Preliminary

Short Title, Extent and Commencement

(1) This Act may be called the Scheduled Castes and the Scheduled Tribes (Prevention of Atrocities) Act, 1989.

(2) It extends to the whole of India except the State of Jammu and Kashmir.

(3) It shall come into force on such date as the Central Government may, by notification in the Official Gazette, appoint.

Definitions

(1) In this Act, unless the context otherwise requires:
   - (a) "atrocity" means an offence punishable under Section 3;
   - (b) "Code" means the Code of Criminal Procedure, 1973 (2 of 1974);
   - (c) "Scheduled Castes and Scheduled Tribes" shall have the meanings assigned to them respectively under clause (24) and clause (25) of Article 366 of the Constitution;
   - (d) "Special Court" means a Court of Session specified as a Special Court in section 14;
   - (e) "Special Public Prosecutor" means a Public Prosecutor specified as a Special Public Prosecutor or an advocate referred to in section 15;
   - (f) words and expressions used but not defined in this Act and defined in the Code or the Indian Penal Code (45 of 1860) shall have the meanings assigned to them respectively in the Code, or as the case may be, in the Indian Penal Code.

(2) Any reference in this Act to any enactment or any provision thereof shall, in relation to an area in which such enactment or such provision is, not in force, be construed as a reference to the corresponding law, if any, in force in that area.

Chapter II
Offences of Atrocities

Punishments for Offences of Atrocities

(1) Whoever, not being a member of a Scheduled Caste or a Scheduled Tribe:

(i) forces a member of a Scheduled Caste or a Scheduled Tribe to drink or eat any inedible or obnoxious substance;

(ii) acts with intent to cause injury, insult or annoyance to any member of a Scheduled Caste or a Scheduled Tribe by dumping excreta, waste matter, carcasses or any other obnoxious substance in his premises or neighbourhood;

(iii) forcibly removes clothes from the person of a member of a Scheduled Caste or a Scheduled Tribe or parades him naked or with painted face or body or commits any similar act which is derogatory to human dignity;

(iv) wrongfully occupies or cultivates any land owned by, or allotted to, or notified by any competent authority to be allotted to, a member of a Scheduled Caste or a Scheduled Tribe or, gets the land allotted to him transferred;

(v) wrongfully dispossesses a member of a Scheduled Caste or a Scheduled Tribe from his land or premises or interferes with the enjoyment of his rights over any land, premises or water;

(vi) compels or entices a member of a Scheduled Caste or a Scheduled Tribe to do "begar" or other similar forms of forced or bonded labor other than any compulsory service for public purposes imposed by Government;

(vii) forces or intimidates a member of a Scheduled Caste or a Scheduled Tribe not to vote or to vote to a particular candidate or to vote in a manner other than that provided by law;

(viii) institutes false, malicious or vexatious suit or criminal or other legal proceedings against a member of a Scheduled Caste or a Scheduled Tribe;

(ix) gives any false or frivolous information to any public servant and thereby causes such public servant to use his lawful power to the injury or annoyance of a member of a Scheduled Caste or a Scheduled Tribe;

(x) intentionally insults or intimidates with intent to humiliate a member of a Scheduled Caste or a Scheduled Tribe in any place within public view;
(xi) assaults or uses force to any woman belonging to a Scheduled Caste or a Scheduled Tribe with intent to dishonor or outrage her modesty;
(xii) being in a position to dominate the will of a woman belonging to a Scheduled Caste or a Scheduled Tribe and uses that position to exploit her sexually to which she would not have otherwise agreed;
(xiii) corrupts or fouls the water of any spring, reservoir or any other source ordinarily used by members of the Scheduled Caste or the Scheduled Tribes so as to render it less fit for the purpose for which it is ordinarily used;
(xiv) denies a member of a Scheduled Caste or a Scheduled Tribe any customary right of passage to a place of public resort or obstructs such member so as to prevent him from using or having access to a place of public resort to which other members of public or any section thereof have a right to use or access to;
(xv) forces or causes a member of a Scheduled Caste or a Scheduled Tribe to leave his house, village or other place of residence, shall be punishable with imprisonment for a term which shall not be less than six months but which may extend to five years and with fine.

(2) Whoever, not being a member of a Scheduled Caste or a Scheduled Tribe:
(i) gives or fabricates false evidence intending thereby to cause, or knowing it to be likely that he will thereby cause, any member of a Scheduled Caste or a Scheduled Tribe to be convicted of an offence which is capital by the law for the time being in force shall be punished with imprisonment for life and with fine; and if an innocent member of a Scheduled Caste or a Scheduled Tribe be convicted and executed in consequence of such false or fabricated evidence, the person who gives or fabricates such false evidence, shall be punished with death;

(ii) gives or fabricates false evidence intending thereby to cause, or knowing it to be likely that he will thereby cause, any member of a Scheduled Caste or a Scheduled Tribe to be convicted of an offence which is not capital but punishable with imprisonment for a term of seven years or upwards, shall be punishable with imprisonment for a term which shall not be less than six months but which may extend to seven years or upwards and with fine;

(iii) commits mischief by fire or any explosive substance intending to cause or knowing it to be likely that he will thereby cause damage to any property belonging to a member of a Scheduled Caste or a Scheduled Tribe shall be punishable with imprisonment for a term which shall not be less than six months but which may extend to seven years and with fine;

(iv) commits mischief by fire or any explosive substance intending to cause or knowing it to be likely that he will thereby cause destruction of any building which is ordinarily used as a place of worship or as a place for human dwelling or as a place for custody of the property by a member of a Scheduled Caste or a Scheduled Tribe, shall be punishable with imprisonment for life and with fine;

(v) commits any offence under the Indian Penal Code (45 of 1860) punishable with imprisonment for a term of ten years or more against a person or property on the ground that such person is a member of a Scheduled Caste or a Scheduled Tribe or such property belongs to such member, shall be punishable with imprisonment for life and with fine;

(vi) knowingly or having reason to believe that an offence has been committed under this Chapter, causes any evidence of the commission of that offence to disappear with the intention of screening the offender from legal punishment, or with that intention gives any information respecting the offence which he knows or believes to be false, shall be punishable with the punishment provided for that offence; or

(vii) being a public servant, commits any offence under this section, shall be punishable with imprisonment for a term which shall not be less than one year but which may extend to the punishment provided for that offence.

Punishment for Neglect of Duties

Whoever, being a public servant but not being a member of a Scheduled Caste or a Scheduled Tribe, willfully neglects his duties required to be performed by him under this Act, shall be punishable with imprisonment for a term which shall not be less than six months but which may extend to one year.

Enhanced Punishment for Subsequent Conviction

Whoever, having already been convicted of an offence under this Chapter is convicted for the second offence or any offence subsequent to the second offence, shall be punishable with imprisonment for a term which shall not be less than one year but which may extend to the punishment provided for that offence.

Application of Certain Provisions of the Indian Penal Code

Subject to the other provisions of this Act, the provisions of Section 34, Chapter III, Chapter IV, Chapter V, Chapter V–A, Section 149 and Chapter XXIII of the Indian Penal Code (45 of 1860), shall, so far as may be, apply for the purposes of this Act as they apply for the purposes of the Indian Penal Code.

Forfeiture of Property of Certain Persons

(1) Where a person has been convicted of any offence punishable under this Chapter, the Special Court may, in addition to awarding any punishment, by order in writing, declare that any property, movable or immovable or both, belonging to the person which has been used for the commission of that offence, shall stand forfeited to Government.

(2) Where any person is accused of any offence under this Chapter, it shall be open to the Special Court trying him to pass an order that all or any of the properties, movable or immovable or both, belonging to him, shall, during the period of such trial, be attached, and where such trial ends in conviction, the property so attached shall be liable to forfeiture to the extent it is required for the purpose of realization of any fine imposed under this Chapter.

Presumption as to Offences

In a prosecution for an offence under this Chapter, if it is proved that:

(a) the accused rendered any financial assistance to a person accused of, or reasonably suspected of committing, an offence under this Chapter, the Special Court shall presume, unless the contrary is proved, that such person had, abetted the offence;

(b) a group of persons committed an offence under this Chapter and if it is proved that the offence committed was a sequel to any existing dispute regarding land or any other matter, it shall be presumed that the offence was committed in furtherance of the common intention or in prosecution of the common object.

Conferment of Powers

(1) Notwithstanding anything contained in the Code or in any other provision of this Act, the State Government may, if it considers it necessary or expedient so to do:
   (a) for the prevention of and for coping with any offence under this Act, or
   (b) for any case or class or group of cases under this Act, in any district or part thereof, confer, by notification in the Official Gazette, on any officer of the State Government, the powers exercisable by a police officer under the Code in such district or part thereof

or, as the case maybe, for such case or class or group of cases, and in particular, the powers of arrest, investigation and prosecution of persons before any Special Court.

(2) All officers of police and all other officers of Government shall assist the officer referred to in sub-Section (1) in the execution of the provisions of this Act or any rule, scheme or order made thereunder.

(3) The provisions of the Code shall, so far as may be, apply to the exercise of the powers by an officer under sub-Section (1).

Chapter III
Externment

Removal of Person Likely to Commit Offence

(l) Where the Special Court is satisfied, upon a complaint or a police report that a person is likely to commit an offence under Chapter II of this Act in any area included in "Scheduled Areas" or "Tribal Areas" as referred to in Article 244 of the Constitution, it may, by order in writing, direct such person to remove himself beyond the limits of such area, by such route and within such time as may be specified in the order, and not to return to that area from which he was directed to remove himself for such period, not exceeding two years, as may be specified in the order.

(2) The Special Court shall, along with the order under sub-Section (1), communicate to the person directed under that sub-Section the grounds on which such order has been made.

(3) The Special Court may revoke or modify the order made under sub-Section (1), for the reasons to be recorded in writing, on the representation made by the person against whom such order has been made or by any other person on his behalf within thirty days from the date of the order.

Procedure on Failure of Person to Remove Himself from area and Enter Thereon after Removal

(1) If a person to whom a direction has been issued under Section 10 to remove himself from any area:
   (a) fails to remove himself as directed; or
   (b) having so removed himself enters such area within the period specified in the order, otherwise than with the permission in writing of the Special Court under sub-Section (2), the Special Court may cause him to be arrested and removed in police custody to such place outside such area as the Special Court may specify.

(2) The Special Court may, by order in writing, permit any person in respect of whom an order under section 10 has been made, to return to the area from which he was directed to remove himself for such temporary period and subject to such conditions as may be specified in such order and may require him to execute a bond with or without surety for the due observation of the conditions imposed.

(3) The Special Court may at any time revoke any such permission.

(4) Any person who, with such permission, returns to the area from which he was directed to remove himself shall observe the conditions imposed and at the expiry of the temporary period for which he was permitted to return or on the revocation of such permission before the expiry of such temporary period shall remove himself outside such area and shall not return thereto within the unexpired portion specified under Section 10 without a fresh permission.

(5) If a person fails to observe any of the conditions imposed or to remove himself accordingly or having so removed himself enters or returns to such area without fresh permission the Special Court may cause him to be arrested and removed in police custody to such place outside such area as the Special Court may specify.

Taking Measurements and Photographs, etc. of Persons Against Whom Order Under Section 10 is Made

(1) Every person against whom an order has been made under Section 10 shall, if so required by the Special Court, allow his measurements and photographs to be taken by a police officer.

(2) If any person referred to in sub-Section (1) when required to allow his measurements or photographs to be taken, resists or refuses to allow the taking of such measurements or photographs, it shall be lawful to use all necessary means to secure the taking thereof.

(3) Resistance to or refusal to allow the taking of measurements or photographs under sub-Section (2) shall be deemed to be an offence under Section 186 of the Indian Penal Code (45 of 1860).

(4) Where an order under Section 10 is revoked, all measurements and photographs (including negatives) taken under sub-Section (2) shall be destroyed or made over to the person against whom such order is made.

Penalty for Non-compliance of Order Under Section 10

Any person contravening an order of the Special Court made under Section 10 shall be punishable with imprisonment for a term which may extend to one year and with fine.

Chapter IV
Special Courts

Special Court

For the purpose of providing for speedy trial, the State Government shall, with the concurrence of the Chief Justice of the High Court, by notification in the Official Gazette, specify for each district a Court of Session to be a Special Court to try the offences under this Act.

Special Public Prosecutor

For every Special Court, the State Government shall, by notification in the Official Gazette, specify a Public Prosecutor or appoint an advocate who has been in practice as an advocate for not less than seven years, as a Special Public Prosecutor for the purpose of conducting cases in that Court.

Chapter V
Miscellaneous

Power of State Government to Impose Collective Fine

The provisions of Section 10-A of the Protection of Civil Rights Act, 1955 (22 of 1955) shall, so far as may be, apply for the purposes of imposition and realisation of collective fine and for all other matters connected therewith under this Act.

Preventive Action to be Taken by the Law and Order Machinery

(1) A District Magistrate or a Sub-divisional Magistrate or any other Executive Magistrate or any police officer not below the rank of a Deputy Superintendent of Police may, on receiving information and after such enquiry as he may think necessary, has reason to believe that a person or a group of persons not belonging to the Scheduled Castes or the Scheduled Tribes, residing in or frequenting any place within the local limits of his jurisdiction is likely to commit an offence or has threatened to commit any offence under this Act and is of the opinion that there is sufficient ground for proceeding, declare such an area to be an area prone to atrocities and take necessary action for keeping the peace and good behaviour and maintenance of public order and tranquility and may take preventive action.

(2) The provisions of Chapters VIII, X and XI of the Code shall, so far as may be, apply for the purposes of sub-Section (1).

(3) The State Government may, by notification in the Official Gazette, make one or more schemes specifying the manner in which the officers referred to in sub-Section (1) shall take appropriate action specified in such scheme or schemes to prevent atrocities and to restore the feeling of security amongst the members of the Scheduled Castes and the Scheduled Tribes.

Section 438 of the Code not to Apply to Persons Committing an Offence Under the Act

Nothing in Section 438 of the Code shall apply in relation to any case involving the arrest of any person on an accusation of having committed an offence under this Act.

Section 360 of the Code and the Provisions of the Probation of Offenders Act not to Apply to Persons Guilty of an Offence Under the Act

The provisions of Section 360 of the Code and the provisions of the Probation of Offenders Act, 1958 (20 of 1958) shall not apply to any person above the age of eighteen years who is found guilty of having committed an offence under this Act.

Act to Override Other Laws

Save as otherwise provided in this Act, the provisions of this Act shall have effect notwithstanding anything inconsistent therewith contained in any other law for the time being in force or any custom or usage or any instrument having effect by virtue of any such law.

Duty of Government to Ensure Effective Implementation of the Act

(1) Subject to such rules as the Central Government may make in this behalf, the State Government shall take such measures as may be necessary for the effective implementation of this Act.

(2) In particular, and without prejudice to the generality of the foregoing provisions, such measures may include:
   (i) the provision for adequate facilities, including legal aid, to the persons subjected to atrocities to enable them to avail themselves of justice;
   (ii) the provision for travelling and maintenance expenses to witnesses including the victims of atrocities, during investigation and trial of offences under this Act;
   (iii) the provision for the economic and social rehabilitation of the victims of the atrocities;
   (iv) the appointment of officers for initiating or exercising supervision over prosecutions for the contravention of the provisions of this Act;
   (v) the setting up of committees at such appropriate levels as the State Government may think fit to assist that Government in formulation or implementation of such measures;
   (vi) provision for a periodic survey of the working of the provisions of this Act with a view to suggesting measures for the better implementation of the provisions of this Act;
   (vii) the identification of the areas where the members of the Scheduled Castes and the Scheduled Tribes are likely to be subjected to atrocities and adoption of such measures so as to ensure safety for such members.

(3) The Central Government shall take such steps as may be necessary to coordinate the measures taken by the State Governments under sub-Section (1).

(4) The Central Government shall, every year, place on the table of each House of Parliament a report on the measures taken by itself and by the State Governments in pursuance of the provisions of this Section.

Protection of Action Taken in Good Faith

No suit, prosecution or other legal proceedings shall lie against the Central Government or against the State Government or any officer or authority of Government or any other person for anything which is in good faith done or intended to be done under this Act.

Power to Make Rules

(1) The Central Government may, by notification in the Official Gazette, make rules for carrying out the purposes of this Act.

(2) Every rule made under this Act shall be laid, as soon as may be after it is made, before each House of Parliament, while it is in session for a total period of thirty days which may be comprised in one session or in two or more successive sessions, and if before the expiry of the session immediately following the session or the successive sessions aforesaid, both Houses agree in making any modification in the rule or both Houses agree that the rule should not be made, the rule shall thereafter have effect only in such modified form or be of no effect, as the case may be; so, however, that any such modification or annulment shall be without prejudice to the validity of anything previously done under that rule.

Source: http://hrw.org/reports/1999/india/India994–16.htm

APPENDIX 10

The Scheduled Castes and Scheduled Tribes: (Prevention of Atrocities) Rules, 1995

G.S.R. 316 (E), dated 31 March, 1995. In exercise of the powers conferred by sub-Section (1) of Sec. 23 of the Scheduled Castes and the Scheduled Tribes (Prevention of Atrocities) Act. 1989 (33 of 1989), the Central Government hereby makes the following rules, namely:

Short Title and Commencement

(1) These rules may be called the Scheduled Castes and the Scheduled Tribes (Prevention of Atrocities) Rules, 1995.

(2) They shall come into force on the date of their publication in the Official Gazette.

Definitions

In these rules, unless the context otherwise requires:

(a) "Act" means the Scheduled Castes and the Scheduled Tribes (Prevention of Atrocities) Act, 1989 (33 of 1989);

(b) "Dependent", with its grammatical variations and cognate expressions, includes wife, children, whether married or unmarried, dependent parents, widowed sister, widow and children of predeceased son of a victim of atrocity;

(c) "Identified area" means such area where State Government has reason to believe that atrocity may take place or there is an apprehension of reoccurence of an offence under the Act or an area prone to victim of atrocity;

(d) "Non-Government Organisation" means a voluntary organisation engaged in the welfare activities relating to the Scheduled Castes and the Scheduled Tribes and registered under the Societies Registration Act. 1860 (21 of 1860) or under any law for the registration of documents of such Organisation for the time being in force;

(e) "Schedule" means the Schedule annexed to these rules;

(f) "Section" means Section of the Act;

(g) "State Government", in relation to a Union Territory, means the Administrator of that Union Territory appointed by the President under Article 239 of the Constitution;

(h) Words and expressions used herein and not defined but defined in the Act shall have the meanings respectively assigned to them in the Act.

Precautionary and Preventive Measures

With a view to prevent atrocities on the Scheduled Castes and the Scheduled Tribes the State Government shall:

(i) identify the area where it has reason to believe that atrocity may take place or there is an apprehension of reoccurence of an offence under the Act;

(ii) order the District Magistrate and Superintendent of Police or any other officer to visit the identified area and review the law and order situation;

(iii) if deem necessary, in the identified area cancel the arms licenses of the persons, not being member of the Scheduled Castes or Scheduled Tribes, their near relations, servants or employees and family friends and get such arms deposited in the Government Armory;

(iv) seize all illegal firearms and prohibit any illegal manufacture of firearms;

(v) with a view to ensure the safety of person and property, if deem necessary, provide arms licenses to the members of the Scheduled Castes and the Scheduled Tribes;

(vi) constitute a high power State level committee, district and divisional level committees or such number of other committees as deem proper and necessary for assisting the Government in implementation of the provisions of the Act.

(vii) set up a vigilance and monitoring committee to suggest effective measures to implement the provisions of the Act;

(viii)set up Awareness Centers and organise Workshops in the identified area or at some other place to educate the persons belonging to the Scheduled Castes and the Scheduled Tribes about their rights and the protection available to them under the provisions of various Central and State enactments or rules, regulations and schemes framed thereunder;

(ix) encourage Non-Government Organisations for establishing and maintaining Awareness Centers and organising Workshops and provide them necessary financial and other sort of assistance;

(x) deploy special police force in the identified area;

(xi) by the end of every quarter, review the law and order situation, functioning of different committees, performance of Special Public Prosecutors, Investigating Officers and other Officers responsible for implementing the provisions of the Act and the cases registered under the Act.

Supervision of Prosecution and Submission of Report

(1) The State Government on the recommendation of the District Magistrate shall prepare for each District a panel of such number of eminent senior advocates who has been in practice for not less than seven years, as it may deem necessary for conducting cases in the Special Courts. Similarly, in consultation with the Director of Prosecution in charge of the prosecution, a panel of such number of Public Prosecutors as it may deem necessary for conducting cases in the Special Courts, shall also be specified. Both these panels shall be notified in the Official Gazette of the State and shall remain in force for a period of three years.

(2) The District Magistrate and the Director of Prosecution in charge of the prosecution shall review at least twice in a calendar year, in the month of January and July, the performance of Special Public Prosecutors so specified or appointed and submit a report to the State Government.

(3) If the State Government is satisfied or has reason to believe that a Special Public Prosecutor so appointed or specified has not conducted the case to the best of his ability and with due care and caution, his name may be, for reasons to be recorded in writing, denotified.

(4) The District Magistrate and the Officer-in-charge of the prosecution at the District level, shall review the position of cases registered under the Act and submit a monthly report on or before 20th day of each subsequent month to the Director of Prosecution and the State Government. This report shall specify the actions taken/proposed to be taken in respect of investigation and prosecution of each case.

(5) Notwithstanding anything contained in sub rule (1) the District Magistrate or the Sub-Divisional Magistrate may, if deem necessary or if so desired by the victim of atrocity

engage an eminent Senior Advocate for conducting cases in the Special Courts on such payment of fees as he may consider appropriate.

(6) Payment of fee to the Special Public Prosecutor shall be fixed by the State Government on a scale higher than the other panel advocates in the State.

Information to Police Officer In-Charge of a Police Station

(1) Every information relating to the commission of an offence under the Act, if given orally to an officer in-charge of a police station shall be reduced to writing by him or under his direction and be read over to the informant, and every such information, whether given in writing or reduced to writing as aforesaid, shall be signed by the persons giving it, and the substance thereof shall be entered in a book to be maintained by that police station.

(2) A copy of the information as so recorded under sub rule (1) above shall be given forthwith, free of cost, to the informant.

(3) Any person aggrieved by a refusal on the part of an officer in charge of a police station to record the information referred in sub rule (1) may send the substance of such information, in writing and by post, to the Superintendent of Police concerned who after investigation either by himself or by a police officer not below the rank of Deputy Superintendent of Police, shall make an order in writing to the officer in-charge of the concerned police station to enter the substance of that information to be entered in the book to be maintained by the police station.

Spot Inspection by Officers

(1) Whenever the District Magistrate or the Sub-Divisional Magistrate or any other executive Magistrate or any police officer not below the rank of Deputy Superintendent of Police receives an information from any person or upon his own

knowledge that an atrocity has been committed on the members of the Scheduled Castes or the Scheduled Tribes within his jurisdiction he shall immediately himself visit the place of occurrence to assess the extent of atrocity, loss of life, loss and damage to the property and submit a report forthwith to the State Government.

(2) The District Magistrate or the Sub-Divisional Magistrate or any other executive Magistrate and the Superintendent of Police, Deputy Superintendent of Police after inspecting the place or area on the spot:
   (i) draw a list of victims, their family members and dependents entitled for relief;
   (ii) prepare a detailed report of the extent of atrocity, loss and damage to the property of the victims;
   (iii) order for intensive police patrolling in the area;
   (iv) take effective and necessary steps to provide protection to the witnesses and other sympathisers of the victims;
   (v) provide immediate relief to the victims.

Investigating Officer

(1) An offence committed under the Act shall be investigated by a police officer not below the rank of a Deputy Superintendent of Police. The investigating officer shall be appointed by the State Government, Director General of Police, Superintendent of Police after taking into account his past experience, sense of ability and justice to perceive the implications of the case and investigate it along with right lines within the shortest possible time.

(2) The investigating officer so appointed under sub rule (1) shall complete the investigation on top priority within thirty days and submit the report to the Superintendent of Police who in turn will immediately forward the report to the Director General of Police of the State Government.

(3) The Home Secretary and the Social Welfare Secretary to the State Government, Director of Prosecution the officer-in-charge of Prosecution and the Director General of

Police shall review by the end of every quarter the position of all investigations done by the investigating officer.

Setting Up of the Scheduled Castes and the Scheduled Tribes Protection Cell

The State Government shall set up a Scheduled Castes and the Scheduled Tribes Protection Cell at the State headquarter under the charge of Director of Police, Inspector General of Police. This Cell shall be responsible for:

(i) conducting survey of the identified area;

(ii) maintaining public order and tranquillity in the identified area;

(iii) recommending to the State Government for deployment of special police force or establishment of special police post in the identified area;

(iv) making investigations about the probable causes leading to an offence under the Act;

(v) restoring the feeling of security amongst the members of the Scheduled Castes and the Scheduled Tribes;

(vi) informing the nodal officer and special officer about the law and order situation in the identified area;

(vii) making enquiries about the investigation and spot inspections conducted by various officers;

(viii) making enquiries about the action taken by the Superintendent of Police in the cases where an officer in-charge of the police station has refused to enter an information in a book to be maintained by that police station under sub rule (3) of rule 5;

(ix) making enquiries about the wilful negligence by a public servant;

(x) reviewing the position of cases registered under the Act, and

(xi) submitting a monthly report on or before 20th day of each subsequent month to the State Government, nodal officer about the action taken proposed to be taken, in respect of the above.

Nomination of Nodal Officer

The State Government shall nominate a nodal officer of the level of a Secretary to the Government preferably belonging to the Scheduled Castes or the Scheduled Tribes, for coordinating the functioning of the District Magistrates and Superintendent of Police or other officers authorised by them investigating officers and other officers responsible for implementing the provisions of the Act. By the end of the every quarter, the nodal officer shall review:

(i) the reports received by the State Government under sub rules (2) and (4) of rule 4, rule 6, Cl. (xi) of rule 8.

(ii) the position of cases registered under the Act;

(iii) law and order situation in the identified area;

(iv) various kinds of measures adopted for providing immediate relief in cash or kind or both to the victims of atrocity or his or her dependent;

(v) adequacy of immediate facilities like rationing, clothing, shelter, legal aid, travelling allowance, daily allowance and transport facilities provided to the victims of atrocity of his/her dependents;

(vi) performance of non-Governmental organisations, the Scheduled Castes and the Scheduled Tribes Protection Cell, various committees and the public servants responsible for implementing the provisions of the Act.

Appointment of a Special Officer

In the identified area a Special Officer not below the rank of an Additional District Magistrate shall be appointed to coordinate with the District Magistrate, Superintendent of Police or other officers responsible for implementing the provisions of the Act, various committees and the Scheduled Castes and the Scheduled Tribes Protection Cell.

The Special Officer shall be responsible for:

(i) providing immediate relief and other facilities to the victims of atrocity and initiate necessary measures to prevent or avoid reoccurence of atrocity;

(ii) setting up an awareness center and organising workshop in the identified area or at the District headquarters to educate the persons belonging to the Scheduled Castes and the Scheduled Tribes about their rights and the protection available to them under the provisions of various Central and State enactments or rules and schemes, etc., framed therein;

(iii) coordinating with the non-governmental organisations and providing necessary facilities and financial and other type of assistance to non-governmental organisations for maintaining centres or organising workshops.

Travelling Allowances, Daily Allowance, Maintenance Expenses and Transport Facilities to the Victim of Atrocity, his or her Dependent and Witnesses

(1) Every victim of atrocity or his/her dependent and witnesses shall be paid to and for rail fare by second class in express/mail/passenger train or actual bus or taxi fare from his/her place of residence or actual bus or taxi fare from his/her place of residence or place of stay to the place of investigation or hearing of trial of an offence under the Act.

(2) The District Magistrate or the Sub-Divisional Magistrate or any other Executive Magistrate shall make necessary arrangements for providing transport facilities or reimbursement of full payment thereof to the victims of atrocity and witnesses for visiting the investigating officer, Superintendent of Police/Deputy Superintendent of Police, District Magistrate or any other Executive Magistrate.

(3) Every woman witness, the victim of atrocity or her dependent being a woman or a minor, a person more than sixty years of age and a person having 40 per cent or more disability shall

be entitled to be accompanied by an attendant of her/his choice. The attendant shall also be paid travelling and maintenance expenses as applicable to the witness or the victim of atrocity when called upon during hearing, investigation and trial of an offence under the Act.

(4) The witness, the victim of atrocity or his/her dependent and the attendant shall be paid daily maintenance expenses for the days he/she is away from the place of his/her residence or stay during investigation, hearing and trial of an offence, at such rates but not less than the minimum wages, as may be fixed by the State Government for the agricultural laborers.

(5) In additional to daily maintenance expenses the witness, the victim of atrocity (or his/her dependent) and the attendant shall also be paid diet expenses at such rates as may be fixed by the State Government from time to time.

(6) The payment of travelling allowance, daily allowance, maintenance expenses and reimbursement of transport facilities shall be made immediately or not later than three days by the District Magistrate or the Sub-Divisional Magistrate or any other Executive Magistrate to the victims, their dependents/attendant and witnesses for the days they visit the investigating officer or in-charge police station or hospital authorities or Superintendent of Police, Deputy Superintendent of Police or District Magistrate or any other officer concerned or the Special Court.

(7) When an offence has been committed under Sec. 3 of the Act, the District Magistrate or the Sub-Divisional Magistrate or any other Executive Magistrate shall reimburse the payment of medicines, special medical consultation, blood transfusion, replacement of essential clothing, meals and fruits provided to the victim(s) of atrocity.

Measures to be taken by the District Administration

(1) The District Magistrate and the Superintendent of Police shall visit the place or area where the atrocity has been

committed to assess the loss of life and damage to the property and draw a list of victim, their family members and dependents entitled for relief.

(2) Superintendent of Police shall ensure that the First Information Report is registered in the book of the concerned police station and effective measures for apprehending the accused are taken.

(3) The Superintendent of Police, after spot inspection, shall immediately appoint an investigation officer and deploy such police force in the area and take such other preventive measures as he may deem proper and necessary.

(4) The District Magistrate or the Sub-Divisional Magistrate or any other Executive Magistrate shall make arrangements for providing immediate relief in cash or in kind or both to the victims of atrocity, their family members and dependents according to the scale as in the schedule annexed to these Rules (Annexure-I read with Annexure-II). Such immediate relief shall also include food, water, clothing, shelter, medical aid, transport facilities and other essential items necessary for human beings.

(5) The relief provided to the victim of the atrocity or his/her dependent under sub rule (4) in respect of death, or injury to, or damage to property shall be in addition to any other right to claim compensation in respect thereof under any other law for the time being in force.

(6) The relief and rehabilitation facilities mentioned in sub rule (4) above shall be provided by the District Magistrate or the Sub-Divisional Magistrate or any other Executive Magistrate in accordance with the scales provided in the Schedule annexed to these rules.

(7) A report of the relief and rehabilitation facilities provided to the victims shall also be forwarded to the Special Court by the District Magistrate or the Sub-Divisional Magistrate or the Executive Magistrate or Superintendent of Police. In case the Special Court is satisfied that the payment of relief was not

made to the victim or his/her dependent in time or the amount of relief or compensation was not sufficient or only a part of payment of relief or compensation was made, it may order for making in full or part the payment of relief or any other kind of assistance.

Selection of Officers and other State Members for Completing the Work Relating to Atrocity

(1) The State Government shall ensure that the administrative officers and other staff members to be appointed in an area prone to atrocity shall have the right aptitude and understanding of the problems of the Scheduled Castes posts and police station.

(2) It shall also be ensured by the State Government that persons from the Scheduled Castes and the Scheduled Tribes are adequately represented in the administration and in the police force at all levels, particularly at the level of police posts and police station.

Specific Responsibility of the State Government

The State Government shall make necessary provisions in its annual budget for providing relief and rehabilitation facilities to the victims of atrocity. It shall review at least twice in a calendar year, in the month of January and July the performance of the Special Public Prosecutor specified or appointed under Sec. 15 of the Act, various reports received, investigation made and preventive steps taken by the District Magistrate, Sub-Divisional Magistrate and Superintendent of Police, relief and rehabilitation facilities provided to the victims and the reports in respect of lapses on behalf of the concerned officers.

Contingency Plan by the State Government

(1) The State Government shall prepare a model contingency plan for implementing the provisions of the Act and notify

the same in the Official Gazette of the State Government. It should specify the role and responsibility of various departments and their officers at different levels, the role and responsibility of Rural/Urban Local Bodies and Non-Government Organisations. Inter alia this plan shall contain a package of relief measures including the following:

(a) scheme to provide immediate relief in cash or in kind or both;
(b) allotment of agricultural land and house sites;
(c) the rehabilitation packages;
(d) scheme for employment in Government or Government undertaking to the dependent or one of the family members of the victim;
(e) pension scheme for widows, dependent children of the deceased, handicapped or old age victims of atrocity;
(f) mandatory compensation for the victims;
(g) scheme for strengthening the socioeconomic condition of the victim;
(h) provisions for providing brick/stone masonry house to the victims;
(i) such other elements as health care, supply of essential commodities, electrification, adequate drinking water facility, burial/cremation ground and link roads to the Scheduled Castes and the Scheduled Tribes.

(2) The State Government shall forward a copy of the contingency plan or a summary thereof and a copy of the scheme, as soon as may be, to the Central Government in the Ministry of Welfare and to all the District Magistrates, Sub-Divisional Magistrates, Inspectors General of Police and Superintendents of Police.

Constitution of State-level Vigilance and Monitoring Committee

(1) The State Government shall constitute high power vigilance and monitoring committee of not more than 25 members consisting of the following:

(i) Chief Minister/Administrator Chairman (in case of a State under President's Rule Governor Chairman).

(ii) Home Minister, Finance Minister and Welfare Minister Members (in case of a State under the President's Rule Advisors Members);

(iii) all elected Members of Parliament and State Legislative Assembly and Legislative Council from the State belonging to the Scheduled Castes and the Scheduled Tribes Members

(iv) Chief Secretary, the Home Secretary, the Director General of Police, Director/Deputy Director, National Commission for the Scheduled Castes and the Scheduled Tribes Members;

(v) the Secretary in-charge of the welfare and development of the Scheduled Castes and the Scheduled Tribes Convener.

(2) The high power vigilance and monitoring committee shall meet at least twice in a calendar year, in the month of January and July to review the implementation of the provisions of the Act, relief and rehabilitation facilities provided to the victims and other matters connected therewith, prosecution of cases under the Act, rule of different officers/agencies responsible for implementing the provisions of the Act and various reports received by the State Government.

Constitution of District Level Vigilance and Monitoring Committee

(1) In each district within the State, the District Magistrate shall set up a vigilance and monitoring committee in his district to review the implementation of the provisions of the Act, relief and rehabilitation facilities provided to the victims and other matters connected therewith, prosecution of cases under the Act, role of different officers/agencies responsible for implementing the provisions of the Act and various reports received by the District Administration.

(2) The district level vigilance and monitoring committee shall consist of the elected Members of the Parliament and State Legislative Assembly and Legislative Council, Superintendent of Police, three-group "A" Officers, Gazetted Officers of the State Government belonging to the Scheduled Castes and the Scheduled Tribes, not more than 5 non-official members belonging to the Scheduled Castes and the Scheduled Tribes and not more than 3 members from the categories other than the Scheduled Castes and the Scheduled Tribes having association with Non-Government Organisations. The District Magistrate and District Social Welfare Officer shall be Chairman and Member Secretary respectively.

(3) The district level committee shall meet at least once in three months.

Material for Annual Report

The State Government shall every year before the 31 March, forward the report to the Central Government about the measures taken for implementing provisions of the Act and various schemes/plans framed by it during the previous calendar year.

Annexure I
Schedule
[See rule 12 (4)]

Norms for Relief Amount

S. No.	*Name and Section Number of Offense*	*Minimum Amount of Relief*
1.	Drink or eat inedible or obnoxious substance [Sec. 3 (1)(i)]	Rs 25,000 or more depending upon the nature and gravity of the offense to each victim and also commensurate with the indignity, insult and defamation suffered by the victim. Payment to be made as follows: 25 per cent when the charge sheet is sent to the court; 75 per cent when accused are convicted by the lower court.
2.	Causing injury insult or annoyance [Sec. 3 (1)(ii)]	
3.	Derogatory Act [Sec. 3 (1)(iii)]	

Cont'd...

Cont'd...

4.	Wrongful occupation or cultivation of land, etc. [Sec. 3 (1)(iv)]	At least Rs 25,000 or more depending upon the nature and gravity of the offense. The land/premises/water supply shall be restored where necessary at Government cost. Full payment to be made when charge sheet is sent to the Court
5.	Relating to land, premises and water [Sec. 3 (1)(v)]	
6.	Begar or forced of bonded labour [Sec. 3 (1)(vi)]	At least Rs 25,000 to each victim. Payment of 25 per cent at First Information Report stage and 75 per cent on conviction in the lower court.
7.	Relating to right to franchise [Sec. 3 (1)(vii)]	Up to Rs 20,000 to each victim depending upon the nature and gravity of offense.
8.	False, malicious or vexatious legal proceedings [Sec. 3 (1)(viii)]	Rs 25,000 or reimbursement of actual legal expenses and damages whichever is less after conclusion of the trial of the accused.
9.	False and frivolous information [Sec. 3 (1)(ix)]	
10.	Insult, intimidation and humiliation [Sec. 3 (1)(x)]	Up to Rs 25,000 to each victim depending upon the nature of the offense. Payment of 25 per cent when charge sheet is sent to the court and the rest on conviction.
11.	Outraging the modesty of a woman [Sec. 3 (1)(xi)]	Rs 50,000 to each victim of the offense. 50 per cent of the amount may be paid after medical examination and remaining 50 per cent at the conclusion of the trial.
12.	Sexual exploitation of a woman [Sec. 3 (1)(xii)]	
13.	Fouling of water [Sec. 3 (1)(xiii)]	Up to Rs 1,00,000 or full cost of restoration of normal facility, including cleaning when the water is fouled. Payment may be made at the stage as deemed fit by District Administration.
14.	Denial of customary rights of passage [Sec. 3 (1)(xiv)]	Up to Rs 1,00,000 or full cost of restoration of right of passage and full compensation of the loss suffered, if any. Payment of 50 per cent when charge sheet is sent to the court and 50 per cent on conviction in lower court.

Cont'd...

Cont'd...

15.	Deserting one from their place of residence [Sec. 3 (1)(xv)]	Restoration of the site/right to stay and compensation of Rs 25,000 to each victim and reconstruction of the house at Govt. cost, if destroyed. To be paid in full when charge sheet is sent to the lower court.
16.	Giving false evidence [Sec. 3(2)(i) and (ii)]	At least Rs 1,00,000 or full compensation of the loss or harm sustained. 50 per cent to be paid when charge sheet is sent to Court and 50 per cent on conviction by the lower court.
17.	Committing offences under the Indian Penal Code punishable with imprisonment for a term of 10 years or more [Sec. 3(2)]	At least Rs 50,000 depending upon the nature and gravity of the offense to each victim and or his dependents. The amount would vary if specifically provided for otherwise in the Schedule.
18.	Victimisation at the hands public servant [Sec. 3 (2)]	Full compensation on account of damages or loss or harm sustained. 50 per cent to be paid when charge sheet is sent to the Court and 50 per cent on conviction by lower court.
19.	Disability ... (a) 100 per cent incapacitation. (i) Non-earning member of a family. (ii) Earning member of a family. (b) Where incapacitation is less than 100 per cent	—At least Rs 1,00,000 to each victim of offense. 50 per cent on FIR and 25 per cent at charge sheet and 25 per cent on conviction by the lower court. —At least Rs 2,00,000 to each victim of offense. 50 per cent to be paid on FIR/medical examination stage, 25 per cent when charge sheet sent to court and 25 per cent at conviction in lower court. —The rates are laid down in (i) and (ii) above shall be reduced in the same proportion, the stages of payment also being the same. However, not less than Rs 15,000 to a non-earning member and not less than Rs 30,000 to an earning member of the family.
20.	Murder/Death (a) Non-earning member of a family. (b) Earning member of a family.	—At least Rs 1,00,000 to each case. Payment of 75 per cent after postmortem and 25 per cent on conviction by the lower court. At least Rs 2,00,000 to each case. Payment of 75 per cent after postmortem and 25 per cent on conviction by the lower court.

Cont'd...

Cont'd...

21.	Victim of murder, death, massacre, rape, mass rape and gang rape, permanent incapacitation and dacoity.	In addition to relief amount paid under above items, relief may be arranged within three months of date of atrocity as follows: (i) Pension to each widow and/or other dependents of deceased SC/ST at Rs 1,000 per month, or employment to one member of the family of the deceased, or provision of agricultural land, a house, if necessary by outright purchase. (ii) Full cost of the education and maintenance of the children of the victims. Children may be admitted to the Ashram Schools/residential schools. (iii) Provision of utensils, rice, wheat, dals, pulses, etc., for a period of three months.
22.	Complete destruction/burnt houses.	Brick/stone masonry house to be constructed or provided at Government cost where it has been burnt or destroyed.

Source: http://hrw.org/reports/1999/india/India994–18.htm#TopOfPage

APPENDIX 11

Dalit Christian Liberation Movement (DCLM), Memorandum Presented at the Meeting of the Catholic Bishops Conference of India (CBCI)

Held in Chennai, 21 January 2000

Your Grace Most Rev. Dr Alan D' Lastic, Archbishop and President of the CBCI, The office bearers, Archbishops and Bishops

Our fraternal greetings on behalf of the Dalit Christian Liberation Movement (DCLM). We are very happy to get this important opportunity to meet the gathering of Bishops from all over India and speak on dalit Christians problems, which we are sure, has drawn your attention these days. Inviting us to speak to this body shows your new concern about it. We have yet to see the historical moment when casteism and its forms of discrimination against dalit Christians are eradicated completely in our Indian Church. We indeed hope that our meeting today with the whole Hierarchy of the Indian Church to voice our people's concern will soon pave the way for this.

In the past one decade a lot of concern has been expressed by the CBCI and other quarters in the Church on the question of discrimination against dalit Christians. Though it brings some hope, much remain in words, as declarations, prayerful wishes and as promises. The consciousness about the discriminations within the church was deepened in recent years, thanks to the open struggles of dalit Christians, which emerged into a movement. We could see concern expressed on various occasions and in different forms by the CBCI, CRI and others. Most notable may be the 10-point programmes announced by the Tamil Nadu Bishops Council (TNBC) to bring about equality and development to dalit Christians. But it may be honestly said that much of these remain vague without force, direction and commitment in implementation and even as a sort of make believe initiative. This is what we are painfully concerned about today.

The changes brought about are very meagre. So we have to address your grace the Archbishops and Bishops to make the agony, sentiments, views and expectation of our people known. We have to be frank, rather doubly frank, in expressing these because the problem is so severe and urgent.

First of all we wish to emphasise that the oppression and discriminations suffered by dalit Christians within our Church is as serious and appalling as the persecution of minorities in our country. With this perspective we have to approach the problem of dalits in the Church. This has to be a top priority as they are a majority in the Catholics population.

Broadly speaking, we face the problems of untouchability, marginalisation in our institutions (in admissions and appointments), marginalisation in vocation, in sharing of power and authority in the Church. Each problem needs specific attention, policy changes and action programmes.

The external forms of untouchability and their practice still exist among Christians, within the Church, in the graveyard, in the festivals, in marriage alliances, etc. The most unfortunate thing is that the caste Christians, practising these inhuman acts are often supported by their own caste priests and nuns, who even encourage them to attack dalit Christians. That is the main reason for caste practice continuing in the Church. Incidents in the past and also in recent years prove that in those areas and villages where large number of priests and nuns have been ordained (few example: Thatchoor in Madras diocese, Eraiyur in Pondy diocese, Varadarajanpet in Kumbakonam diocese), the caste Christians are more active in oppressing dalit Christians and resisting vigorously when they demand dignity, equality, and justice. Most of the caste priests, nuns and some in hierarchical positions use their money, authority and institutional power against dalit Christians at times of crisis, instead of supporting their just cause. We are saying this from many experience.

The marginalisation of dalit Christians in our Christian minority institutions (in admissions and appointment) all along the several decades has very severely affected their social and economic mobility and progress. The degree of marginalisation is alarming and appalling since dalits are a majority in the Catholic

Church, but they are only about 6 per cent as students and employees in most institutions. Their exclusion or marginalisation in employment has caused enormous economic loss to the community over decades. If this continues how can poverty be alleviated in the community? The marginalisation in appointments is very severe in our Girls Schools and Women Colleges and needs specific attentions. It will take decades to improve this situation for dalit Christians even if the institutions now take a policy of reservation for them and sincerely follow up. So, what is needed in a vigorous and strict implementation of reservation.

We have to look at the question of reservation to dalit Christians in our own institutions a little deeply. It is high time that we realise that only reservation can safeguard the dalits' interest and opportunities against the caste politics and caste domination. Whether the government does it or not for dalit Christians, the Church needs to do it for them because, they are severely marginalised within the Church. It is worse than in society as the minority caste Christians enjoy the bigger share of the cake and the majority dalit Christians get too little. So the policy of reservation is all the more needed for dalit Christians in the church. When we speak of this, eyebrows are raised. But it is important to note that the minority right is also a sort of reservation given for different reason. When that does not reach the majority dalit Christians it is logical to ask for reservation for them within. Reservation is needed to set right the longstanding and historical inequality and backlogs. It is not at all helpful to talk about justice without implementing some concrete rules of distributive justice.

So, the Church cannot put the whole burden on the government, because she is owning institutions, properties, financial and material resources, powers and authority of secular nature for helping minorities, but from which dalit Christian are excluded and alienated. The reservation we ask from the government is a case of constitutional equality irrespective of religion. But reservation for dalit Catholics in the Church is necessary as there is a clear case of inequality within. Our elegant preaching for equality and liberation to the oppressed only goes to strengthen the plea for reservation to the oppressed. We cannot set right inequality without some norms of distributive justice. We may call it reservation "option", "preference" or priority. But the thing is it must be done and done without further delay.

Even though favourable views, concerns and solidarity are expressed, recommendation are declared by the hierarchies, religious heads, priests and nuns, we find that the main or core issues are sidelined. The rights and opportunities are denied to us in the day-to-day matters. Concrete policies and steps are lacking at every level. Enforcement is important, but that is what is lacking very much. With this background and understanding of the reality we fervently appeal for, suggest and demand the following steps and measures.

- We appeal to the Bishops to see that the priests, nuns and authorities stop supporting their caste Christians against dalit Christians and instead they openly oppose any practice of casteism and close down the churches and services in those places. It is not right to think that it is the responsibility of only the dalits to oppose these.
- The number of dalit Bishops among the Indian Bishops is alarmingly negligible and it is seen as a grave injustice at the higher level itself. It is a matter of conscience for us to see now itself how many among the nearly 140 gathered here are dalit Bishops. It is doubtful whether it will be even 6 per cent. But the dalit Catholics are a majority among the Catholics. So, we strongly appeal that special drive is made to see that about 85 dalit Bishops are appointed in the next 5 to 10 years to bring equality. To enable this, some socially conscious Bishops, committed to dalits cause may go in for voluntary retirement.
- We request that dalit priests are appointed in Bishop vacancies that already exist, especially now in Tamil Nadu. (We may note here with regret that dalit priests were not considered for the post of Auxiliary Bishops appointed recently in Tamil Nadu). We are not asking for dalit Bishops with any narrow sense of possessiveness, but for the dignity and credibility of the Church in truly upholding

equality in the caste society. It is also high time that a dalit Bishop is appointed as Cardinal. A coordination between the CBCI, the Apostolic Nuncio to India and the Vatican can be evolved for the special drive and time bound steps.

- Similarly in the religious congregations, there has to be equitable number of superiors, provincials, etc. and heads of Institutions appointed from dalit priests and nuns. We have appealed to the CRI regarding this and we request the intervention of the CBCI for the same.
- We request the CBCI to take steps to constantly follow up the congregations and institutions and see that the dalits are given priority in admissions and appointments. About 60 per cent of the Catholics admitted to courses or appointed to various posts in our institutions have to be dalit Catholics, which is a fair and just target. Whenever representation is made by the dalit Christians or their movement, the Bishops can take it with the concerned heads of institutions or congregations and intervene to help. If necessary they could take up the matter with the respective world superiors or Generals to seek remedy. There has to be insistence for policy formulations on these lines. We expect CBCI to come up with its own policy statements that are appropriate and adequate so that others can follow the model.
- As a special case we request that considerable number of seats are reserved for dalit Catholics in St. John's Medical College, Bangalore and any other Catholic Medical Colleges. A large number of Doctors (even second generation of doctors) have come up among the other dalits, thanks to the reservation for them by the government. We could rarely see doctors among dalit Catholics. Other Catholics have been fully benefiting so far from St. John's Medical College, as only Catholics are admitted. Now it is time that dalit Catholics get more chances there.
- We request that primary (or) basic education is made free for dalit Catholics in our institutions just as the

government does. CBCI may give necessary directions to all our institutions and religious congregations.

- Educational scholarships and fee concessions for rural dalit Catholics is very necessary to make any considerable progress. Without this their entry in the educational field, especially higher courses, will be very slow and they end up at the fringe of our institutions. Many of our institutions are well established and rich with buildings and facilities. But the dalit Catholics cannot have access to or benefit from these without supplementary financial assistance to them. We request that in our hostels and orphanages 50 per cent concession is given for poor dalits.
- We wish to recommend to the kind consideration of all the bishops and superiors that hereafter only technical institutes are started, keeping in mind the interest and scope of the rural dalits. Mere academic courses may be given less priority.
- Power sharing with dalit Catholics is a crucial issue today and no reason will be accepted by them for their continued exclusion in this respect. They can no more depend on the charity, generosity or benevolent action of others. What is relevant is empowerment of dalits, which essentially means for them sharing power at all levels. The marginalisation in vocations to priesthood and religious, in the hierarchical posts of Bishops and diocesan officials/administrators, heads of institutions, in the national organisations such as NBCLC, in vital or strategic organisational positions, etc., is a matter of serious concern today. In particular, in the diocesan social service societies, organisations such as IGSSS, CARITAS India, which are dealing with funds, in the management of local and foreign funds, the representation of dalit priests, nuns and dalit lay people is almost nil. The general complaint is that resources have not reached the dalits proportionately. These must be quickly attended to. At least 50 per cent representation to dalits will be a just situation. How long can the majority dalit Catholics remain marginalised,

suffer and be at the loosing end? Why should they alone suffer forever? Power sharing with dalits is a vital step for long-term changes and for sustaining the change process.

- Enforcing and reinforcing are important but, that is what is lacking in the matters regarding dalit Christians. The line of communication, authority and mechanisms to enforce must be clearly known.
- We request the CBCI to constitute an apex body representing CBCI and CRI officials, dalit leaders, dalit priests and nuns, which can take up the issues of dalit Christians, follow up and resolve them. It can have regional bodies to deal with representation of local issues. These bodies should have mandatory power to take action or impose some sanctions wherever needed. These bodies, the lines of communications, action and enforcement of decisions have to be transparent, with due representation of dalits, so that solving problems will be possible. The whole difficulty in finding solutions and making progress is that each Bishop, diocese, congregation, institution and authority functions as separate kingdom with each one's own interpretation of dalit Christians issues and the solutions. Our greatest frustration is running from pillar to post with no one responsible to us. So we have to make this important practical suggestion.
- There has to be a more concerted effort by the whole Church to get the constitutional reservation for dalit Christians. We appeal to the CBCI for the same. It can take steps to demand from the State Governments MBC status for dalit Christians till they are included in the SC list by the Central Government.

We expect that this body announces a clear agenda, as a special gesture of Jubilee 2000, which will really help to establish a just Church for dalits.

In conclusion, we have to state with all respect and reverence, that the CBCI and the Regional Bishops Councils have not made judicious use of their authority, administrative capacity, institutional power and the minority right to solve the problems of dalit Christians. Also in terms of time, energy, human and material resources, very little is used, which is not even in the least proportion to the serious sectoral problem of dalits who form a big majority in the Catholic Church.

We are glad that the CBCI is concerned with the task of nation building and the role of the Christian minorities. We wish to respectfully remind that empowering the oppressed dalit community is a prime task of our nation building and only together with the empowered dalit Christians the Church can make a substantial contribution for nation building and play a leading role in the task.

It is with pain we have to say that our Indian Catholic Church has not so far taken steps to attend to the problems of dalit Christian in the normal course of things, and we see the caste culture as the basic reason. Now it is called to make a special effort as the affected people have become articulate. We in fact think that we need not say more as we believe that all the Bishops know these very well. But why things are not done? That is where our struggle comes in. We have to solve things peacefully, but peaceful solution consists of sincere, serious and speedy steps to solve all the problems and that has to come from the authorities, the dominant and the powerful. So, the question is whether you as the Apex Hierarchy want to do and avoid our struggle or you don't want to do and leave us to struggle even more. Hope this august Body will decide.

Prof. Dr M. Mary John
President, DCLM and Executive Member

APPENDIX 12

Major Developments – Post-1990s

- 1998, 10–11 October: First World Dalit Convention, Kuala Lumpur, Malaysia.
- 1998, 10 December: National Campaign on Dalit Human Rights launched.
- 2000, International Dalit Solidarity Network formed.
- 2000, 16–17 September: International Conference on Dalit Human Rights, London.
- 2001, 31 August – 7 September: World Conference Against Racism, Durban
- 2001, 8–10 December: National Conference of Dalit Organisations (NACDOR-I) organised.
- 2002, 12–13 January: Bhopal Conference and adoption of Bhopal Declaration.
- 2002, 23 December: UN Committee on Elimination of Racial Discrimination condemns caste.
- 2003, 16–18 May: International Dalit Conference, Vancouver.
- 2004, 29 November-1 December: International Consultation on Caste-based Discrimination, Kathmandu.
- 2005, 19 April: UN Commission on Human Rights adopts decision to appoint two Special Rapporteuers to tackle caste-based discrimination.
- 2006, 13 November: Process of organising NACDOR-II, launched.
- 2006, 20–21 November: First International Conference on Human Rights of Dalit Women.
- 2009, April 20–24: Durban Review Conference, also known as Durban II, held.

Bibliography

Ahmed, Rafiuddin, *The Bengal Muslims, 1871–1906, A Quest for Identity,* Oxford University Press, New Delhi, 1981.

Aloysius, G., *Religion as Emancipatory Identity, A Buddhist Movement Among the Tamils Under Colonialism,* New Age International Publishers, Delhi, 1998.

Ambedkar, B.R., *Dr Babasaheb Ambedkar Writings and Speeches,* Government of Maharashtra, Bombay, Vols. 1–18, Edited by Vasant Moon, 1990-2003.

Baago, Kaj, *Pioneers of Indigenous Christianity,* The Christian Institute for the Study of Religion and Society, Bangalore, and Christian Literature Society, Madras, 1969.

Bandyopadhyaya, Jayantanuja, *Class and Religion in Ancient India,* Anthem Press, New Delhi, 2007.

Basham, A.L., *The Wonder That Was India,* Rupa, New Delhi, 1994.

Baxi, Upendra, *The Future of Human Rights,* Oxford University Press, New Delhi, 2008.

Chatterjee, Debi, *Ideas And Movements Against Caste in India: Ancient to Modern Times,* Print-o-Graph, Calcutta, 1998.

——, *Sociology of National Integration,* Minerva Associates, Calcutta, 1993.

——, *Up Against Caste: Comparative Study Of Ambedkar And Periyar,* Rawat Publications, Jaipur, 2006.

Clarke, Sathianathan, *Dalits and Christianity: Subaltern Religion and Liberation Theology in India,* Oxford University Press, Delhi, 1998.

Dangle, Arjun, ed., *Poisoned Bread: Translations from Modern Marathi Dalit Literature,* Orient Longman, Bombay, 1992.

Dasgupta, Shashibhusan, *Obscure Religious Cults,* Firma K.L. Mukhopadhyaya, Calcutta, 1969.

Deliege, R., *The Untouchables of India,* Berg Publishers, Oxford, 1999, Translated from the French original by Nora Scott.

Devi, Vidya, *Dalit and Social Justice,* MD Publications, New Delhi, 2008.

Dhaka, Sunita and Rajvir S. Dhaka, *Behind the Veil: Dalit Women in Panchayati Raj,* Abhijeet, Delhi, 2005.

Diehl, Carl Gustav, *Church and Shrine, Intermingling Patterns of Culture in the Life of Some Christian Groups in South India,* Uppasala, Stockholm, 1965.

Embree, Ainslie, T., ed., *Sources of Indian Tradition*, Penguin, New Delhi, 1992.

Ghurye, G.S., *Caste and Race in India,* Popular Prakashan, Bombay, 1969.

Goswami, B., *Constitutional Safeguards for Scheduled Castes and Scheduled Tribes,* New Delhi, Rawat Publications, 2003.

Hutton, J.H., *Caste in India,* Oxford University Press, Bombay, 1983.

Jain, P.C., Shashi Jain and Sudha Bhatnagar, ed., *Scheduled Caste Women*, Rawat Publications, Jaipur and New Delhi, 1997.

Joe, Arun C., *Constructing Dalit Identity*, Rawat Publications, Jaipur and New Delhi, 2007.

Kamble, N.D., *The Scheduled Castes*, Ashish Publishing House, New Delhi, 1982.

Keer, Dhananjay, *Dr Ambedkar: Life and Mission,* A.V.Keer, Bombay, 1954.

Ketkar, S.V., *History of Caste in India,* Ithaca, New York, 1909.

Kosambi, D.D., *The Civilisation of Ancient India in Historical Outline*, Vikas Publishing House, New Delhi, 1981.

Kothari, Rajni, ed., *Caste in Indian Politics,* Orient Longman, New Delhi, 1976.

Kumar, Narender, *Dalit Policies, Politics and Parliament,* Shipra Publications, Delhi, 2004.

Kumar, Vivek, *Dalit Leadership in India,* Kalpaz Publications, Delhi, 2002.

Louis, Prakash, *The Political Sociology of Dalit Assertion*, Gyan Books, New Delhi.

Massey, James, *Dalits in India: Religion as a Source of Bondage or Liberation With Special Reference to Christians*, Manohar, New Delhi, 1995.

Mathew, Joseph, *Ideology, Protest and Social Mobility, Case Study of Mahars and Pulayas*, Inter-India Publications, New Delhi, 1986.

Moffatt, M., *An Untouchable Community in South India: Structure and Concensus*, Princeton University Press, Princeton, 1979.

Nandi, Ramendra Nath, *Social Roots of Religion in Ancient India*, K.P.Bagchi, Calcutta.

Omvedt, Gail, *Dalits and the Democratic Revolution: Dr Ambedkar and the Democratic Movement in Colonial India*, Sage, New Delhi, 1994.

——, *Cultural Revolt in a Colonial Society: The Non-Brahman Movement in Western India 1873–1930*, Scientific Socialist Education Trust, Bombay, 1976.

Pai, Sudha, *Dalit Assertion and the Unfinished Democratic Revolution: The Bahujan Samaj Party in Uttar Pradesh: Cultural Subordination and the Dalit Challenge*, Sage Publications, New Delhi, 2002.

Paswan, Sanjay and Pramanshi Jaideva, ed., *Encyclopaedia of Dalits in India*, Kalpaz, Delhi, 2002, 14 Vols.

Prashad, Vijay, *Untouchable Freedom: A Social History of A Dalit Community*, Oxford University Press, Delhi, 2000.

Purane, K.D., *Untouchability and the Law: The Ground Reality*, Gyan Books, New Delhi, 2000.

Rajawat, Mamta, ed., *Dalit Women: Issues and Perspectives*, Anmol, New Delhi, 2005.

Ram, Nandu, ed., *Ambedkar, Dalits and Buddhism: Collection of Dr Ambedkar Memorial Annual Lectures*, Manak, New Delhi, 2008.

Ram, Nandu, *Beyond Ambedkar: Essays on Dalits in India*, Har-Anand, New Delhi, 1995.

Shah, Ghanshyam, ed., *Dalit Identity and Politics*, Sage, New Delhi, 2001.

Shah, Ghanshyam, ed, *Dalits and the State,* Concept, New Delhi, 2002.

Shinde, Prem K. ed., *Dalits and Human Rights,* Isha Books, Delhi, 2005, 3 vols.

Thorat, Sukhadeo and Aryama, ed., *Ambedkar in Retrospect: Essays on Economics, Politics and Society,* Rawat Publications, Jaipur and New Delhi, 2007.

Thorat, Sukhadeo and Narender Kumar, *B.R. Ambedkar: Perspectives on Social Exclusion and Inclusive Policies,* Oxford University Press, New Delhi, 2008.

Webster John C.B., *The Dalit Christians: A History,* ISPCK, Delhi, 1992.

Index